ANGULAR
AND
MACHINE LEARNING
Pocket Primer

LICENSE, DISCLAIMER OF LIABILITY, AND LIMITED WARRANTY

ANGULAR
AND
MACHINE LEARNING

Pocket Primer

Oswald Campesato

MERCURY LEARNING AND INFORMATION

Dulles, Virginia
Boston, Massachusetts
New Delhi

Publisher: David Pallai
MERCURY LEARNING AND INFORMATION
22841 Quicksilver Drive
Dulles, VA 20166
info@merclearning.com
www.merclearning.com
(800) 232-0223

O. Campesato. *Angular and Machine Learning Pocket Primer*.
ISBN: 9781683924708

Library of Congress Control Number: 2020934206

202122 321 Printed on acid-free paper in the United States of America

Our titles are available for adoption, license, or bulk purchase by institutions, corpo-
rations, etc. For additional information, please contact the Customer Service Dept. at
(800) 232-0223(toll free).

Digital versions of our titles are available at: www.academiccourseware.com and other
electronic vendors. *Companion files are available from the publisher by writing to
info@merclearning.com.*

*I'd like to dedicate this book to my parents –
may this bring joy and happiness into their lives.*

CONTENTS

PREFACE

What is the Goal?

The goal of this book is to introduce advanced beginners to basic machine learning and incorporate that knowledge into Angular 8 applications. This book is intended to be a fast-paced introduction to some basic features of machine learning and an overview of several popular machine learning classifiers. It includes code samples that are part of a university course taught by the author of this book.

This book will save you the time required to search for code samples, which is a potentially time-consuming process. If you're not sure whether you can absorb the material in this book, glance through the code samples to get a feel for the level of complexity.

At the risk of stating the obvious, please keep in mind the following point: *you will not become an expert in machine learning or Angular 8 by reading this book.*

What Will I Learn from This Book?

The first three chapters contain a short tour of basic Angular functionality, such as UI components and forms in Angular applications. The fourth chapter introduces you to machine learning concepts, such as supervised and unsupervised learning, followed by the major types of machine learning algorithms (regression, classification, and clustering), along with a section discussing linear regression. The fifth chapter is devoted to classification algorithms, such as kNN, Naïve Bayes, decision trees, random forests, and SVM (Support Vector Machines).

The sixth chapter introduces basic TensorFlow concepts, followed by TensorFlow.js (i.e., TensorFlow in modern browsers) and some examples of Angular applications combined with machine learning. The appendix contains an introduction to Keras, along with some basic code samples.

Although Jupyter is popular, all the code samples in this book are Python scripts. However, you can quickly learn about the useful features of Jupyter through various online tutorials. In addition, it's worth looking at Google Colaboratory: it is entirely online, is based on Jupyter notebooks, and offers free GPU usage.

How Much Keras Knowledge is Needed for This Book?

Some exposure to Keras is helpful, and you can read the appendix if Keras is new to you. If you also want to learn about Keras and logistic regression, there is an example in Chapter 3. This example requires some theoretical knowledge involving activation functions, optimizers, and cost functions, all of which are discussed in Chapter 4.

Please keep in mind that Keras is well-integrated into TensorFlow 2 (in the tf.keras namespace), and it provides a layer of abstraction over the "pure" TensorFlow that will enable you to develop prototypes more quickly.

Do I Need to Learn the Theory Portions of This Book?

Once again, the answer depends on the extent to which you plan to become involved in machine learning. In addition to creating a model, you will use various algorithms to see which ones provide the level of accuracy (or some other metric) that you need for your project. If you fall short, the theoretical aspects of machine learning can help you perform a "forensic" analysis of your model and your data, and ideally assist in determining how to improve your model.

How Were the Code Samples Created?

The code samples in this book were created and tested using Python 3 and Keras that's built into TensorFlow 2 on a Macbook Pro with OS X 10.12.6 (macOS Sierra). The code samples were derived primarily from the author for his *Deep Learning and Keras* graduate course. In some cases, there are code samples that incorporate short sections of code from discussions in online forums. The key point to remember is that the code samples follow the "Four Cs": they must be Clear, Concise, Complete, and Correct to the extent that it's possible to do so, given the size of this book.

Launching the Code Samples: Please Read This

Since the code samples require more than 10 GB of disk space, which is greater than the capacity of a DVD, all the node_modules subdirectories have been deleted. Hence, you need to run the following command from the top-level directory of each Angular application:

```
npm install
```

The version numbers for the Angular CLI and NodeJs are displayed in the section "Installing the Angular CLI" in Chapter 1, and they are displayed below for your convenience:

```
Angular CLI: 8.3.21
Node: 13.3.0
OS: darwin x64
Angular:
...
```

Package	Version
@angular-devkit/architect	0.803.21
@angular-devkit/core	8.3.21
@angular-devkit/schematics	8.3.21
@schematics/angular	8.3.21
@schematics/update	0.803.21
rxjs	6.4.0

You might have different versions of the Angular CLI and Node, and if they are close to the version numbers displayed above, they will probably work as well.

Another point to keep in mind: several code samples in Chapter 3 were created with an additional manual invocation of npm, which means that the file package.json is slightly different in those directories. Therefore, do not copy package.json from one code sample to other code samples.

In the event that you do overwrite `package.json` with another copy of this file, the code samples that involve the extra command line invocation will have the following comment in `app.component.ts`:

```
// remember: npm install jquery -save
```

If the file `app.component.ts` does not have this type of comment line, then you only need to invoke `npm install` once from the command line.

I Received An Error After Launching npm: What Can I Do?

One potential error that can occur when you launch `npm install` in the code samples is shown here:

```
An unhandled exception occurred: Could not find module
"@angular-devkit/build-angular"
```

The first step involves removing the file `package-lock.json`:

```
rm package-lock.json
```

The second step is to install the package (introduced in Angular 6) listed in the preceding error message as a dependency, which involves the following command:

```
npm install --save-dev @angular-devkit/build-angular
```

The third step involves the standard `npm` invocation:

```
npm install
```

There are other errors that can occur for various reasons (such as different versions of the Angular CLI), and in those situations, perform an Internet search. There's a good chance that someone else has encountered the same error and has a solution for that error.

What are the Technical Prerequisites for This Book?

For the machine learning aspect of this book, you need some familiarity with Python, and also know how to launch Python code from the command line (in a Unix-like environment for Mac users). In addition, a mixture of basic linear algebra (vectors and matrices), probability/statistics, (mean, median, and standard deviation) and basic concepts in calculus (such as derivatives) will help you learn the material in this book. Some knowledge of NumPy and Matplotlib is also helpful, and the assumption is that you are familiar with their basic functionalities (such as NumPy arrays).

For the Angular aspect of this book, you need some familiarity with TypeScript as well as RxJS and Observables. Since RxJS is a JavaScript-based implementation of FRP (Functional Reactive Programming), some knowledge of the latter would be very useful.

One other prerequisite is important for understanding the code samples in the second half of this book: some familiarity with neural networks, including the concepts of hidden layers and activation functions (even if you don't fully understand them). Knowledge of cross entropy is also helpful for some of the code samples.

What are the Non-Technical Prerequisites for This Book?

Although the answer to this question is more difficult to quantify, it's very important to have strong desire to learn about machine learning, along with the motivation and discipline to read and understand the code samples.

Even simple machine language APIs can be a challenge to understand the first time you encounter them, so be prepared to read the code samples several times.

How Do I Set Up a Command Shell?

If you are a Mac user, there are three ways to do so. The first method is to use Finder to navigate to Applications > Utilities, and then double click on the Utilities application. Next, if you already have a command shell available, you can launch a new command shell by typing the following command:

```
open /Applications/Utilities/Terminal.app
```

A second method for Mac users is to open a new command shell on a Macbook from a command shell that is already visible simply by clicking command+n in that command shell, and your Mac will launch another command shell.

If you are a PC user, you can install Cygwin (open source, available at *https://cygwin.com/*) that simulates bash commands, or use another toolkit such as MKS (a commercial product). Please read the online documentation that describes the download and installation process. Note that custom aliases are not automatically set if they are defined in a file other than the main start-up file (such as .bash_login).

Companion Files

All the code samples and figures in this book may be obtained by writing to the publisher at info@merclearning.com.

What are the "Next Steps" After Finishing This Book?

The answer to this question varies widely, mainly because the answer depends heavily on your objectives. If you are interested primarily in Angular, then you can learn more advanced Angular features that you can incorporate in new Angular applications.

If you are primarily interested in machine learning, there are many resources available, and you can perform an Internet search for those resources. The aspects of machine learning for you to learn depend on who you are: the needs of a machine learning engineer, data scientist, manager, student, and software developer are all different.

O. Campesato
March 2020

## CHAPTER 1

QUICK INTRODUCTION TO ANGULAR

This chapter provides a fast introduction to Angular-based applications. While many of the code samples are straightforward, you need to invest additional time and effort to acquire a deeper understanding of Angular. The purpose of the code samples is to illustrate some fundamental features of Angular. Although some fine-grained details are discussed, you will need to consult some online tutorials to gain a thorough understanding of the features of Angular.

Another important factor is your learning style: you might prefer to read the details regarding the "scaffolding" for Angular applications before you delve into the first code sample. However, it's perfectly acceptable to skim the introductory portion of this chapter, quickly "get into the weeds" with the Angular sample code, and afterward review the initial portion again.

The first part of this chapter discusses some of the design goals of Angular and its various features, such as components, modules, and one-way data binding. The second part of this chapter discusses the Angular CLI, which is a command-line tool for generating Angular applications.

NOTE *The Angular applications in this book are based on Angular 8, using the ng command line utility for creating Angular applications.*

There are several points to keep in mind before you read this short book. First, the code samples highlight basic coding techniques in Angular applications. Hence, you will not find an in-depth and highly detailed description of the Angular concepts, design goals, and architecture that are available in 600-page books. However, you can fill some of those technical gaps via online articles.

Second, you can learn the Angular concepts in the various applications without having previous experience with Angular, but obviously some knowledge of Angular would be helpful.

Third, this chapter contains some Angular applications for generating SVG-based graphics and D3-based animation effects. Due to space constraints, this chapter does not contain an introduction to SVG or D3. Fortunately, there are many online tutorials that provide detailed information regarding the features of SVG and D3. If you are not interested in either of these technologies, feel free to skip the associated code samples, since there will be no loss of continuity.

What You Need to Understand for Angular Applications

Two important technologies in Angular are TypeScript and RxJS. In very casual terms, TypeScript might remind you of combining JavaScript with a classical object-oriented approach. If you have an affinity for Java, you will probably be more comfortable with the "look-and-feel" of TypeScript than JavaScript.

RxJS is JavaScript-based FRP (Functional Reactive Programming) that supports many intermediate operators, such as `filter()`, `map()`, `take()`, and other useful operators. The following subsections contain some additional details regarding TypeScript and RxJS.

Learn TypeScript

Knowledge of TypeScript is highly recommended, along with a basic proficiency in NodeJS (i.e., the `npm` utility) and ES6. The Angular applications have been created with the Angular CLI (discussed later) that uses `node` v12.6.0 and `npm` 6.9.0, but it's likely that slightly lower versions will work as well. Determine the version on your machine with the following commands:

```
node -v
npm -v
```

If necessary, navigate to the NodeJS home page to download a more recent version of the node executable. If you have not worked with Node, read an online tutorial to learn how to use basic `npm` commands.

The code samples include basic concepts about ES6 and TypeScript, and their respective home pages contain plenty of information to help you get started. In particular, learn basic concepts regarding Typescript classes and template strings. As you will see in subsequent chapters, Angular applications rely heavily on dynamic templates, which frequently involve the interpolation (via the "{{}}" syntax) of variables. In addition, the following website provides an online "playground," along with links for documentation and code samples about TypeScript:

https://www.typescriptlang.org/play/.

Angular takes advantage of ES6 features such as components and classes, as well as features that are part of TypeScript, such as annotations and its type system. TypeScript is preferred over ES6 because TypeScript supports all the features of ES6 and TypeScript provides an optional type inferencing system that can catch many coding errors.

Learn RxJS and Observables

If you have worked with ES6, then you probably know about functions such as the `filter()` function (which is handy for Angular `Pipes`) and the `map()` function (often used with `Observables` and HTTP requests in earlier versions of Angular). Other functions, such as `merge()` and `flatten()`, can also be useful, and you can learn about them and other functions on an as-needed basis.

In RxJS, the preceding functions are called "intermediate operators," and you will frequently encounter them in RxJS `Observables`. In highly simplified terms, you can define an `Observable` involving one or more intermediate operators, and then invoke the `Observable` via a so-called "terminal operator."

Different languages can support different methods as terminal operators, and in the case of RxJS, the `subscribe()` method is a terminal operator. RxJS `Observables` are more powerful than `Promises`, and knowledge of the latter will simplify your transition to RxJS `Observables`. After you learn the basic features of RxJS, the following (albeit more advanced) article contains very good information regarding the RxJS `unsubscribe()` method:

https://blog.bitsrc.io/6-ways-to-unsubscribe-from-observables-in-angular-ab912819a78f.

Promises versus Observables

In Chapter 2 and Chapter 3, you will see examples of Angular applications that involve `Observables`. Although you can find online code samples that use `Promises`, Angular with TypeScript favors `Observables`. This book does not provide tutorial-like information regarding `Observables` (or `Promises`), but you can learn about the advantages of `Observables` over `Promises` at

https://www.syncfusion.com/blogs/post/angular-promises-versus-observables.aspx.

There are many other online tutorials available regarding `Observables`, and if necessary, you can read them on an as-needed basis in parallel with the code samples in the next two chapters. Fortunately, the code samples involve only a few features of `Observables`, so you do not need to become highly proficient with `Observables` for this book.

You can develop Angular applications in Electron, Webstorm, and Visual Studio Code. Check their respective websites for pricing and feature support.

A High-Level View of Angular

Angular was designed as a platform that supports Angular applications in a browser, server-side rendering, and Angular applications on mobile devices. The first aspect – rendering Angular applications in browsers – is the focus of this book. The second aspect – Angular Universal (a.k.a., server-side rendering) – is not discussed in this book, but in essence, server-side rendering creates the "first view" of an Angular application on a server instead of a browser. Since browsers do not need to construct this view, they can render a view more quickly and create a faster perceived load time. The third aspect – Angular applications on mobile devices – is outside the scope of this book.

Angular has a component-based architecture, where components are organized in a tree-like structure (the same is true of Angular modules). Angular also supports powerful technologies that you will learn in order to become proficient in writing Angular applications. The simplest way to create an Angular application is to use the Angular CLI (discussed in detail later) that generates the required files for an Angular application. Some of the important features of Angular are listed here:

- one-way data binding
- "tree shaking"
- change detection
- style encapsulation

The first two features are briefly discussed below. You can consult the online tutorials regarding style encapsulation.

One-way Data Binding in Angular

Angular provides declarative one-way binding as the default behavior (but Angular 4 enables you to switch to two-way binding if you wish to do so). One-way binding acts as a unidirectional change propagation that provides an improvement in performance as well as a reduction in code complexity. Angular also supports stateful, reactive, and immutable models. The meaning of the previous statement will become clearer as you work with Angular applications.

Angular applications involve defining a top-level ("root") module that references a `Component` that in turn specifies an HTML element (via a mandatory `selector` property) that is the "parent" element of the `Component`. The definition of the `Component` involves a so-called "decorator" that contains a `selector` property and also a `template` property (or a `templateUrl` property).

The `template` property contains a mixture of HTML and custom mark-up that you can place in a separate file and then reference that file via the `templateUrl` property. In addition, the `Component` is immediately followed by a TypeScript class definition that contains "backing code" that is associated with component-related variables that appear in the `template` property. These details will become much clearer after you have worked with some Angular applications.

NOTE *The* `templateUrl` *property and* `styleUrls` *property refer to files, whereas the* `template` *property and* `styles` *property refer to inline code.*

A High-Level View of Angular Applications

Angular applications consist of a combination of built-in components and custom components (the latter are written by you), each of which is typically defined in a separate TypeScript file (with a `ts` extension). Each component uses one or more `import` statements to include its dependencies.

There are various types of dependencies available in Angular, such as directives and pipes. A *custom directive* is essentially the contents of a TypeScript file that defines a component. Thus, a custom directive consists of `import` statements, a `Component` decorator, and an exported TypeScript class.

Angular provides *built-in directives*, such as *ngIf (for if logic) and *ngFor (used in for loops). These two directives are also called "structural directives" because they modify the content of an HTML page. Angular *built-in pipes* include the date and numeric values (currency, decimals, numbers, and percent), whereas *custom pipes* are defined by you.

In addition, TypeScript classes use a *decorator* (which is a built-in function) that provides metadata to a class, its members, or its method arguments. Decorators are easy to identify because they always have an @ prefix. Angular provides a number of built-in decorators, such as @ Component and @NgModule.

This concludes the high-level introduction to Angular features. The next portion of this chapter introduces the Angular CLI, which is used throughout this book to create Angular applications.

The Angular CLI

The Angular CLI is the official Angular application generator from Google. The Angular CLI is a command line tool called ng that generates complete Angular applications, which includes test-related code and also launches npm install in order to install the required files in node_ modules. The home page for the Angular CLI is cli.angular.io.

The Angular CLI generates a configuration file called package.json to manage the "core" dependencies and their version numbers. After generating an Angular application, navigate to the node_modules subdirectory, and you will see an assortment of Angular subdirectories that contain files that are required for Angular applications.

Installing the Angular CLI

You need to perform several steps in order to install the Angular CLI: uninstall older versions (if you have any installed) of the CLI, then install the latest version of the CLI, and then create a new Angular application.

Step 1: uninstall the previous CLI (if you installed an older version) with the following:

```
sudo npm uninstall -g angular-cli
npm cache clean
```

Step 2: install the new CLI with this command (note the new package name):

```
[sudo] npm install -g @angular/cli
```

The preceding command installs the `ng` executable, whose location you can find via the following command:

```
which ng
```

If the preceding command displays a blank line, that means that the directory that contains the `ng` executable is not included in the `PATH` environment variable. In this case, type the following command in a command shell:

```
export PATH=/Users/owner/.npm-global/bin:$PATH
```

Note that preceding command is valid for Mac OS X, Linux, `bash`, `ksh`, `zsh`, and any other Unix shells that are derived from the Bourne shell. If you are using Windows or a BSD-like shell (such as `csh`), search online to find the correct syntax for the preceding command for your system.

Now display the versions of the various components of the CLI by invoking the following command in a command shell:

```
ng version
```

As this book goes to print, the output of the preceding command will be something similar to what is shown below (version numbers might be slightly different for you):

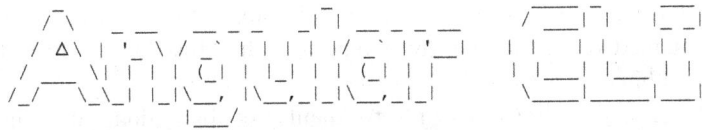

```
Angular CLI: 8.3.21
Node: 13.3.0
OS: darwin x64
Angular:

...
```

```
Package                         Version
------------------------------------------------------------
@angular-devkit/architect       0.803.21
@angular-devkit/core            8.3.21
@angular-devkit/schematics      8.3.21
@schematics/angular             8.3.21
@schematics/update              0.803.21
rxjs                            6.4.0
```

Features of the Angular CLI (optional)

Although this section contains useful information, you don't need these details to create an Angular application (which you will see in the next section). After you have created some basic Angular applications and you want to incorporate additional functionality, you can return to this section and read about the Angular CLI options.

In order to see the various options of the `ng` executable, type the following command from a command shell (make sure that your PATH environment variable include the location of the `ng` executable, as discussed in a previous section):

```
$ ng help
```

Available Commands:

- `add` — Adds support for an external library to your project.
- `analytics` — Configures the gathering of the Angular CLI usage metrics. See *v8.angular.io/cli/usage-analytics-gathering*.
- `build` (b) — Compiles an Angular app into an output directory named `dist/` at the given output path. Must be executed from within a workspace directory.
- `config` — Retrieves or sets Angular configuration values in the angular.json file for the workspace.
- `doc` (d) — Opens the official Angular documentation (angular.io) in a browser, and searches for a given keyword.
- `e2e` (e) — Builds and serves an Angular app, then runs end-to-end tests using Protractor.
- `generate` (g) — Generates and/or modifies files based on a schematic.
- `help` — Lists available commands and their short descriptions.
- `lint` (l) — Runs linting tools on Angular app code in a given project folder.

- `new (n)` — Creates a new workspace and an initial Angular app.
- `run` — Runs an Architect target with an optional custom builder configuration defined in your project.
- `serve (s)` — Builds and serves your app, rebuilding on file changes.
- `test (t)` — Runs unit tests in a project.
- `update` — Updates your application and its dependencies. See update.angular.io/.
- `version (v)` — Outputs the Angular CLI version.
- `xi18n` — Extracts i18n messages from the source code.
- `version (v)` — Outputs the Angular CLI version.
- `xi18n` — Extracts i18n messages from the source code.

The `ng g` option is equivalent to the `ng generate` option, which enables you to generate an Angular custom `Component`, an Angular `Pipe` (discussed in Chapter 3), and other options. The `ng x18n` option extracts i18n messages from the source code. The next section shows you an example of generating an Angular custom `Component` in an application, and the contents of the files that are automatically generated for you.

The default prefix is `app` for components (e.g., `<app-root></app-root>`), but you can specify a different prefix with this invocation:

```
ng new app-root-name -prefix abc
```

NOTE *Angular applications created via* ng *always contain the* src/app *directory.*

Information about upgrading the Angular CLI is here:

https://github.com/angular/angular-cli.

Documentation for the Angular CLI is here:

http://cli.angular.io.

Now that you have an understanding of some of the features of the `ng` utility, let's create our first Angular application, which is the topic of the next section.

A "Hello World" Angular Application

As you will discover, it's possible to create many basic Angular applications with a small amount of custom code. When you are ready to create medium-sized applications, you can take advantage of the component-based nature of Angular applications in order to incrementally add new components (and modules).

Now let's create a new project called `HelloWorld` by navigating to a suitable directory on your machine and then invoking the following command:

```
ng new HelloWorld
```

The Angular CLI generates everything except for your custom code. Second, the Angular CLI enables you to generate new components, routers, and so forth, which are possible with starter applications. Third, the Angular CLI is based purely on TypeScript, and the generated application includes the JSON files `tsconfig.json`, `tslint.json`, `typedoc.json`, and `typings.json`.

Now launch the `HelloWorld` application as follows:

```
cd HelloWorld
ng serve
```

Launch a new browser session, navigate to `localhost:4200`, and you will see the same display as the content of Figure 1.1.

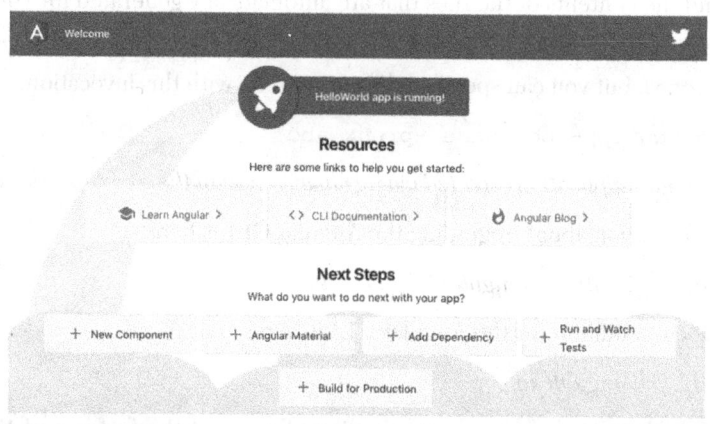

FIGURE 1.1 A Hello World Angular Application

NOTE *Full color figures are available in the companion files.*

The Anatomy of an Angular Application

The `ng` command that you launched in the previous section created an Angular application that contains more than 35,000 files, most of which are in the `node_modules` subdirectory. Fortunately, you only need to be aware of a handful of files when you need to create your own Angular applications.

Here is the list of files and directories in the root directory of the `HelloWorld` Angular application:

- `tslint.json`
- `README.md`
- **`angular.json`**
- `browserslist`
- `e2e`
- `karma.conf.js`
- `node_modules`
- `package-lock.json`
- **`package.json`**
- **`src`**
- `tsconfig.app.json`
- `tsconfig.json`
- `tsconfig.spec.json`
- `tslint.json`
- `.gitignore`
- `.editorconfig`

The most relevant files are package.json and angular.json and the most important directory for creating custom code in the `src` directory (all of these are shown in bold in the preceding list). In general, you will not need to modify either of these files. As you will see later in this chapter, you need to perform an extra step from the command line when you need to work with D3-based graphics.

The Main Files in the src/app Subdirectory (Overview)

The `src` subdirectory contains a combination of subdirectories and files, as shown here:

```
app
assets
environments
favicon.ico
index.html
main.ts
polyfills.ts
styles.css
test.ts
```

Notice that the preceding list contains the TypeScript file `main.ts`, which will be discussed later in this chapter.

Next, the `src/app` subdirectory contains your custom code and the `src/assets` subdirectory contains other assets, such as JSON files. Later you will see an example of an Angular application that reads the content of `authors.json` that is located in the `src/assets` subdirectory.

The following list displays the contents of the `src/app` subdirectory:

```
app.component.css
app.component.html
app.component.spec.ts
app.component.ts
app.module.ts
```

Unless it's noted differently, you can delete the contents of `app.component.html` for every code sample in this book. The file `app.component.ts` contains TypeScript code that is specific to your Angular application, and the file `app.module.ts` specifies any dependencies in your Angular application, which can include Angular modules as well as custom modules (you'll see examples of such in Chapter 3).

The three TypeScript files `main.ts`, `app.component.ts`, and `app.module.ts` are the bootstrap file, the main module, and the main component class, respectively, for Angular applications.

Here is the condensed one-sentence explanation about the purpose of these three files: Angular uses `main.ts` as the initial "entry point" to bootstrap the Angular module `AppModule` (defined in `app.module.ts`), which in turn references the main component `AppComponent` (defined in `app.component.ts`), as well as any other custom components (and modules) that you have imported into `AppModule`.

The Contents of the Three Main Files

The preceding section briefly described the sequence in which files are processed in Angular applications. The code samples this book involve custom code in the TypeScript file `app.component.ts` and sometimes involve updating the contents of the file `app.module.ts`, but there is no need to modify the file `main.ts`. The following subsections display the contents of these three files, along with a brief description of their contents.

The main.ts Bootstrap File

Listing 1.1 displays the contents of main.ts in the src subdirectory (not the src/app subdirectory) that imports and bootstraps the top-level Angular module AppModule. Although you won't need to modify this file in the code samples in this book, it's worth briefly taking a one-time look at the contents of this file.

This file acts as an "entry point" from which a sequence of files is accessed and then launched. As you will soon see, Angular applications have a component-based architecture, which might seem more complex than alternate frameworks. However, as you become more familiar with this architecture, you will see that this architecture enables teams of developers to work in parallel on different parts of a complex application.

LISTING 1.1 main.ts

```
import { enableProdMode } from '@angular/core';
import { platformBrowserDynamic } from '@angular/platform-
browser-dynamic';

import { AppModule }        from './app/app.module';
import { environment }        from './environments/
environment';

if (environment.production) {
  enableProdMode();
}

platformBrowserDynamic().bootstrapModule(AppModule)
  .catch(err => console.error(err));
```

The first line of code in Listing 1.1 is an import statement that is needed for the conditional logic later in the code listing. The second import statement appears in many Angular code samples, and it's necessary for launching Angular applications on desktops and laptops.

The third import statement involves the top-level module of Angular applications, which in turn contains all the custom components and services that are included in this Angular module. The fourth import statement contains environment-related information that is used in the next conditional logic snippet: if the current application is in production mode, the enableProdMode() function is executed.

The final line of code is the actual bootstrapping process that involves rendering the code in `app.component.ts` in a browser.

The app.component.ts File

Listing 1.2 displays the content of `app.component.ts,` which illustrates the typical properties of an Angular application.

LISTING 1.2 app.component.ts

```
import { Component } from '@angular/core';

@Component({
  selector:    'app-root',
  templateUrl: './app.component.html',
  styleUrls:   ['./app.component.css']
})
export class AppComponent {
  title = 'HelloWorld';
}
```

Listing 1.2 starts with an `import` statement for the Angular `@Component` decorator in order to define the metadata for the class `AppComponent`. At a minimum, the metadata involves two properties: `selector` and either `template` or `templateUrl`. Except for the routing-related components, both of these properties are required in custom components. In this example, the `selector` property specifies the custom element `app-root` (which you can change) that is in the HTML Web page `index.html`.

The `templateURL` property specifies a file that contains HTML markup that will be inserted in the custom element `app-root`. An alternative is the `template` property, which contains the HTML markup that will be inserted in the custom element `app-root`. The final line of code in Listing 1.2 is an `export` statement that makes the `AppComponent` class available for import in other TypeScript files, such as `app.module.ts,` which is shown in Listing 1.3 in the next section.

Although the property `templateUrl` specifies an HTML Web page with mark-up, the Angular code samples in this book use the `template` property to define the layout of the HTML web page for Angular applications (that's why the HTML Web page `app.component.html` in the code samples in this book is empty).

The app.module.ts File

Listing 1.3 displays the content of app.module.ts, which displays the dependencies of various modules in an Angular application.

LISTING 1.3 app.module.ts

```
import { BrowserModule } from '@angular/platform-browser';
import { NgModule }       from '@angular/core';
import { AppComponent }   from './app.component';

@NgModule({
  declarations: [
    AppComponent
  ],
  imports: [
    BrowserModule
  ],
  providers: [],
  bootstrap: [AppComponent]
})
export class AppModule { }
```

Listing 1.3 contains import statements that import BrowserModule and NgModule that are part of Angular. The third import statement imports the class AppComponent that is the top-level component illustrated in Listing 1.2 in the previous section.

> **NOTE** *Angular dependencies always contain the "@" symbol, whereas custom dependencies specify a relative path to your custom TypeScript files.*

Next, the @NgModule decorator contains an object with various properties (discussed in the next section). These properties specify the metadata for the class AppModule that is exported in the final line of code in Listing 1.3. The metadata in AppModule involves the following array-based properties of values: imports, providers, declarations, exports, and bootstrap.

In Listing 1.3, the array properties declarations, imports, and bootstrap are non-null, whereas the providers property is an empty array. This metadata is required in order for Angular to "bootstrap" the code in AppComponent, which in turn contains the details of what is rendered (e.g., an <h1> element) and where it is rendered (e.g., as a child of the app-root element in index.html).

Now let's take a look at the contents of the HTML Web page `index. html`, which is the main Web page for our Angular application.

The index.html Web Page

Listing 1.4 displays the content of `index.html` for a new Angular application that is generated from the command line via the `ng` utility.

LISTING 1.4 index.html

```html
<!doctype html>
<html lang="en">
<head>
  <meta charset="utf-8">
  <title>HelloWorld</title>
  <base href="/">

    <meta  name="viewport"  content="width=device-width,
initial-scale=1">
    <link  rel="icon"  type="image/x-icon"  href="favicon.
ico">
</head>
<body>
  <app-root></app-root>
</body>
</html>
```

Listing 1.4 is minimalistic: only the custom `<app-root>` element (which is specified in the `selector` property in `app.component.ts`) gives you an indication that this Web page is part of an Angular application.

NOTE   *The Angular CLI automatically inserts JavaScript dependencies in* `index.html` *during the "build" of the project.*

Before we delve into the TypeScript files in an Angular application, let's take a quick detour to understand how `import` statements work in Angular applications. However, feel free to skip the next section if you are already familiar with the `import` and `export` statements in Angular.

Exporting and Importing Packages and Classes (optional)

Every TypeScript class that is imported in a TypeScript file must be exported in the TypeScript file where that class is defined. You will see many examples of import and export statements: in fact, this is true of every Angular application in this book.

There are two common types of import statements: one type involves importing packages from Angular modules, and the other type involves importing custom classes (written by you). Here is the syntax for both types:

```
import {some-package-name} from 'some-angular-module';
import {some-class }       from 'my-custom-class';
```

Here is an example of both types of import statements:

```
import { NgModule }     from '@angular/core';
import {EmpComponent}   from './emp.component';
```

In the preceding code snippet, the NgModule package is imported from the @angular/core module that is located in the node_modules directory. The EmpComponent class is a custom class that is defined and exported in the TypeScript file emp.component.ts.

In the second import statement, the "./" prefix is required whenever a custom class is imported from a TypeScript file: notice the omission of the ".ts" suffix.

Working with Components in Angular

As you have already learned, an Angular application is a tree of nested components, where the top-level component is the application. The components define the UI elements, screens, and routes. In general, organize Angular applications by placing each custom component in a TypeScript file, and then import that same TypeScript file in the "main" file (which is often named app.component.ts) that contains the top-level component.

The MetaData in Components

Angular components are often a combination of an @Component decorator and a class definition that can optionally contain a constructor. A simple example of an @Component decorator is here:

```
import { Component }   from '@angular/core';
import {EmpComponent} from './emp/emp.component';

@Component({
    selector: 'app-container',
```

```
    template:  `<tasks>{{message}}</tasks>`,
    directives: [EmpComponent]
})
```

The preceding @Component decorator contains several properties, some of which are mandatory and others that are optional. Let's look at both types in the preceding code block.

The selector property is mandatory, and it specifies the HTML element (whether it's an existing element or a custom element) that serves as the "root" of an Angular application.

Next, the template property (or a templateUrl property) is mandatory, and it contains a mixture of markup, interpolated variables, and TypeScript code. One important detail: the template property requires "backticks" when its definition spans multiple lines.

The directives property is an optional property that specifies an array of components that are treated as nested components. In this example, the directives property specifies the component EmpComponent that is also imported (via an import statement) near the beginning of the code block. Notice that the import statement does not contain the "@" symbol, which means that EmpComponent is a custom component defined in the file emp/emp.component.ts.

Stateful versus Stateless Components in Angular

In high-level terms, a *stateful* component retains information that is relevant to other parts of the same Angular application. Stateless components do not maintain the application state, nor do they request or fetch data: they pass data via property bindings from another component (such as its parent).

The code samples in this book include a combination of stateful components, stateless components, and sometimes also "value objects", which are instances of custom classes that "model" different entities (such as an employee, customer, student, and so forth).

You will see an example of a presentational component in Chapter 2. In the meantime, a good article that delves into stateful and stateless components is here:

https://toddmotto.com/stateful-stateless-components#stateful.

Syntax, Attributes, and Properties in Angular

Angular introduced the square bracket "[]" notation for attributes and properties, as well as the round parentheses "()" notation for functions that handle events. This new syntax is actually valid HTML5 syntax. Here is an example of a code snippet that specifies an attribute and a function:

```
<foo [bar]= "x+1" (baz)="doSomething()">Hello World</
foo>
```

An example that specifies a property and a function is here:

```
<button [disabled]="!inputIsValid" (click)="authenti-
cate()">Login </button>
```

An example of a data-related element with a custom element is here:

```
<my-chart [data]="myData" (drag)="handleDrag()"></
my-chart>
```

The new syntax in the preceding code snippet eliminates the need for many built-in directives, as you will see later in this chapter.

Attributes versus Properties in Angular

Keep in mind the following distinction: a property can specify a complex model, whereas an attribute can only specify a string. For example, in Angular 1.x, you can write the following:

```
<my-directive foo="{{something}}"></my-directive>
```

The corresponding code in Angular (which does not require interpolation) is here:

```
<my-directive [foo]="something"></my-directive>
```

Before delving into code samples that show you how to create graphics and animation effects, let's look at the Angular lifecycle methods.

Angular Lifecycle Methods

Angular applications have lifecycle methods that are executed in a pre-defined sequence. Hence, you can place custom code in those methods in order to handle various events (such as `application`, `start`, `run`, and so forth). The "Lifecycle Hook" interfaces are defined in the @angular/core library, and they are listed here:

- OnInit
- OnDestroy
- DoCheck
- OnChanges
- AfterContentInit
- AfterContentChecked
- AfterViewInit
- AfterViewChecked

Each interface has a single method whose name is the interface name prefixed with ng. For example, the OnInit interface has a method named ngOnInit. Angular invokes these lifecycle methods in the following order:

- ngOnChanges: called when an input or output binding value changes
- ngOnInit: after the first ngOnChanges
- ngDoCheck: developer's custom change detection
- ngAfterContentInit: after component content initialized
- ngAfterContentChecked: after every check of component content
- ngAfterViewInit: after component's view(s) are initialized
- ngAfterViewChecked: after every check of a component's view(s)
- ngOnDestroy: just before the directive is destroyed

Since Angular invokes the constructor of a component when that component is created, the constructor is a convenient location to initialize the state for that component. However, child components must be initialized before accessing any properties or data that is defined in those child components. In this scenario, place custom code in the ngOnInit lifecycle method to access the data from the child components.

The complete set of Angular lifecycle events is here:

https://angular.io/docs/ts/latest/guide/lifecycle-hooks.html.

A Simple Example of Angular Lifecycle Methods

Copy the directory LifeCycle from the companion disc into a convenient location. Recall that the node_modules directory was removed in order to fit the entire set of Angular applications on the companion disc.

Please read the section "Launching the Code" in the preface that explains how to generate the node_modules subdirectory.

Listing 1.5 displays the content of app.component.ts, which shows you the sequence in which some Angular lifecycle methods are invoked.

LISTING 1.5 app.component.ts

```
import {Component} from '@angular/core';

@Component({
  selector: 'app-root',
  template: '<h2>Angular Lifecycle Methods</h2>',
})
export class AppComponent{
  ngOnInit() {
    // invoked after child components are initialized
    console.log("ngOnInit");
  }
  ngOnDestroy() {
    // invoked when a component is destroyed
    console.log("ngOnDestroy");
  }
  ngDoCheck() {
    // custom change detection
    console.log("ngDoCheck");
  }
  ngOnChanges(changes) {
    console.log("ngOnChanges");
    // Invoked after bindings have been checked
    // but only if one of the bindings has changed.
    //
    // changes is an object of the format:
    // {
    //   'prop': PropertyUpdate
    // }
  }
  ngAfterContentInit() {
    // Component content has been initialized
    console.log("ngAfterContentInit");
  }
  ngAfterContentChecked() {
    // Component content has been checked
    console.log("ngAfterContentChecked");
  }
```

```
   ngAfterViewInit() {
   // Component views are initialized
     console.log("ngAfterViewInit");
   }
   ngAfterViewChecked() {
   // Component views have been checked
     console.log("ngAfterViewChecked");
   }
}
```

Listing 1.5 contains all the Angular lifecycle methods, and each method contains console.log() so that you can see the order in which the methods are executed.

Launch the application by navigating to the src subdirectory of the LifeCycle application, and invoke the following command:

ng serve

Navigate to localhost:4200 in a Chrome browser session and open Chrome Inspector, after which you will see the following output in the Console tab:

```
ngOnInit
ngDoCheck
ngAfterContentInit
ngAfterContentChecked
ngAfterViewInit
ngAfterViewChecked
ngDoCheck
ngAfterContentChecked
ngAfterViewChecked
```

The preceding lifecycle methods are useful if you need to execute some custom code in a specific method. The next section shows you how to add CSS3 animation effects in Angular applications.

CSS3 Animation Effects in Angular

This section enhances the code sample in an earlier section by adding a CSS3 animation effect. If you are unfamiliar with CSS3, there are many online tutorials available. If you have no interest in Angular applications with custom CSS3 code, feel free to skip this section.

Now copy the directory SimpleCSS3Anim from the companion files into a convenient location. Listing 1.6 displays the content of app.component.ts, which illustrates how to change the color of list items whenever users hover over each list item with their mouse.

LISTING 1.6 app.component.ts

```
import {Component} from '@angular/core';

@Component({
    selector: 'app-root',
    template: `
      <h2>Employee Information</h2>
      <ul>
        <li *ngFor="let emp of employees">
        {{emp.fname}} {{emp.lname}} lives in {{emp.city}}
        </li>
      </ul>
      `,
    styles: [`
      @keyframes hoveritem {
          0%   {background-color: red;}
          25%  {background-color: #880;}
          50%  {background-color: #ccf;}
          100% {background-color: #f0f;}
      }

      li:hover {
          width: 50%;
          animation-name: hoveritem;
          animation-duration: 4s;
      }
      `]
})
export class AppComponent {
  employees = [];

  constructor() {
    this.employees = [
            {"fname":"Jane","lname":"Jones","city":"San Francisco"},
      {"fname":"John","lname":"Smith","city":"New York"},
```

```
        {"fname":"Dave","lname":"Stone","city":"Seattle"},
        {"fname":"Sara","lname":"Edson","city":"Chicago"}
      ];
    }
}
```

Listing 1.6 contains the `styles` property, which contains a `@keyframes` definition for creating an animation effect involving color changes. The `styles` property also contains an `li:hover` selector that references the `@keyframes` definition and specifies a time duration of 4 seconds for the animation effect. The colors that you see are specified in the `@keyframes` definition. If you have worked with CSS3 animation effects, then `@keyframes` is probably very familiar to you.

Launch the Angular application and navigate to `localhost:4200` in a browser session. When the list of names is displayed, move your mouse slowly over each name and watch how they change color. The text display is shown below, but you need to launch the application to see the color-related transformations:

```
Employee Information
```

- Jane Jones lives in San Francisco
- John Smith lives in New York
- Dave Stone lives in Seattle
- Sara Edson lives in Chicago

Instead of using CSS3 to perform animation effects, you can also do so via Angular functionality, which is illustrated in the next section.

Animation Effects via the "Angular Way"

This section enhances the code in the previous section by creating an animation effect by means of Angular-specific functionality instead of CSS3-based functionality. This section also requires an understanding of how to instantiate a custom TypeScript class, which in this section is the custom `Emp` class that is defined in Listing 1.7.

Now copy the directory `SimpleAnimation` from the companion disc into a convenient location. Listing 1.7 displays the content of `app.component.ts`, which illustrates how to move the position of the `<li>` elements whenever users hover over them with their mouse.

LISTING 1.7 app.component.ts

```typescript
// part #1: new import statement
import { Component, Input } from '@angular/core';

import {trigger, state, style, transition, animate} from
'@angular/animations';

// part #2: new Emp class
class Emp {
  constructor(public fname: string,
              public lname: string,
              public city:  string,
              public state = 'inactive') {

  }


  toggleState() {
     this.state = (this.state==='active' ? 'inactive' :
'active');
        console.log(this.fname+"  "+"new  state  =  "+this.
state);
   }
}
@Component({
   selector: 'app-root',

   // part #3: new animations property
   animations: [
     trigger('empState', [
       state('inactive', style({
         backgroundColor: '#eee',
         transform: 'scale(1)'
       })),
       state('active',    style({
         backgroundColor: '#cfd8dc',
       transform: 'scale(1.1)'
       })),
        transition('inactive => active', animate('100ms
ease-in')),
        transition('active => inactive', animate('100ms
ease-out'))
```

```
      ])
    ],
    template: `
      <h2>Employee Information</h2>
      <ul>
        <li *ngFor="let emp of employees"
                  [@empState]="emp.state"
                  (mousemove)="emp.toggleState()">
          {{emp.fname}} {{emp.lname}} lives in {{emp.city}}
        </li>
      </ul>

  })
export class AppComponent {
  employees = [];

  constructor() {
    // part #5: array of Emp objects
    this.employees = [
      new Emp("Jane","Jones","San Francisco"),
      new Emp("John","Smith","New York"),
      new Emp("Dave","Stone","Seattle"),
      new Emp("Sara","Edson","Chicago")
    ];
  }
}
```

Listing 1.7 consists of five modifications to the code in Listing 1.6. Specifically, the section labeled "part #1" is a new `import` statement that replaces the original `import` statement. The section labeled "part #2" is the newly added `Emp` class that holds data for each employee.

The section labeled "part #3" is the new `transitions` property that defines the behavior when an animation event is triggered (which occurs during a `mousemove` event "over" an `<li>` element). The portion in bold (which is not labeled, but is "part #4") in the `ngFor` element essentially binds the `mousemove` event to the `toggleState()` method in the `Emp` class. Finally, the section labeled "part #5" is an array of `Emp` objects that replaces the original array in which each employee is represented as a JSON string.

Launch this Angular application from the command line via `ng serve`, navigate to `localhost:4200`, and then move your mouse over each person's name and observe the "fading" effect. The output in your browser will look like this:

```
Employee Information
```

- Jane Jones lives in San Francisco
- John Smith lives in New York
- Dave Stone lives in Seattle
- Sara Edson lives in Chicago

Although this example is simple, you can extend this code with your own custom modifications to create other CSS3-based animation effects.

Now open the Inspector option in your browser (Chrome or Firefox) and you will see the following type of output:

```
Dave new state = active
Dave new state = inactive
John new state = active
John new state = inactive
Jane new state = inactive
Jane new state = active
Jane new state = inactive
Jane new state = active
Jane new state = inactive
John new state = active
Dave new state = active
Dave new state = inactive
Sara new state = active
Sara new state = inactive
```

A Basic SVG Example in Angular

This section shows you how to specify a custom component that contains SVG code for rendering an SVG element. This example serves as the basis for the SVG code in the next section, which involves dynamically creating and appending an SVG element to the DOM.

Copy the directory SVGEllipse from the companion files into a convenient location. Listing 1.8 displays the content of app.component.ts, which references an Angular custom component in order to render an SVG ellipse.

LISTING 1.8 *app.component.ts*

```
import {Component} from '@angular/core';

@Component({
   selector: 'app-root',
   template: `<div><my-svg></my-svg></div>`
})
export class AppComponent {}
```

Listing 1.8 is very straightforward: the code defines a component whose `template` property contains a custom `<my-svg>` element inside a `<div>` element.

Listing 1.9 displays the contents of `MyEllipse.ts` that contains the SVG code for rendering three overlapping ellipses in SVG.

LISTING 1.9 *MyEllipse.ts*

```
import {Component} from '@angular/core';

@Component({
   selector: 'my-svg',
   template: `
     <svg width="500" height="300">
       <ellipse cx="100" cy="100"
                rx="50" ry="30"
                fill="red"/>
       <ellipse cx="180" cy="100"
                rx="80" ry="40"
                fill="blue"/>
       <ellipse cx="140" cy="140"
                rx="80" ry="40"
                fill="yellow"/>
     </svg>
})
export class MyEllipse{}
```

Listing 1.9 is also straightforward: the `template` property contains the code for an SVG `<svg>` element with the `width` and `height` attributes, which in turn contains a nested SVG `<ellipse>` element with hard-coded values for the required attributes `cx`, `cy`, `rx`, `ry`, and `fill`.

Listing 1.10 displays the contents of `app.module.ts` with the new contents shown in bold.

LISTING 1.10 app.module.ts

```
import {Component}        from '@angular/core';
import { NgModule }       from '@angular/core';
import { BrowserModule } from '@angular/platform-browser';
import { AppComponent }   from './app.component';
import { MyEllipse }      from './MyEllipse;

@NgModule({
   imports:        [ BrowserModule ],
   declarations: [ AppComponent, MyEllipse ],
   bootstrap:      [ AppComponent ]
})
export class AppModule { }
```

Listing 1.10 contains generic code that you are familiar with from previous examples in this chapter, as well as a new `import` statement (shown in bold) involving the `MyEllipse` class. The other modification in Listing 1.10 is the inclusion of the `MyEllipse1` class (shown in bold) in the `declarations` array.

Launch the Angular application in the usual fashion, and in a browser session you will see three colored ellipses in SVG, as shown in Figure 1.2.

In case you are interested, the following links explain how to create SVG gradients and also how to create SVG Gradient Effects in Angular applications:

FIGURE 1.2 Rendering Ellipses in SVG in an Angular Application

https://developer.mozilla.org/en-US/docs/Web/SVG/Tutorial/Gradients

and

https://medium.com/@OlegVaraksin/how-to-proper-use-svg-gradients-in-angularjs-2-3241672e4de2#.oah0e9z1k

Detecting Mouse Positions in Angular Applications

This section shows you how to detect a mouse position inside an SVG
<svg> element. Copy the directory SVGMouseMove from the companion
files into a convenient location. Listing 1.11 displays the content of app.
component.ts, which illustrates how to detect a mousemove event and
to display the coordinates of the current mouse position.

LISTING 1.11 app.component.ts

```
import {Component} from '@angular/core';

@Component({
    selector: 'app-root',
    template: `<div><mouse-move></mouse-move></div>`
})
class AppComponent {}
```

Listing 1.11 contains a template property that consists of a <div> element that contains a nested <mouse-move> element, where the latter is
the value of the selector property in the custom component MouseMove
that is defined in the custom TypeScript file mousemove.ts.

In essence, the component AppComponent "delegates" the handling of
the mousemove events to the MouseMove component, which defines the
mouseMove() function in order to handle such events.

Listing 1.12 displays the content of mousemove.ts, which illustrates
how to detect a mousemove event and display the coordinates of the current mouse position.

LISTING 1.12 mousemove.ts

```
import {Component} from '@angular/core';

@Component({
  selector: 'mouse-move',
  template: `<svg id="svg" width="600px" height="400px"
            (mousemove)="mouseMove($event)">
        </svg>
`
})
export class MouseMove{
    mouseMove(event) {
```

```
        console.log("Position  x:  "+event.clientX+"  y:
"+event.clientY);
    }
}
```

Listing 1.12 contains the `mouseMove()` method whose lone argument `event` is an object that contains information about the mouse event (such as its location). The `mouseMove()` method contains a `console.log()` statement that simply displays the x-coordinate and the y-coordinate of the location of the mouse click event.

Notice the two new code snippets (shown in bold) in `app.module.ts` displayed in Listing 1.13, which includes the `MouseMove` class.

LISTING 1.13 app.module.ts

```
import { NgModule }       from '@angular/core';
import { BrowserModule } from '@angular/platform-browser';
import { AppComponent }  from './app.component';
import { MouseMove }      from './Mousemove';

@NgModule({
  imports:       [ BrowserModule ],
  declarations:  [ AppComponent, MouseMove ],
  bootstrap:     [ AppComponent ]
})
export class AppModule { }
```

Listing 1.13 imports the `MouseMove` class and adds this class to the `declarations` property (both of which are shown in bold).

Now launch this Angular application, and in new browser session, navigate to `View -> Developer -> JavaScript Console` (for a Chrome browser) to display the console. As you move your mouse around the screen, you will see the following type of output displayed in the console:

```
Position x: 506 y: 254 mousemove.ts:12:13
Position x: 505 y: 255 mousemove.ts:12:13
Position x: 505 y: 258 mousemove.ts:12:13
Position x: 504 y: 259 mousemove.ts:12:13
Position x: 503 y: 261 mousemove.ts:12:13
Position x: 502 y: 262 mousemove.ts:12:13
Position x: 501 y: 263 mousemove.ts:12:13
Position x: 505 y: 263 mousemove.ts:12:13
```

```
Position x: 510 y: 262 mousemove.ts:12:13
Position x: 515 y: 261 mousemove.ts:12:13
Position x: 520 y: 260 mousemove.ts:12:13
Position x: 526 y: 259 mousemove.ts:12:13
```

The next section combines SVG graphs with mouse movement in order to render a set of "follow the mouse" SVG ellipses.

Angular and Follow-the-Mouse in SVG

The code sample in this section relies on mouse-related events in order to create dynamic graphics effects. Copy the directory SVGFollowMe from the companion files into a convenient location.

Listing 1.14 displays the content of app.component.ts, which illustrates how to reference a custom Angular component that renders an SVG <ellipse> element at the current mouse position.

LISTING 1.14 app.component.ts

```
import {Component} from '@angular/core';

@Component({
    selector: 'app-root',
    template: `<div><mouse-move></mouse-move></div>`
})
export class AppComponent {}
```

As you can see, the template property in Listing 1.14 specifies a <div> element that contains a custom <mouse-move> element.

Listing 1.15 displays the content of MouseMove.ts, which illustrates how to reference a custom Angular component that renders an SVG <ellipse> element at the current mouse position.

LISTING 1.15 MouseMove.ts

```
import {Component} from '@angular/core';

@Component({
 selector: 'mouse-move',
 template: `<svg id="svg" width="600" height="400"
            (mousemove)="mouseMove($event)">
```

```
        </svg>

})
export class MouseMove {
    radiusX = "25";
    radiusY = "50";

    mouseMove(event) {
        var svgns = "http://www.w3.org/2000/svg";
        var svg   = document.getElementById("svg");
        var colors = ["#ff0000", "#88ff00", "#3333ff"];

        var sum = Math.floor(event.clientX+event.clientY);

        var  ellipse   =   document.createElementNS(svgns,
"ellipse");
        ellipse.setAttribute("cx", event.clientX);
        ellipse.setAttribute("cy", event.clientY);
        ellipse.setAttribute("rx", this.radiusX);
        ellipse.setAttribute("ry", this.radiusY);
        ellipse.setAttribute("fill", colors[sum % colors.
length]);
        svg.appendChild(ellipse);
    }
}
```

Listing 1.15 contains a `template` property that defines an SVG `<svg>` element. The `(mousemove)` event handler is executed whenever users move their mouse, which in turn executes the custom method `mouse-Move()` that is defined in the `MouseMove` class.

Notice that the `mouseMove` method accepts an `event` argument, which is an object that provides the coordinates of the location of each mouse-move event. The coordinates of the current point are specified by `event.clientX` and `event.clientY`, which are the x-coordinate and the y-coordinate, respectively, of the current mouse position.

The next code block in the `mouseMove` method dynamically creates an SVG `<ellipse>` method, sets the values of the five required attributes for an ellipse (see the previous section for the details), and then appends the newly created SVG `<ellipse>` method to the DOM. This functionality creates a "follow-the-mouse" effect that you can see when you launch the Angular application code in this section.

Note that the final line of code in the `mouseMove` method appends an SVG `<ellipse>` element directly to the DOM, which is better to avoid if it's possible to do so; however, this code sample is for the purpose of illustration.

Listing 1.16 displays the content of `app.module.ts`, with the new content of `app.component.ts` shown in bold.

LISTING 1.16 app.module.ts

```
import { BrowserModule } from '@angular/platform-browser';
import { NgModule }      from '@angular/core';
import { AppComponent }  from './app.component';
import { MouseMove }     from './MouseMove';

@NgModule({
  declarations: [ AppComponent, MouseMove ],
  imports: [
    BrowserModule
  ],
  providers: [],
  bootstrap: [AppComponent]
})
export class AppModule { }
```

The code in Listing 1.16 follows a familiar pattern: start with the "baseline" code, add an `import` statement that references an exported TypeScript class (which is `MouseMove` in this example), and also add that same TypeScript class to the `declarations` array.

Launch the Angular application in the usual manner, and then slowly move your mouse and watch you will see different colored SVG ellipses rendered near your mouse. Figure 1.3 shows a sample of the output that can be generated in this application.

In case you are looking for ideas for enhancing this code sample, modify the code in `MouseMove.ts` so that new SVG ellipses are "centered" underneath your mouse.

FIGURE 1.3 Ellipses in a "Follow-the-Mouse" in SVG in an Angular Application

Angular and SVG Charts

This section creates a child component and uses mouse-related events to create dynamic graphics effects. As you will see, the graphics effects are very rudimentary; however, they provide a starting point from which you can add custom enhancements.

Now copy the directory SVGCharts from the companion disc into a convenient location. Listing 1.17 displays the content of app.component. ts, whose template code specifies a <div> element that contains a custom <mycharts> element (as a child element) in which the SVG-based charts will be rendered.

NOTE *When you launch this application you will see a blank screen. However, each time you click inside the screen, you will see a different bar chart, scatter chart, and line graph.*

LISTING 1.17 app.component.ts

```
import { Component } from '@angular/core';

@Component({
    selector: 'app-root',
    template: '<div><mycharts></mycharts></div>'
})
export class AppComponent { }
```

Listing 1.17 displays the content of app.component.ts, whose template property specifies a custom <mycharts> element as a child of a <div> element. As you will see, the charts and graphs in this code sample are rendered inside the <mycharts> element.

Listing 1.18 displays the content of app.module.ts, which specifies the custom component MyGraphics that contains the SVG-based code.

LISTING 1.18 app.module.ts

```
import { BrowserModule } from '@angular/platform-browser';
import { NgModule }      from '@angular/core';
import { AppComponent }  from './app.component';
import { MyGraphics }    from './MyGraphics';

@NgModule({
    declarations: [
```

```
      AppComponent,
      MyGraphics
   ],
   imports: [
      BrowserModule
   ],
   providers: [],
   bootstrap: [AppComponent]
})
export class AppModule { }
```

Listing 1.18 contains a code snippet to import the MyGraphics class and also updates the declarations property to include the MyGraphics class. The remaining code in Listing 1.18 is the same as the code that you have seen in previous code samples.

Listing 1.19 displays the contents of MyGraphics.ts that contains the SVG-based code for rendering a line graph, scatter plot, and a bar chart.

LISTING 1.19 MyGraphics.ts

```
import { BrowserModule } from '@angular/platform-browser';
import {Component} from '@angular/core';

@Component({
  selector: 'mycharts',
  template: `<svg id="svg" width="600" height="600"
           (click)="drawCharts($event)">
           </svg>

})
export class MyGraphics {
    public scatterWidth:number   = 400;
    public scatterHeight:number  = 400;
    public scatterCount:number   = 40;
    public offsetX:number        = 0;
    public offsetY:number        = 0;
    public clickCount:number     = 0;
    public radius:number         = 5;
    public barCount:number       = 15;
    public barWidth:number       = 30;
    public barHeight:number      = 50;
```

```
public maxBarHeight:number  = 200;
public barHeights:any       = [];
public polyPts:any          = "";

publiccolors=["#ff0000","#00ff00","#ffc800","#0000ff"];
public svgns  = "http://www.w3.org/2000/svg";

private generateBarHeights() {
   for(let i=0; i<this.barCount; i++) {
        this.barHeights[i]   =   ""+Math.random()*this.
maxBarHeight;
     }
   }

   drawCharts(event) {
      this.generateBarHeights();
      this.drawBarChart();
      this.drawScatterPlot();
      this.drawLineGraph();
      this.clickCount += 1;
   }

   private drawBarChart() {
     var svg = document.getElementById("svg");
      var gElem = document.createElementNS(this.svgns,
"g");
     svg.appendChild(gElem);

     for(let i=0; i<this.barCount; i++) {
         var rect = document.createElementNS(this.svgns,
"rect");
         rect.setAttribute("x",       ""+i*this.barWidth);
            rect.setAttribute("y",         ""+(200-this.
barHeights[i]));
           rect.setAttribute("width",  ""+this.barWidth);
        rect.setAttribute("height", ""+this.barHeights[i]);

            rect.setAttribute("fill",  this.colors[i%this.
colors.length]);
          gElem.appendChild(rect);
     }
     svg.appendChild(gElem);
   }
```

```
    private drawLineGraph() {
        var svg = document.getElementById("svg");
         var gElem = document.createElementNS(this.svgns,
"g");
        svg.appendChild(gElem);

        // construct a line graph
        for ( let i = 0; i < this.barCount; i++) {
             this.polyPts += (i*this.barWidth).toString() +
"," +

                            (600-this.barHeights[i]) + " ";
        }

        var polyline = document.createElementNS(this.svgns,
"polyline");
        polyline.setAttribute("points", ""+this.polyPts);
        polyline.setAttribute("style",
                    "fill:none;stroke:blue;stroke-width:3");
        gElem.appendChild(polyline);
        svg.appendChild(gElem);
    }

  private drawScatterPlot() {
        var svg = document.getElementById("svg");
         var gElem = document.createElementNS(this.svgns,
"g");
        svg.appendChild(gElem);

        // construct circles
        for(let i=0; i<this.scatterCount; i++) {
           var circle = document.createElementNS(this.svgns,
"circle");
            this.offsetX = this.scatterWidth*Math.random();
            this.offsetY = 200*Math.random();
            circle.setAttribute("cx", ""+this.offsetX);
          circle.setAttribute("cy", ""+(200+this.offsetY));
            circle.setAttribute("r",  ""+this.radius);

            circle.setAttribute("fill", this.colors[i%this.
colors.length]);
            gElem.appendChild(circle);
```

```
    }
    svg.appendChild(gElem);
  }
}
```

Listing 1.19 starts with the usual `import` statements, followed by a template property that specifies an SVG `<svg>` element whose `width` and `width` attributes are both 600 pixels (and you can specify different values if you need to do so). Notice that the SVG `<svg>` element also specifies an Angular (`click`) attribute, as shown here:

```
template: `<svg id="svg" width="600" width ="600"
             (click)="drawCharts($event)">
          </svg>
```

When users click anywhere inside the SVG `<svg>` element, the `drawCharts()` method is executed, whose content is reproduced here:

```
drawCharts(event) {
    this.generateBarHeights();
    this.drawBarChart();
    this.drawScatterPlot();
    this.drawLineGraph();
    this.clickCount += 1;
}
```

Notice that the `drawCharts()` method also receives an `event` argument, which is actually an object that contains information about the location of the mouse event. This method invokes five other methods, starting with the `generateBarHeights()` method that populates the `barHeights` array with a set of random numbers that represent the height of each bar element in the bar chart.

Next, the `drawCharts()` method invokes the `drawBarChart()` method, which starts by obtaining a reference to the existing `<svg>` element (specified in the `template` property), creating a new SVG `<g>` element called `gElem`, and then appending the newly created SVG `<g>` element to the SVG `<svg>` element, as shown here:

```
var svg = document.getElementById("svg");
var gElem = document.createElementNS(this.svgns, "g");
svg.appendChild(gElem);
```

Although it's not absolutely necessary, it's a good idea to place the bar chart inside an <g> element as a way to "modularize" the graphics (the same thing is done for the scatter plot and the line graph).

The next code block consists of a `for` loop that creates an SVG <rect> element, populates its attributes appropriately, and then appends the SVG <rect> element to the existing SVG <g> element, as shown here:

```
for(let i=0; i<this.barCount; i++) {
    var  rect  =  document.createElementNS(this.svgns,
"rect");
    rect.setAttribute("x",       ""+i*this.barWidth);
  rect.setAttribute("y",     ""+(200-this.barHeights[i]));
    rect.setAttribute("width",  ""+this.barWidth);
    rect.setAttribute("height", ""+this.barHeights[i]);

    rect.setAttribute("fill", this.colors[i%this.colors.
length]);
    gElem.appendChild(rect);
}
svg.appendChild(gElem);
```

Next, the `drawCharts()` method invokes the `drawScatterPlot()` method, that also starts with the same code block as `drawBarChart()` that pertains to the SVG <svg> element. This method also contains a `for` loop that creates a set of SVG <circle> elements, populates their attributes appropriately, and then appends them to the third <g> element.

Finally, the `drawCharts()` method invokes the `drawLineGraph()` method, which also starts with the same code block as `drawBarChart()` that pertains to the SVG <svg> element. This method contains a `for` loop that updates the string `polyPts` with the x-coordinate and y-coordinate of the top-level vertex of each bar element, as shown here:

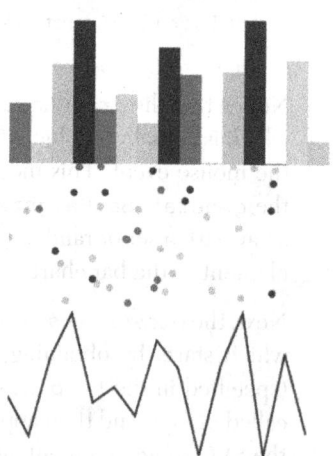

FIGURE 1.4 An SVG bar chart, scatter plot, and line graph in an Angular Application

```
for ( let i = 0; i < this.barCount; i++) {
```

```
      this.polyPts += (i*this.barWidth).toString() + "," +
                          (600-this.barHeights[i]) + " ";
}
```

The next portion of the `drawLineGraph()` method creates a new SVG `<polyline>` element, sets its `points` attribute equal to the content of `polyPts`, and then appends the SVG `<polyline>` element to the SVG `<svg>` element.

Launch this Angular application, and then, in the new browser session, click anywhere on the screen and you will see a rudimentary bar chart, scatter plot, and line graph, as shown in Figure 1.4.

D3 Animation and Angular

The previous two sections showed you examples of Angular applications with SVG, and this section shows you how to create D3 animation effects with Angular. Note that the code sample in this section also appends the SVG elements directly to the DOM.

In case you don't already know, D3 is an open source toolkit that provides a JavaScript-based layer of abstraction over SVG. Fortunately, the attributes of every SVG element have the same name in D3 (so you can leverage your knowledge of SVG in D3, or vice versa).

Copy the directory `D3Anim` from the companion disc into a convenient location. Listing 1.20 displays the content of `app.component.ts`, which illustrates how to use D3 to render basic SVG graphics in an Angular application.

LISTING 1.20 app.component.ts

```
import { Component, ViewChild, ElementRef } from '@
angular/core';
import * as d3 from 'd3';

// remember: npm install d3 --save

@Component({
  selector: 'app-root',
  template: `<app-root><mysvg></mysvg></app-root>`,
  styleUrls: ['./app.component.css']
})
```

```
export class AppComponent {
  constructor() {
    var width = 800, height = 500, duration=2000;
    var radius = 30, moveCount = 0, index = 0;
    var circleColors = ["red", "yellow", "green", "blue"];

    var svg = d3.select("body")
                .append("svg")
                .attr("width",  width)
                .attr("height", height);

    svg.on("mousemove", function() {
      index = (++moveCount) % circleColors.length;


      var circle = svg.append("circle")
                             .attr("cx",  (width-100)*Math.
random())
                             .attr("cy",  (height-100)*Math.
random())
                      .attr("r",  radius)
                      .attr("fill", circleColors[index])
                      .transition()
                      .duration(duration)
                      .attr("transform", function() {
                          return "scale(0.5, 0.5)";
                          //return "rotate(-20)";
                      })
    });
  }
}
```

Listing 1.20 starts with two `import` statements, followed by a comment statement that serves as a reminder that you need to install d3 in this Angular application.

Next, the `template` property contains a `<div>` element that is available in the `ngAfterContentInit` method, which in turn simply invokes the `createSVG()` method that populates an SVG `<svg>` element with four 2D shapes: a circle, an ellipse, a rectangle, and a line segment.

Note the `@ViewChild` decorator that defines the variable `mysvg` that has type `ElementRef`. This variable "links" the `<div>` element in the `template` property with the variable `svgElement` that is defined in the `createSVG()` method:

```
let svgElement = this.mysvg.nativeElement;
```

Notice how the various SVG elements are dynamically created and how their mandatory attributes (which depend on the SVG element in question) are assigned values via the `attr()` method, as shown here (and in the preceding code block, as well):

```
// append a circle
svg.append("circle")
   .attr("cx", cx)
   .attr("cy", cy)
   .attr("r",  radius1)
   .attr("fill", colors[0]);
```

After you learn the mandatory attribute names for the SVG elements, you can use the preceding syntax to create and append such elements to the DOM.

Listing 1.21 displays the content of `app.module.ts`, with the new code shown in bold.

LISTING 1.21 app.module.ts

```
import { BrowserModule }      from '@angular/platform-
browser';
import { NgModule }          from '@angular/core';
import { AppComponent }      from './app.component';
import { NO_ERRORS_SCHEMA } from '@angular/core';

@NgModule({
  declarations: [
    AppComponent
  ],
  imports: [
    BrowserModule
  ],
  providers: [],
  schemas: [NO_ERRORS_SCHEMA],
  bootstrap: [AppComponent]
})
export class AppModule { }
```

Listing 1.21 contains code that is already familiar to you, along with the following new `import` statement:

```
import { NO_ERRORS_SCHEMA } from '@angular/core';
```

The preceding code snippet allows us add any element that is created in the D3-based code without generating an error message. Notice that the `schemas` property in Listing 1.21 must also be updated to include `NO_ERRORS_SCHEMA`.

Launch this Angular application and then in the new browser session click anywhere on the screen and you will see a "cascade" of animated circles.

Launch the Angular application in the usual manner. Then, slowly move your mouse and observe the different colored SVG ellipses rendered near your mouse. Figure 1.5 shows a sample of the output that can be generated in this application.

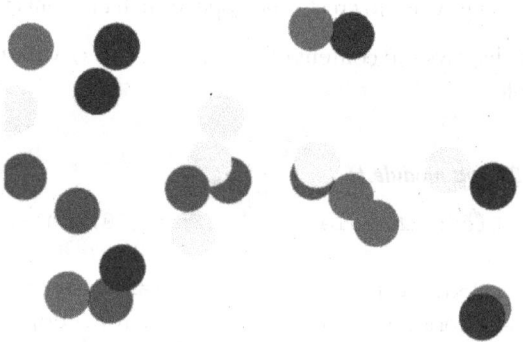

FIGURE 1.5 Rendering Circles with D3 in an Angular Application

You can also find many similar code samples involving SVG and Angular (with an older beta-version Angular code) here:

https://github.com/ocampesato/angular2-svg-graphics.

D3 and SVG Animation in Angular

The following code block illustrates how to add D3-based animation effects to the SVG `<circle>` element in the `D3Angular` Angular application:

```
svg.on("mousemove", function() {
  index = (++moveCount) % circleColors.length;
```

```
var circle = svg.append("circle")
             .attr("cx", (width-100)*Math.random())
             .attr("cy", (height-100)*Math.random())
             .attr("r",  radius)
             .attr("fill", circleColors[index])
             .transition()
             .duration(duration)
             .attr("transform", function() {
                 return "scale(0.5, 0.5)";
                //return "rotate(-20)";
             })
});
```

The code inside the preceding event handler is executed during each `mousemove` event, accompanied by the dynamic creation of an SVG `<ellipse>` element. The new functionality involves the `transition()` method, the `duration()` method, and setting the `transform` attribute, all of which are shown in bold in the preceding code block.

As you can see, the `transform` attribute is set to a `scale()` value, which sets the width and height to `50%` of their initial value during an interval of 2 seconds (which equals `2000` milliseconds), thereby creating an animation effect.

Summary

This chapter started with a description overview of Angular and its hierarchical component-based structure. Next, you learned about the Angular CLI utility `ng` and how to create an Angular "Hello World" application with the `ng` utility.

You also learned about the TypeScript files `app.component.ts` and `app.module.ts`, which contain the TypeScript code for Angular applications. Next you learned about creating Angular applications for rendering SVG-based ellipses and charts, followed by D3-based animation effects.

UI CONTROLS, USER INPUT, AND PIPES

This chapter contains Angular applications with an assortment of UI Controls, along with code samples that involve user input. Note that the Angular applications in this chapter render UI Controls using standard HTML syntax instead of using functionality that is specific to Angular.

The first part of this chapter contains a simple example of displaying a hard-coded list of strings, followed by an Angular application that supports click events on a button. The second part of this chapter shows you how to manage lists of items, which includes displaying, adding, and deleting items from a list. You will also learn about Controls and ControlGroups.

The third section contains two examples of displaying a list of user names: the first retrieves user names that are stored as strings in a JavaScript array, and the second retrieves user names that are stored in object literals in a JavaScript array. The third section goes a step further: you will learn how to define a custom user component that contains user-related information (also contained in a JavaScript array). Later in this chapter, you will learn how to make an HTTP GET request to retrieve data (such as user-related information) that you can use to populate a list of items.

The third part of this chapter discusses Angular Pipes. You will see an Angular application that uses async pipes, which can eliminate the need for defining instance variables and also reduce the likelihood of memory leaks in Angular applications.

Now let's create a simple Angular application that displays a hard-coded list of strings via the ngFor directive, as discussed in the next section.

The ngFor Directive in Angular

The code sample in this section displays a hard-coded list of strings via the ngFor directive. This simple code sample is a starting point from which you can create more complex (and more interesting) Angular applications.

Copy the directory SimpleList from the companion files into a convenient location. Listing 2.1 displays the content of app.component.ts, which illustrates how to display a list of items using the *ngFor directive in Angular.

LISTING 2.1 app.component.ts

```
import {Component} from '@angular/core';

@Component({
  selector: 'app-root',
  template: `<div *ngFor="let item of items">
             {{item}}
             </div>`
})
export class AppComponent {
  items = [];

  constructor() {
    this.items = ['one','two','three','four'];
  }
}
```

Listing 2.1 contains a Component annotation that in turn contains the standard selector property. Next, the template property consists of a <div> element that contains the ngFor directive that iterates through the items array and displays each item in that array. Notice that the items array is initialized as an empty array in the AppComponent class, and then its value is set to an array consisting of four strings in the constructor method.

Launch the application in this section and you will see the following output in a browser session:

```
one
two
three
four
```

The next section contains a code sample involving a <button> element, which is probably one of the most common UI controls in HTML Web pages. The file app.component.ts contains the required custom code, and the file app.component.ts contains auto-generated code that does not require any modification.

Displaying a Button in Angular

Copy the directory ButtonClick from the companion files into a convenient location. The file app.component.ts in this section contains all the custom code for this Angular application. Listing 2.2 displays the content of app.component.ts, which illustrates how to render a <button> element and respond to click events by displaying the number of times that users have clicked the <button> element during the current session.

LISTING 2.2 app.component.ts

```
import { Component } from '@angular/core';

@Component({
    selector: 'app-root',
    template: `<div>
                <button (click)="clickMe()">ClickMe</button>
                <p>Click count is now {{clickCount}}</p>
                </div>`,
    styles: [` button {
                color: red;
            }`
            ]
})
export class AppComponent {
    clickCount = 0;

    clickMe() {
        ++this.clickCount;
        console.log("click count: "+this.clickCount);
    }
}
```

Listing 2.2 starts with an import statement followed by the required selector property. Next, the template property contains a <button>

element that responds to click events and a <p> element whose contents are updated whenever users click on the <button> element. As you can see, the value of the term (click) is the clickMe() function (defined in the AppComponent class) that increments and then displays the value of the clickCount variable.

In addition, the styles property specifies a value of red for the <button> element. The styles property is an example of component style, which means that the styles only apply to the template of the given component. In effect, Angular applies CSS locally instead of globally by generating unique attributes that are visible when you click on the Elements tab in Chrome Inspector.

More detailed information regarding component styles in Angular is at

https://angular.io/docs/ts/latest/guide/component-styles.html.

The next portion of Listing 2.2 is the definition of the AppComponent class that contains the clickCount variable that is incremented in the clickMe() function. Now launch the Angular application whose output is displayed in Figure 2.1 (after it has been clicked three times).

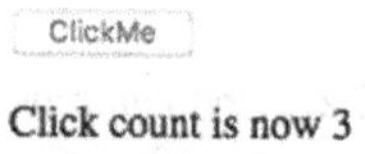

> ClickMe
>
> Click count is now 3

FIGURE 2.1 A <button> Element that Responds to Click Events

Since the file app.module.ts contains auto-generated code that does not require any modification, there is no need to display its contents because they have already been discussed in Chapter 1.

Element versus Property

In Listing 2.2, the selector property matched the element <app-root></app-root> in the HTML page index.html:

```
selector: 'app-root'
```

However, you can also specify a property instead of an element. For example, suppose that index.html contains the following element:

```
<div app-root>Loading. . .</div>
```

In this scenario, you also need to modify the selector property as follows (notice the square brackets):

```
selector: '[app-root]'
```

The next section contains an Angular application that keeps track of the radio button that users have clicked. After that, we'll see how to use the `<button>` element to add new user names to a list of users.

Once again, the file `app.module.ts` contains auto-generated code that does not require any modification, so there is no need to display its contents because they have already been discussed in Chapter 1.

Angular and Radio Buttons

Copy the directory `RadioButtons` from the companion files into a convenient location. Listing 2.3 displays the content of `app.component.ts`, which illustrates how to render a set of radio buttons and keeps track of the radio button that users have clicked.

LISTING 2.3 app.component.ts

```
import {Component} from '@angular/core';

@Component({
  selector: 'app-root',
  template: `
  <h2>{{radioTitle}}</h2>
  <label *ngFor="let item of radioItems">
    <input type="radio" name="options"
           (click)="model.options = item"
           [checked]="item === model.options">
      {{item}}
  </label>
    <p><button        (click)="model.options='option1'">Set
Option #1</button>

})
export class AppComponent {
  radioTitle = "Radio Buttons in Angular";
  radioItems = ['option1','option2','option3','option4'];
  model = { options: 'option3' };
}
```

Listing 2.3 defines the `AppComponent` component whose `template` property contains three parts: a `<label>` element, an `<input>` element, and a `<button>` element. The `<label>` element contains an `ngFor` directive that displays a set of radio buttons by iterating through the `radioItems` array that is defined in the `AppComponent` class.

By default, the first radio button is highlighted. However, when users click on the `<button>` element, the `(click)` attribute of the `<input>` element sets the *current* item to the value of `model.options`, and then the `[checked]` attribute of the `<input>` element sets the *checked* item to the current value of `model.options`. As you can see, the `<input>` element in Listing 2.3 contains functionality that is more compact than using JavaScript to achieve the same results.

Radio Buttons in Angular

○ option1 ○ option2 ◉ option3 ○ option4

Set Option #1

Now launch the Angular application, and you will see the output that is displayed in Figure 2.2.

FIGURE 2.2 A Set of Radio Buttons that Respond to Click Events

The file `app.module.ts` contains auto-generated code that does not require any modification, so we'll skip the discussion of its contents.

Adding Items to a List in Angular

The code sample in this section shows you how to update a list of strings whenever users click on a button. Copy the directory `AddListButton` from the companion files into a convenient location. Listing 2.4 displays the content of `app.component.ts`, which illustrates how to append strings to an array of items whenever users click on a button.

LISTING 2.4 app.component.ts

```
import {Component} from '@angular/core';

@Component({
    selector: 'app-root',
    template: `
        <div>
            <input #fname>
            <button (click)="clickMe(fname.value)">ClickMe
            </button>
            <ul>
                <li *ngFor="let user of users">
```

```
            {{user}}
          </li>
        </ul>
      </div>`
})
export class AppComponent {
    users = ["Jane", "Dave", "Tom"];

    clickMe(user) {
        console.log("new user = "+user);
        this.users.push(user);
/*
        // prevent empty user or duplicates
        if(user is non-null) {
          if(user is duplicate) {
            // display alert message
          } else {
            // display alert message
          }
        } else {
          // display alert message
        }
*/
    }
}
```

Listing 2.4 contains code that is similar to that in Listing 2.3, which displays a list of strings. In addition, the template property in Listing 2.4 contains an `<input>` element so that users can enter text. When users click on the `<button>` element, the `clickMe()` method is invoked with `fname.value` as a parameter, which is a reference to the text in the `<input>` element.

Notice the use of the `#fname` syntax as an identifier for an element, which in this case is an `<input>` element. Thus, the text that users enter in the `<input>` element is referenced via `fname.value`. The following code snippet provides this functionality:

```
<input #fname>
<button (click)="clickMe(fname.value)">ClickMe</button>
```

The `clickMe()` method in the `AppComponent` component contains a `console.log()` statement to display the user-entered text (which is optional) and then appends the new text to the array `user`. The final section in Listing 2.4 consists of a commented-out block of pseudocode that prevents users from entering an empty string or a duplicate string. This code block involves "pure" JavaScript, and the actual code is left as an exercise for you.

Now launch the Angular application, and you will see the output that is displayed in Figure 2.3 when you enter the string "Sara" and click the button element.

In addition, the file `app.module.ts` contains auto-generated code that does not require any modification.

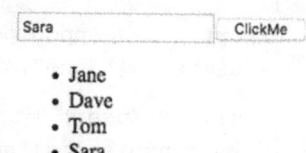

FIGURE 2.3 Adding a Text String to a List

Deleting Items from a List in Angular

This section enhances the code in the previous section by adding a new `<button>` element next to each list item. Now copy the directory `DelListButton` from the companion files into a convenient location. Listing 2.5 displays the content of `app.component.ts`, which illustrates how to delete individual elements from an array of items whenever users click on a button that is adjacent to each array item.

LISTING 2.5 app.component.ts

```
import {Component} from '@angular/core';

@Component({
    selector: 'app-root',
    template: `
     <div>
        <input #fname>
        <button  (click)="clickMe(fname.value)">ClickMe</
        button>
        <ul>
          <li *ngFor="let user of users">
             <button (click)="deleteMe(user)">Delete</
             button>
             {{user}}
          </li>
        </ul>
     </div>`
})
```

```
export class AppComponent {
    users = ["Jane", "Dave", "Tom"];

    deleteMe(user) {
        console.log("delete user = "+user);
        var index = this.users.indexOf(user);

        if(index >=0 ) {
            this.users.splice(index, 1);
        }
    }
    clickMe(user) {
        console.log("new user = "+user);
        this.users.push(user);
/*
        // prevent empty user or duplicates
        if(user is non-null) {
          if(user is duplicate) {
            // display alert message
          } else {
            // display alert message
          }
        } else {
          // display alert message
        }
*/

    }
}
```

Listing 2.5 contains an ngFor directive that displays a list of "pairs" of items, where each "pair" consists of a <button> element followed by a user that is defined in the users array.

When users click on any <button> element, the "associated" user is passed as a parameter to the deleteMe() method, which simply deletes that user from the users array in the AppComponent class. The content of deleteMe() is standard JavaScript code for removing an item from an array. You can replace the block of pseudocode in Listing 2.5 with the same code that you added in Listing 2.4 that prevents users from entering an empty string or a duplicate string.

The file app.module.ts contains auto-generated code that does not require any modification, so there is no need to discuss its contents.

Angular Directives and Child Components

The code sample in this section shows you how to create a child component in Angular that you can reference in an Angular application. Copy the directory `ChildComponent` from the companion files into a convenient location. Listing 2.6 displays the content of `app.component.ts`, which illustrates how to import a custom component (written by you) in an Angular application.

LISTING 2.6 app.component.ts

```
import {Component}    from '@angular/core';

@Component({
    selector: 'app-root',
    template: `<div>Goodbye<child-comp></child-comp>
    World!</div>`
})
export class AppComponent {}
```

Listing 2.6 contains a `template` property that consists of a `<div>` element that contains a nested `<child-comp>` element, where the latter is the value of the `selector` property in the child component `ChildComponent`.

Notice that Listing 2.6 does *not* import the `ChildComponent` class: this class is imported in `app.module.ts` in Listing 2.8 (shown later).

Listing 2.7 displays the contents of `child.component.ts` in the `app` subdirectory.

LISTING 2.7 child.component.ts

```
import {Component} from '@angular/core';

@Component({
    selector: 'child-comp',
    template: `<div>Hello World from ChildComponent!</
    div>`
})
export class ChildComponent{}
```

Listing 2.7 is straightforward: the `template` property specifies a text string that will be displayed inside the `<child-comp>` element that is nested inside the `<div>` element in Listing 2.7.

Listing 2.8 displays the modified contents of `app.module.ts`, which *must* import the class `ChildComponent` from `child.component.ts` and also specify the class `ChildComponent` in the `declarations` property. These additions to the default contents of `app.module.ts` are shown in bold in Listing 2.8.

LISTING 2.8 app.module.ts

```
import { NgModule }       from '@angular/core';
import { BrowserModule } from '@angular/platform-browser';
import { AppComponent }   from './app.component';
import { ChildComponent } from './child.component';

@NgModule({
  imports:      [ BrowserModule ],
  declarations: [ AppComponent, ChildComponent ],
  bootstrap:    [ AppComponent ]
})
export class AppModule { }
```

Listing 2.8 contains a new `import` statement (shown in bold) that imports the `ChildComponent` component from the Typescript file `child.component.ts`. The second modification is the inclusion of `ChildComponent` (shown in bold) in the `declarations` array.

As you can see, Listing 2.8 involves two very simple updates in order to include a child component in an Angular application. With practice, you will become familiar with the sequence of steps that are discussed in this section.

The Constructor and Storing State in Angular

This section contains a code sample that shows how to initialize a variable in a constructor and then reference the value of that variable via interpolation in the `template` property. Now copy the directory `StateComponent` from the companion files into a convenient location. Listing 2.9 displays the content of `app.component.ts`, which shows you how to display various attributes of an "employee."

LISTING 2.9: app.component.ts

```
import {Component} from '@angular/core';

@Component({
  selector: 'app-root',
```

```
    template: '<h3>My name is {{emp.fname}} {{emp.lname}}</
    h3>'
})
export class AppComponent {
    public emp    = {fname:'John',lname:'Smith',city:'San
    Francisco'};
    public name = 'John Smith'

    constructor() {
        this.name = 'Jane Edwards'
        this.emp   = {fname:'Sarah',lname:'Smith',city:'San
        Francisco'};
    }
}
```

Listing 2.9 contains a `constructor()` method that initializes the variable name as well as the literal object `emp`. The `emp` variable is shown in bold in the template property and in two other places inside the `AppComponent` class.

Question: Which name will be displayed when you launch the application?

Answer: The value that is assigned to the `emp` variable in the `constructor`. This behavior is the same as OO-oriented languages such as Java.

Launch this application, and you will see the following output displayed in a Web browser:

My name is Sarah Smith

Keen-eyed readers will notice that we "slipped in" the TypeScript keyword `public` in the declaration of the `emp` and `name` variables. Other possible keywords include `private` and `protected`; all three keywords have the same semantics that they have in Java. If you are unfamiliar with these keywords, you can find online TypeScript tutorials that will explain their purpose. Another handy TypeScript syntax for TypeScript variables that is discussed in the next section.

Private Arguments in the Constructor: a Shortcut

TypeScript provides a short-hand notation for initializing private variables via a constructor. For example, consider the following TypeScript code block:

```
class MyStuff {
    private firstName: string;
```

```
constructor(firstName: string) {
    this.firstName = firstName;
}
}
```

A simpler and equivalent TypeScript code block is shown below:

```
class MyStuff {
    constructor(private firstName: string) {
    }
}
```

TypeScript support for the `private` keyword in a constructor is a convenient feature that reduces some boilerplate code and also eliminates a potential source of error (i.e., misspelled variable names).

As another example, the `constructor()` method in the following code snippet populates an `employees` object with data retrieved from an `EmpService` component (which is defined elsewhere and not important here):

```
constructor(private empService: EmpService) {
    this.employees = this.empService.getEmployees();
}
```

The next section shows you how to use the `*ngIf` directive for conditional logic in Angular applications.

Conditional Logic in Angular

Although previous examples contain a `template` property with a single line of text, Angular enables you to specify multiple lines of text. If you place interpolated variables inside a pair of matching "back ticks," Angular will replace ("interpolate") the variables with their values.

Now copy the directory `IfLogic` from the companion files into a convenient location. Listing 2.10 displays the content of `app.component.ts`, which illustrates how to use the `*ngIf` directive.

LISTING 2.10 app.component.ts

```
import {Component} from '@angular/core';

@Component({
    selector: 'app-root',
```

```
template: `
   <h3>Hello everyone!</h3>
   <h3>My name is {{emp.fname}} {{emp.lname}}</h3>
   <button (click)="moreInfo()">More Details</button>
   <div *ngIf="showMore === true">
      <h3>I live in {{emp.city}}</h3>
   </div>

   <div (click)="showDiv = !showDiv">Toggle Me</div>
   <div *ngIf="showDiv"
        style="color:white;background-color:blue;
        width:25%">Content1</div>
   <div *ngIf="showDiv"
        style="background-color:red;width:25%;">Content2</
        div>

})
export class AppComponent {
  public  emp  =  {fname:'John',lname:'Smith',city:'San
  Francisco'};
  public showMore = false;

  moreInfo() {
    this.showMore = true;
  }
}
```

Listing 2.10 contains some new code in the template property: a <but-
ton> element that invokes the method moreInfo() whenever users click
on the button. After the click event, a <div> element with city-related
information inside an <h3> element is rendered. Notice that this <div>
element is only rendered when showMore is true, which is controlled
via the ngIf directive that checks for the value of showMore. The initial
value of showMore is false, and right after users click the <button> element, its value is set to true, after which the <div> element is displayed.

The new code in AppComponent involves a Boolean variable showMore
(whose initial value is false) and the method moreInfo() that initializes
showMore to true.

The file app.module.ts contains auto-generated code that does not
require any modification, so we'll omit its contents in this section.

Handling User Input

The code sample in this section shows you how to handle user input and introduces the notion of a *service* in Angular. This code sample contains custom code in the file app.component.ts and some updates to the file app.module.ts, along with these three custom files (all of which are discussed in this section):

- todoservice.ts
- todolist.ts
- todoinput.ts

As you will see later, the "source of truth" for a dynamically updated list of to-do items is the TypeScript todos array that is defined in todoservice. ts; this array is accessed indirectly in the other two TypeScript classes. This coding style conforms to object-oriented programming (OOP). If you are unfamiliar with OOP, it's worthwhile to learn this methodology and also highly recommended for moderate and large Angular applications.

Before we look at the custom code, recall that Angular enables you to create a reference to an HTML element, as shown here:

```
<input type="text" #user>
```

The #user syntax creates a reference to the <input> element that enables you to reference {{user.value}} to see its value or {{user. type}} to see the type of the input. Moreover, you can use this reference in the following code block:

```
<p (click)="user.focus()">
  Get the input focus
</p>
<input type="text" #user (keyup)>
{{user.value}}
```

Whenever users click on the <input> element, the focus() method is invoked, and the (keyup) property updates the value in the input during the occurrence of a keyup event.

Now copy the directory TodoInput from the companion files into a convenient location. Listing 2.11 displays the content of app.component. ts, which illustrates how to reference a component that appends user input to an array in Angular.

LISTING 2.11: app.component.ts

```
import {Component}   from '@angular/core';

@Component({
    selector: 'app-root',
    template: `<div>
                <todo-input></todo-input>
                <todo-list></todo-list>
               </div>`
})
export class AppComponent {}
```

Listing 2.11 contains a standard import statement. The template property specifies a <div> element that contains placeholders for the TodoInput and TodoList components.

Listing 2.12 displays the content of todoinput.ts, which illustrates how to display an <input> field and a <button> element in order to capture user input in Angular.

LISTING 2.12 todoinput.ts

```
import {Component}   from '@angular/core';
import {TodoService } from './todoservice';

@Component({
 selector: 'todo-input',
 template: `
   <div>
     <input type="text" #myInput>
     <button (click)="mouseEvent(myInput.value)">Add Item
     </button>
   </div>`
})
export class TodoInput{
    constructor(public todoService:TodoService) {}

    mouseEvent(value) {
       if((value != null) && (value.length > 0)) {
          this.todoService.todos.push(value);
          console.log("todos: "+this.todoService.todos);
       } else {
```

```
        console.log("value must be non-null");
    }
  }
}
```

Listing 2.12 contains a `template` property that consists of a `<div>` element that contains an `<input>` element for user input, followed by a `<button>` element for handling mouse click events.

The `TodoInput` class defines an empty constructor that also initializes an instance of the custom `TodoService` that is imported near the beginning of `todoinput.ts`. This instance contains an array `todos` that is updated with new to-do items whenever users click on the `<button>` element, provided that the new to-do item is not an empty string.

Now let's look at the custom files, starting with Listing 2.13, which displays the content of `todolist.ts` that keeps track of the items in a to-do list.

LISTING 2.13 todolist.ts

```
import {Component}   from '@angular/core';
import {TodoService} from './todoservice';

@Component({
  selector: 'todo-list',
  template: `<div>
            <ul>
            <li *ngFor="let todo of todoService.todos">
                {{todo}}
              </li>
            </ul>
            </div>`
})
export class TodoList {
    constructor(public todoService:TodoService) {}
}
```

Listing 2.13 contains a `template` property whose contents are a `<div>` element that contains an unordered list of items called `todos` (and defined in Listing 2.14), along with an empty constructor that initializes an instance of the `TodoService` custom component. This instance is used in the `template` property in order to iterate through the elements in the `todos` array.

Listing 2.14 displays the content of `todoservice.ts`, which keeps track of the current contents of a to-do list.

LISTING 2.14 todoservice.ts

```
export class TodoService {
    todos = [];
}
```

Listing 2.14 contains a `todos` array that is updated with new to-do items when users click on the `<button>` element in the root component.

Finally, update the contents of `app.module.ts` to include the class shown in bold in Listing 2.15.

LISTING 2.15 app.module.ts

```
import { NgModule }        from '@angular/core';
import { BrowserModule } from '@angular/platform-browser';
import { AppComponent }   from './app.component';
import { TodoInput }      from './todoinput';
import { TodoList }       from './todolist';
import { TodoService }    from './todoservice';

@NgModule({
   imports:        [ BrowserModule ],
   providers:      [ TodoService ],
   declarations:   [ AppComponent, TodoInput, TodoList ],
   bootstrap:      [ AppComponent ]
})
export class AppModule { }
```

As you probably expected, Listing 2.15 imports three to-do-related classes and adds them to the `providers` property and the `declarations` property (shown in bold). Although the number of custom modifications to `app.module.ts` in this section is greater than in the Angular applications that you have seen earlier in this chapter, the updates make sense and are straightforward.

The output for this Angular application is similar to Figure 2.3, so it will not be reproduced here. Keep in mind that although the output looks similar, the important point regarding the code sample in this section is its focus on Angular services. It defines them following the methodology of object oriented programming.

Click Events in Multiple Components

An Angular application can contain multiple components, each of which can declare event handlers with the same name. The Angular application in this section shows you how to add click events to different elements in an Angular application.

Copy the directory ClickItems from the companion files into a convenient location. Listing 2.16 displays the content of app.component.ts, which declares an onClick() event handler for each item in a list of items.

LISTING 2.16 app.component.ts

```
import {Component} from '@angular/core';
import {ClickItem} from './clickitem';

@Component({
   selector: 'app-root',
   styles:   [`li { display: inline; }`],
   template: `
   <div>
     <ul>
      <li><img (click)="onClick(100)"
            width="100" height="100" src="src/sample1.
            png"></li>
      <li><img (click)="onClick(200)"
            width="100" height="100" src="src/sample2.
            png"></li>
      <li><img (click)="onClick(300)"
            width="100" height="100" src="src/sample3.
            png"></li>
     </ul>
   </div>
   `
})
export class AppComponent {
  onClick(id) {
    console.log("you clicked me: "+id);
  }
}
```

The template property in Listing 2.16 displays an unordered list in which each item is a clickable PNG-based image. Whenever users click on one of the images, the `onClick()` method is invoked that simply displays a message via `console.log()`.

Listing 2.17 displays the content of the TypeScript file `clickitem.ts`, which declares an `onClick()` event handler for each item in a list of items.

LISTING 2.17 clickitem.ts

```
import {Component} from '@angular/core';

@Component({
    selector: 'cclick',
    styleUrl: [` li { inline: block } `],
    template: `
      <div>
       <ul>
        <li><img (click)="onClick(100)"
                 width="100"  height="100"  src="assets/
                 sample1.png"></li>
          <li><img (click)="onClick(200)"
                 width="100"  height="100"  src="assets/
                 sample2.png"></li>
          <li><img (click)="onClick(300)"
                 width="100"  height="100"  src="assets/
                 sample3.png"></li>
       </ul>
      </div>

})
export class ClickItem {
  onClick(id) {
    console.log("app.component.ts:  you  clicked  me:
    "+id);
  }
}
```

Listing 2.17 is very similar to Listing 2.16 in terms of functionality, so we won't repeat those details. In addition, the file `app.module.ts` contains the auto-generated code, along with two new code snippets. The first snippet is the following `import` statement that references the file `clickitem.ts`:

```
import { ClickItem }    from './clickitem';
```

The second code snippet specifies the preceding class in the `providers` element, as shown here:

```
providers: [ClickItem],
```

Now launch the application and you will see the three images that are displayed in Figure 2.4.

FIGURE 2.4 Clicking on Images in an Angular Application

Now click on the left-most image, then the middle image, and then the right-most image. Now open the Inspector for the current browser session and you will see these messages:

```
you clicked me: 100
you clicked me: 200
you clicked me: 300
```

Working with @Input, @Output, and EventEmitter

Angular supports the `@Input` and `@Output` annotations in order to pass values between components. The `@Input` annotation is for variables that receive values from a parent component, whereas the `@Output` annotation sends (or "emits") data from a component to its parent component whenever the value of the given variable is modified.

The output from this code sample is "anti-climatic" in the sense that there is a *lot* of code just to produce the following output that is visible in the Inspector tab:

```
constructor parentValue = 77
```

However, the purpose of this code sample is to draw your attention to some of the non-intuitive code snippets (especially in `app.module.ts`).

Now copy the directory `ParentChildEmitters` from the companion files to a convenient location. Listing 2.18 displays the content of `app.component.ts`, which shows you how to update the value of a property of a child component from a parent component.

LISTING 2.18 app.component.ts

```
import {Component}      from '@angular/core';
import {EventEmitter}   from '@angular/core';
import {ChildComponent} from './childcomponent';

@Component({
  selector: 'app-root',
  providers: [ChildComponent],
  template: `
    <div>
      <child-comp [childValue]="parentValue"
        (childValueChange)="reportValueChange($event)">
      </child-comp>
    </div>
  `
})
export class AppComponent {
  public parentValue:number = 77;

  constructor() {
      console.log("constructor  parentValue  =  "+this.
parentValue);
  }

  reportValueChange(event) {
    console.log(event);
  }
}
```

The `template` property in Listing 2.18 has a top-level `<div>` element that contains a `<child-comp>` element that has two attributes, as shown here:

```
<child-comp [childValue]="parentValue"
        (childValueChange)="reportValueChange($event)">
</child-comp>
```

The `[childValue]` attribute assigns the value of `parentValue` to the value of `childValue`. Notice that the variable `parentValue` is defined in `AppComponent`, whereas the variable `childValue` is defined in

`ChildComponent`. This code shows how to pass a value from a parent component to a child component.

Next, the `childValueChange` attribute is assigned the value that is returned from `ChildComponent` to the current ("parent") component. Keep in mind that the attribute `childValueChange` is updated only when the value of `childValue` (in the child component) is modified. This code shows how to pass a value from a child component to a parent component.

Keep in mind the following point: the child component *must* define a variable of type `EventEmitter` (such as `childValueChange`) in order to "emit" a modified value from the child component to the parent component.

The next portion of Listing 2.18 is a simple constructor, followed by the method `reportValueChange` that contains a `console.log()` statement.

Listing 2.19 displays the content of `childcomponent.ts`, which shows you how to update the value of a property of a child component from a parent component.

LISTING 2.19 childcomponent.ts

```
import {Component}    from '@angular/core';
import {Input}        from '@angular/core';
import {Output}       from '@angular/core';
import {EventEmitter} from '@angular/core';

@Component({
  selector: 'child-comp',
  template: `
      <button (click)="decrement();">Subtract</button>
      <input type="text" [value]="childValue">
      <button (click)="increment();">Add</button>
  `
})
export class ChildComponent {
  @Input() childValue:number = 3;
  @Output() childValueChange = new EventEmitter();

  constructor() {
    console.log("constructor    childValue    = "+this.
    childValue);
```

```
    }
    increment() {
      this.childValue++;
      this.childValueChange.emit({
        value: this.childValue
      })
    }
    decrement() {
      this.childValue--;
      this.childValueChange.emit({
        value: this.childValue
      })
    }
  }
```

Listing 2.19 contains a `template` property that specifies three elements: a "decrement" `<button>` element, an `<input>` field where users can enter a number, and an "increment" `<button>` element. The first `<button>` element increments the value `<input>` field, whereas the second `<button>` element decrements the value.

The exported class `ChildComponent` class contains the numeric variable `childValue` that is decorated via `@Input()`, and whose value is set by the parent.

As you can see, the methods `increment()` and `decrement()` increase and decrease the value of `childValue`, respectively. In both cases, the modified value of `childValue` is then "emitted" back to the parent with this code block:

```
this.childValueChange.emit({
    value: this.childValue
})
```

Update the contents of `app.module.ts` as shown in Listing 2.20. Note that the content of Listing 2.20 is different from the content of this file in the previous examples in this chapter.

LISTING 2.20 app.module.ts

```
import { NgModule }          from '@angular/core';
import {CUSTOM_ELEMENTS_SCHEMA} from '@angular/core';
import { BrowserModule } from '@angular/platform-browser';
```

```
import { AppComponent }   from './app.component';
import { ChildComponent } from './childcomponent';

@NgModule({
   imports:       [ BrowserModule ],
   providers:     [ ChildComponent ],
   declarations:  [ AppComponent ],
   bootstrap:     [ AppComponent ],
   schemas:       [CUSTOM_ELEMENTS_SCHEMA]
})
export class AppModule { }
```

When you launch the Angular application in this section, the value that is displayed in the <input> element is 77, which is the value in the parent component, and *not* the value that is assigned in the child component (which is 3). Open the Inspector for the current browser session and you will see the following output:

```
constructor parentValue = 77
```

Keep in mind that if you specify ChildComponent in the declarations property instead of the providers property, you will probably see this error message:

```
"Can't bind to <child-comp> since it isn't a known native
property"
```

Next, Listing 2.20 contains three code snippets shown in bold, all of which are required for this code sample. If you do not include them, you will see the following type of error message in the Inspector tab of your browser:

```
Error: Template parse errors:
Can't bind to 'childValue' since it isn't a known prop-
erty of 'child-comp'.
1. If 'child-comp' is an Angular component and it has 'child-
Value' input, then verify that it is part of this module.
2. If 'child-comp' is a Web Component then add 'CUSTOM_
ELEMENTS_SCHEMA' to the '@NgModule.schemas' of this
component to suppress this message. 3. To allow any
property add 'NO_ERRORS_SCHEMA' to the '@NgModule.sche-
mas' of this component. (" <div> <child-comp [ERROR ->]
[childValue]="parentValue"
(childValueChange)="reportValueChange($event)">       </
child-comp"):
ng:///AppModule/AppComponent.html@2:18
```

Presentational Components

Presentational components receive data as input and generate views as outputs (so they do not maintain application state). Consider the following component:

```
@Component({
  selector: 'student-info',
  template: `<h2>{{studentDetails?.status}}</h2>
    <div class="container">
      <table class="table">
        <tbody>
        <tr *ngFor="let student of students">
            <td>{{student.fname}}</td>
            <td>{{student.lname}}</td>
        </tr>
        </tbody>
      </table>
</div>`
})
export class StudentDetailsComponent {
  @Input()
  studentDetails:StudentDetails;
}
```

The `StudentDetailsComponent` component has primarily presentational responsibilities: the component receives input data and displays that on the screen. As a result, this component is reusable.

By contrast, application-specific components (also called "smart" components) are tightly coupled to a specific Angular application. Thus, a smart component would have a presentation component (but not the converse).

Since data is passed to this component synchronously (not via an `Observable`), the data might not be present initially, which is the reason for including the so-called "Elvis" operator (i.e., the "?" in the template).

Working with Pipes in Angular

Angular supports something called a `pipe` that is somewhat analogous to the Unix pipe "|" command. Angular pipes enable you to specify conditional logic that filters data, which is to say, you can display a subset of data items that is based on your conditional logic.

Angular supports built-in pipes, asynchronous pipes, and support for custom pipes. The next two sections show you some example of built-in pipes, followed by a description of asynchronous pipes. A separate section shows you how to define a custom Angular pipe.

Working with Built-in Pipes

Angular supports various built-in pipes, such as `DatePipe`, `UpperCasePipe`, `LowerCasePipe`, `CurrencyPipe`, and `PercentPipe`. Each of these intuitively named pipes provides the functionality that you would expect: the `DatePipe` supports date values, the `UpperCasePipe` converts strings to uppercase, and so forth.

As a simple example, suppose that the variable food has the value `pizza`. Then the following code snippet displays the string `PIZZA`:

```
<p>I eat too much {{ food | UppercasePipe }} </p>
```

You can also parameterize some Angular pipes, an example of which is shown here:

```
<p>My brother's birthday is {{ birthday | date:"MM/dd/
yy" }} </p>
```

In fact, you can even chain pipes, as shown here:

```
My brother's birthday is {{ birthday | date | uppercase}}
```

In the preceding code snippet, birthday is a custom pipe (written by you). As another example, suppose that an Angular application contains the variable `employees` array that contains JSON-based data. You can display the contents of the array with this code snippet:

```
<div>{{employees | json }}</div>
```

The AsyncPipe

The Angular `AsyncPipe` accepts a `Promise` or `Observable` as input and subscribes to the input automatically, eventually returning the emitted values. Moreover, `AsyncPipe` is stateful: the pipe maintains a subscription to the input `Observable` and keeps delivering values from that `Observable` as they arrive.

The following code block gives you an idea of how to display stock quotes, where the variable `quotes$` is an `Observable`:

```
@Component({
    selector: 'stock-quotes',
    template: `
      <h2>Your Stock Quotes</h2>
      <p>Message: {{ quotes$ | async }}</p>

})
```

Keep in mind that the `AsyncPipe` provides two advantages. First, `AsyncPipe` reduces boilerplate code. Second, there is no need to subscribe or to unsubscribe from an `Observable` (the latter can help avoid memory leaks).

One other point: Angular does not provide pipes for filtering or sorting lists (i.e., there is no `FilterPipe` or `OrderByPipe`) because both can be compute-intensive, which would adversely affect the perceived performance of an application.

The code sample in the next section shows you how to create a custom pipe that displays a filtered list of users based on conditional logic that is defined in custom code.

Creating a Custom Angular Pipe

Copy the directory `SimplePipe` from the companion files into a convenient location. Listing 2.21 displays the content of `app.component.ts`, which illustrates how to define and use a custom pipe in an Angular application that displays a subset of a hard-coded list of users.

LISTING 2.21 *app.component.ts*

```
import { Component } from '@angular/core';
import {User}         from './user.component';
import {MyPipe}       from './pipe.component';

@Component({
  selector: 'app-root',
  template: `
    <div>
      <h2>Complete List of Users:</h2>
      <ul>
```

```
      <li
      *ngFor="let user of userList"
        (mouseover)='mouseEvent(user)'
        [class.chosen]="isSelected(user)">
        {{user.fname}}-{{user.lname}}<br/>
      </li>
      </ul>

      <h2>Filtered List of Users:</h2>
      <ul>
      <li
      *ngFor="let user of userList|MyPipe"
        (mouseover)='mouseEvent(user)'
        [class.chosen]="isSelected(user)">
        {{user.fname}}-{{user.lname}}<br/>
      </li>
      </ul>
    </div>

})
export class AppComponent {
  user:User;
  currentUser:User;
  userList:User[];

  mouseEvent(user:User) {
    console.log("current user: "+user.fname+" "+user.
    lname);
    this.currentUser = user;
  }

  isSelected(user: User): boolean {
    if (!user || !this.currentUser) {
      return false;
    }

    return user.lname === this.currentUser.lname;
//return true;
  }

  constructor() {
    this.userList = [
                new User('Jane','Smith'),
                new User('John','Stone'),
```

```
                    new User('Dave','Jones'),
                    new User('Rick','Heard'),
                  ]
        }
}
```

Listing 2.21 imports the `User` custom class and the `MyPipe` custom class, where the latter is specified in the array of values for the `pipes` property.

Next, the `template` property displays two unordered lists of user names. The first list displayed the complete list, and whenever users hover (with their mouse) over a user in the first list, the current user is set equal to that user via the code in the `mouseEvent()` method (defined in the `AppComponent` class).

Note that the constructor in the `AppComponent` class (shown at the bottom of Listing 2.21) initializes the `userList` array with a set of users, each of which is an instance of the `User` custom component.

The second list displays a filtered list of users based on the conditional logic in the custom pipe called `MyPipe`. Listing 2.22 displays the content of `pipe.component.ts`, which defines the custom pipe `MyPipe` that is referenced in Listing 2.24.

LISTING 2.22 pipe.component.ts

```
import {Component} from '@angular/core';
import {Pipe}      from '@angular/core';

@Pipe({
  name: "MyPipe"
})
export class MyPipe {
  transform(item) {
   return item.filter((item) => item.fname.startsWith("J"));
  //return item.filter((item) => item.lname.endsWith("th"));
  //return item.filter((item) => item.lname.contains("n"));
   }
}
```

Listing 2.22 contains the `MyPipe` class that contains the `transform()` method. There are three examples of how to define the behavior of the pipe, the first of which returns the users whose first name starts with an uppercase `J` (which is admittedly somewhat contrived, but nevertheless illustrative of the pipe-related functionality).

Listing 2.23 displays the contents of the custom component `user.com-ponent.ts` for creating `User` instances, which is also referenced via an import statement in `app.component.ts`.

LISTING 2.23 user.component.ts

```
import {Component} from '@angular/core';

@Component({
  selector: 'my-user',
  template: '<h1></h1>'
})
export class User {
  fname: string;
  lname: string;

  constructor(fname:string, lname:string) {
    this.fname = fname;
    this.lname = lname;
  }
}
```

The content of Listing 2.23 is straightforward: there is a `User` class comprising the fields `fname` and `lname` for the first name and last name, respectively, for each new user, both of which are specified in the constructor whenever a new instance of the `User` class is created.

Finally, we need to update the contents of `app.module.ts`, as shown in Listing 2.24, where the modified contents are shown in bold.

LISTING 2.24 app.module.ts

```
import { NgModule }      from '@angular/core';
import { BrowserModule } from '@angular/platform-browser';
import { AppComponent }  from './app.component';
import { MyPipe }        from './pipe.component';
import { User }          from './user.component';

@NgModule({
  imports:      [ BrowserModule ],
  declarations: [ AppComponent, MyPipe, User ],
  bootstrap:    [ AppComponent ]
})
export class AppModule { }
```

As you can see, Listing 2.24 contains two new `import` statements so that the custom components `MyPipe` and `User` can be referenced in the declarations property. In addition, the `declarations` element includes `MyPipe` and `User` in its array of values.

Launch the application, navigate to `localhost:4200` in a browser session, and after a few moments, you will see the following output:

```
Complete List of Users:
```

- Jane-Smith
- John-Stone
- Dave-Jones
- Rick-Heard

```
Filtered List of Users:
```

- Jane-Smith
- John-Stone

As you can see in the last portion of the preceding output, this Angular application performs a filtering operation that "filters out" the users whose first name does not start with the capital letter `J`.

Now that you understand how to define a basic `Pipe` in Angular, you can experiment with a custom `Pipe` that receives data asynchronously. This type of functionality can be very useful when you need to display data (such as a list or a table) whenever it's updated without the need for "polling" the source of the data.

Additional information regarding Angular pipes is at

https://angular.io/docs/ts/latest/guide/pipes.html.

This concludes the portion of the chapter regarding `Pipes` in Angular. The next section discusses Services in Angular applications.

Reading JSON Data via an Observable in Angular

This section shows you how to read data from a file that contains JSON-based data. Now copy the directory `ReadJSONFile` from the companion files into a convenient location. Listing 2.25 displays the content of `app.component.ts`, which illustrates how to make an `HTTP` request (which returns an `Observable`) to read a `JSON`-based file with `employee` information.

LISTING 2.25 app.component.ts

```
import { Component }    from '@angular/core';
import { Observable}    from 'rxjs';
import { Inject }       from '@angular/core';
import { HttpClient }   from '@angular/common/http';
import { HttpHeaders }  from '@angular/common/http';
declare var $: any;

@Component({
  selector: 'app-root',
  template: `
       <button (click)="httpRequest()">Employee Info</
button>
    <ul>
      <li *ngFor="let emp of employees">
       {{emp.fname}} {{emp.lname}} lives in {{emp.city}}
       </li>
      </ul>

})
export class AppComponent {
  employees : any;

//OLD STYLE: constructor(@Inject(Http) public http:Http)
{}
  constructor(@Inject(HttpClient) public http:HttpCli-
  ent) {}

  httpRequest() {
    this.http.get('assets/employees.json')
      .subscribe(
        // this function runs on success
        data => this.employees = data,
        // this function runs on error
        err => console.log('error reading data: '+err),
        // this function runs on completion
        () => this.userInfo()
      );
  }

  userInfo() {
```

```
   //console.log("employees   =   "+JSON.stringify(this.
employees));
  }
}
```

The `template` property in Listing 2.25 starts with a `<button>` element for making an `HTTP GET` request to retrieve information about employees from a JSON file. The `template` property also contains a `<ul>` element for displaying an unordered list of employee-based data.

The `AppComponent` class contains the variable `employees`, followed by a constructor that initializes the `http` variable that is an instance of the `Http` class. The `httpRequest()` method contains the code for making the `HTTP GET` request that returns an `Observable`. The `subscribe()` method contains the usual code, which in this case also initializes the `employees` array from the contents of the file `employees.json` in the subdirectory `src/assets`.

Listing 2.26 displays the content of `employees.json`, which contains employee related information. This file is located in the `src/assets` subdirectory.

LISTING 2.26 employees.json

```
[
{"fname":"Jane","lname":"Jones","city":"San Francisco"},
{"fname":"John","lname":"Smith","city":"New York"},
{"fname":"Dave","lname":"Stone","city":"Seattle"},
{"fname":"Sara","lname":"Edson","city":"Chicago"}
]
```

Listing 2.27 displays the content of `app.module.ts`, which imports the Angular `HttpClientModule`.

LISTING 2.27 app.module.ts

```
import { NgModule }          from '@angular/core';
import { BrowserModule }     from '@angular/platform-
browser';
import { HttpClientModule } from '@angular/common/http';
import { AppComponent }      from './app.component';

@NgModule({
  imports:      [ BrowserModule, HttpClientModule ],
  declarations: [ AppComponent ],
```

```
bootstrap:    [ AppComponent ]
})
export class AppModule { }
```

Listing 2.27 contains a familiar set of `import` statements, along with `HttpClientModule` that is listed in the array of elements in the `imports` property that is inside the `@NgModule` decorator.

Launch the Angular application, and you will see a button element (not shown here) that you can click, after which you will see the following text:

- Jane Jones lives in San Francisco
- John Smith lives in New York
- Dave Stone lives in Seattle
- Sara Edson lives in Chicago

One other point: earlier versions of Angular required two additional code snippets, neither of which is required for Angular 8 and beyond. In case you encounter Angular applications that use an earlier version of Angular, the redundant code is included below.

The first redundant code snippet is an `import` statement for the `map()` operator, as shown here:

```
import { map } from 'rxjs/operators';
```

The second redundant code snippet involves an invocation of the `map()` operator immediately following the invocation of the `get()` method, as shown here:

```
this.http.get('assets/employees.json')
//.map(res => res.json()) redundant in Angular 8
```

However, the `map()` operator is automatically invoked for us, so it's no longer required; moreover, if you do include this code snippet, you will see an error message.

Upgrading Code from Earlier Angular Versions

Although Angular 8 is mostly backward compatible with earlier versions of Angular, sometimes code modifications are required, especially code that involves `HTTP` requests.

In particular, the previous section showed you that the invocation of the `map()` operator is no longer required in Angular 8. Another change pertains to a redundant `import` statement and a modification to another `import` statement.

Specifically, suppose that you see the following error messages when you compile an Angular 8 application:

```
Error: Can't resolve 'rxjs/Rx'
```

```
Module not found Error: Can't resolve '@angular/http'
Error: Unexpected value 'HttpClient' imported by the
module 'AppModule'. Please add a @NgModule annotation.
```

You need to update the code in `app.component.ts` as well as `app.module.ts` with the appropriate code for Angular 8, as shown here for `app.component.ts`:

```
// import { Observable } from 'rxjs/Observable';    // old
import { Observable }  from 'rxjs';                  // new

// import { Http }       from '@angular/http';       // old
import { Http }         from '@angular/common/http'; // new

import { HttpClient }  from '@angular/common/http'; // new
import { HttpHeaders } from '@angular/common/http'; // new

// import 'rxjs/Rx';                                 // old
```

Here are the changes to `app.module.ts`:

```
//import {HttpModule}    from '@angular/http';       // old
import {HttpClientModule} from '@angular/common/http';
// new

imports: [
  BrowserModule,
  HttpClientModule,            // new
],
declarations: [
  AppComponent,
  HttpClientModule            // new
],
```

The preceding changes to `app.component.ts` and `app.module.ts` are precisely the changes that have been made to the Angular application `ReadJSONFile` (discussed in the previous section) in order to upgrade to an Angular 8 application. In an ideal scenario, these changes will work for your application as well, which will save you some debugging effort.

However, please keep in mind that you might need to make other modifications to the code in your Angular application.

Reading Multiple Files with JSON Data in Angular

This section shows you how to read data from several files that contain JSON-based data. Now copy the directory `ReadMultipleJSONFiles` from the companion files into a convenient location. Listing 2.28 displays the content of `app.component.ts`, which illustrates how to make multiple `HTTP` requests (which returns an `Observable`) to read a `JSON` -based files with `customer` information, `employee` information, and `relative` information.

LISTING 2.28 app.component.ts

```
import { Component } from '@angular/core';
import { Observable } from 'rxjs';
import { HttpClient } from '@angular/common/http';

@Component({
  selector: 'app-root',
  styleUrls: ['./app.component.css'],
  template:`
    <h2>Angular HTTP and Observables</h2>
    <h3>Some of our Employees</h3>
    <ul>
      <li *ngFor="let emp of employees">
        {{emp.fname}} {{emp.lname}} lives in {{emp.city}}
      </li>
    </ul>
    <h3>Some of our Customers</h3>
    <ul>
      <li *ngFor="let cust of customers">
          {{cust.fname}} {{cust.lname}} lives in {{cust.
city}}
      </li>
    </ul>
    <h3>Some of our Relatives</h3>
    <ul>
      <li *ngFor="let rel of relatives">
        {{rel.fname}} {{rel.lname}} lives in {{rel.city}}
      </li>
```

```
      </ul>
})
export class AppComponent {
  public employees : any = [];
  public customers : any = [];
  public relatives : any = [];
  constructor(private http:HttpClient) {
    //this.getCustomers();
    //this.getEmployees();
    //this.getRelatives();
      this.getEveryone();
  }

  getCustomers() {
    this.http.get('assets/customers.json')
      .subscribe(
        // this function runs on success
        data => { this.customers = data },
        // this function runs on error
        err => console.log('error reading customer data:
        '+err),
        // this function runs on completion
        () => console.log('Loading customers completed')
      );
  }

  getEmployees() {
    this.http.get('assets/employees.json')
      .subscribe(
        // this function runs on success
        data => { this.employees = data },
        // this function runs on error
        err => console.log('error reading employee data:
'+err),
        // this function runs on completion
        () => console.log('Loading employees completed')
      );
  }

  getRelatives() {
    this.http.get('assets/relatives.json')
```

```
      .subscribe(
        // this function runs on success
        data => { this.relatives = data },
        // this function runs on error
        err => console.log('error reading relatives data:
'+err),
        // this function runs on completion
        () => console.log('Loading relatives completed')
      );
  }

  getEveryone() {
    this.getCustomers();
    this.getEmployees();
    this.getRelatives();
  }

  infoResults() {
    console.log('inside infoResults');
    console.log('this.customers:',this.customers);
    console.log('this.employees:',this.employees);
    console.log('this.relatives:',this.relatives);
  }
}
```

The `template` property in Listing 2.28 contains three very similar blocks of code that all use `ngFor` to display information about customers, employees, and relatives. Since each code block resembles the code with `ngFor` in Listing 2.25, read the associated description for the details about their contents.

The `AppComponent` class contains the array-based variables `customers`, `employees`, and `relatives`. Next a constructor initializes the `http` variable that is an instance of the `HttpClient` class, as shown here:

```
constructor(private http:HttpClient) {
  //this.getCustomers();
  //this.getEmployees();
  //this.getRelatives();
    this.getEveryone();
}
```

Notice that the constructor contains three commented-out methods. As you will see later, these three methods retrieve data from the JSON-based files customers.json, employees.json, and relatives.json. The getEveryone() method is a convenience method that invokes the other three methods to retrieve all three types of data.

Although these three methods are similar to the code in Listing 2.25, let's take a quick look at the contents of the getCustomers() method:

```
getCustomers() {
    this.http.get('assets/customers.json')
      .subscribe(
        // this function runs on success
        data => { this.customers = data },
        // this function runs on error
            err => console.log('error reading customer
data:'+err),
        // this function runs on completion
        () => console.log('Loading customers completed')
      );
}
```

The preceding code makes an HTTP GET request when the subscribe() method is invoked, and if it's successful, the variable customers is populated with the contents of the file customers.json. In fact, these are the only two lines that you need to modify in the getEmployees() method (which involves the employees.json file) and the getRelatives() method (which involves the relatives.json file).

The httpRequest() method contains the code for making the HTTP GET request that returns an Observable. The subscribe() method contains the usual code, which in this case also initializes the employees array from the contents of the file employees.json in the subdirectory src/assets.

Listing 2.29, Listing 2.30, and Listing 2.31 show the contents of the JSON-based files customers.json, employees.json, and relatives.json, respectively.

LISTING 2.29 customers.json

```
[
{"fname":"Paolo","lname":"Friulano","city":"Maniago"},
{"fname":"Luigi","lname":"Napoli","city":"Vicenza"},
{"fname":"Miko","lname":"Tanaka","city":"Yokohama"},
{"fname":"Yumi","lname":"Fujimoto","city":"Tokyo"}
]
```

LISTING 2.30 employees.json

```
[
{"fname":"Jane","lname":"Jones","city":"San Francisco"},
{"fname":"John","lname":"Smith","city":"New York"},
{"fname":"Dave","lname":"Stone","city":"Seattle"},
{"fname":"Sara","lname":"Edson","city":"Chicago"}
]
```

LISTING 2.31 relatives.json

```
[
{"fname":"Beppi","lname":"Guarda","city":"Vicenza"},
{"fname":"Paolo","lname":"Fermi","city":"Padova"},
{"fname":"Antonio","lname":"Gatto","city":"Brescia"},
{"fname":"Pasquale","lname":"Fritto","city":"Verona"}
]
```

Listing 2.32 displays the contents of app.module.ts that imports the Angular HttpModule.

LISTING 2.32 app.module.ts

```
import { BrowserModule }            from '@angular/
platform-browser';
import { NgModule }         from '@angular/core';
import { AppComponent }     from './app.component';
import { HttpClientModule } from '@angular/common/http';

@NgModule({
  declarations: [
    AppComponent
  ],
  imports: [
    BrowserModule,
    HttpClientModule,
  ],
  providers: [ ],
  bootstrap: [AppComponent]
})
export class AppModule { }
```

Listing 2.32 contains the standard set of import statements, along with HttpClientModule that is listed in the array of imports in the @NgModule decorator.

Launch this Angular application and you will see the following output displayed in a browser session:

```
Angular HTTP and Observables
```

```
Some of our Employees
```
- Jane Jones lives in San Diego
- John Smith lives in New York
- Dave Stone lives in Seattle
- Sara Edson lives in Chicago

```
Some of our Customers
```
- Paolo Friulano lives in Maniago
- Luigi Napoli lives in Vicenza
- Miko Tanaka lives in Yokohama
- Yumi Fujimoto lives in Tokyo

```
Some of our Relatives
```
- Beppi Guarda lives in Vicenza
- Paolo Fermi lives in Padova
- Antonio Gatto lives in Brescia
- Pasquale Fritto lives in Verona

One more thing: the JSON files in Angular applications are located in the src/assets subdirectory, and in this example, there are three JSON files. These files are referenced in each of the three methods getCustomers(), getEmployees(), and getRelatives(), with the following code snippets:

```
this.http.get('assets/customers.json')
this.http.get('assets/employees.json')
this.http.get('assets/relatives.json')
```

As you can probably infer, the prefix assets in the preceding code snippet refers to the subdirectory src/assets in an Angular application. If you see a blank screen when you launch an Angular application, you probably did not place your JSON files in the correct subdirectory.

Reading CSV Files in Angular

The code sample in this section shows you how to read the contents of a CSV file and display the contents of that file. This Angular application will be very useful in Chapter 6 for the machine learning task that involves reading the contents of a dataset from a CSV file.

Now copy the directory ReadWineCSV from the companion files into a convenient location. Listing 2.33 displays the content of app.component.ts, which illustrates how to read the contents of assets/wine.csv and then display the data in tabular form.

LISTING 2.33 app.component.ts

```
import { Component }   from '@angular/core';
import { Inject }      from '@angular/core';
import { HttpClient }  from '@angular/common/http';
import { Observable }  from 'rxjs';

@Component({
  selector: 'app-root',
  styleUrls: ['./app.component.css'],
  template: `
    <table>
      <thead>
       <tr>
         <th>{{headers[0]}}</th>
         <th>{{headers[1]}}</th>
         <th>{{headers[2]}}</th>
       </tr>
      </thead>
      <tbody>
       <tr *ngFor="let record of records;let i = index;">
          <td> <span>{{record[0]}}</span> </td>
          <td> <span>{{record[1]}}</span> </td>
          <td> <span>{{record[2]}}</span> </td>
       </tr>
      </tbody>
    </table>
  `,
})
export class AppComponent {
  public headers: any = [];
  public records: any = [];
  public csvUrl = 'assets/wine.csv';

  constructor(@Inject(HttpClient) public http:HttpClient)
  {
     this.readCsvData ();
  }
```

```
    readCsvData () {
       this.http.get(this.csvUrl, {responseType: 'text'})
          .subscribe(
             data => { this.extractData(data) },
             err => { console.log(err) }
          );
    }

    private extractData(res: any) {
       let csvData = res || '';
       let allTextLines = csvData.split(/\r\n|\n/);

       // headers: Alcohol, Malic acid, class
       this.headers = allTextLines[0].split(',');
       // console.log("headers: "+this.headers)

       let lines = [];

       // skip the header row: start from index 1
       for (let i=1; i < allTextLines.length; i++) {
          // split content based on comma
          let data = allTextLines[i].split(',');

          if (data.length == headers.length) {
             let tarr = [];
             for ( let j = 0; j < headers.length; j++) {
                tarr.push(data[j]);
             }
             lines.push(tarr);
          }
       }
       // console.log("lines: "+lines)
       this.records = lines;
    }
}
```

Listing 2.33 contains an assortment of import statements, some standard properties, and a template property that consists of two parts. The first part displays header-related information, and the second part contains a loop that iterates through the data that was retrieved from the CSV file wine.csv.

The next portion of Listing 2.33 defines a constructor that invokes the readCsvData() method, which in turn makes an HTTP GET request in order to read the contents of the CSV file `wine.csv` in the `src/assets` subdirectory.

After the `HTTP GET` request has been completed, the code invokes the `extractData()` method that contains a loop that creates a one-dimensional array for each row of data in the CSV file `wine.csv`. Each array is appended to the `lines` array, and when the loop has been completed, the `records` array is initialized with the contents of the `lines` array.

Now take a look at the `template` property in Listing 2.33 and you will see a loop in the `<tbody>` element that creates and displays a `<tr>` element for each row in the `records` array.

Listing 2.34 displays the updated contents of `app.module.ts` that contains the usual code that you have seen in previous code samples.

LISTING 2.34 app.module.ts

```
import { BrowserModule }      from '@angular/platform-
browser';
import { NgModule }       from '@angular/core';
import { AppComponent }   from './app.component';
import { HttpClientModule } from '@angular/common/http';

@NgModule({
  declarations: [
    AppComponent
  ],
  imports: [
    BrowserModule,
    HttpClientModule
  ],
  providers: [],
  bootstrap: [AppComponent]
})
export class AppModule { }
```

There are two additions to the auto-generated file `app.module.ts` that are shown in bold in Listing 2.34: the first snippet is an `import` statement and the second snippet references `HttpClientModule` in the `imports` element.

Now launch this Angular application, and in a browser session, you will see the following output:

```
Alcohol Malic acid    class
14.23   1.71     1
13.2    1.78     1
13.16   2.36     1
14.37   1.95     1
13.24   2.59     1
// details omitted for brevity
13.71   5.65     3
13.4    3.91     3
13.27   4.28     3
13.17   2.59     3
14.13   4.1      3
```

The output above is a "bare bones" display consisting of three columns of numeric data. Feel free to define the CSS-related code for a better styling of the output.

Summary

This chapter showed you how to use UI Controls in Angular applications. You saw how to render buttons, render lists of names, and add and delete names from those lists. You also learned about conditional logic and how to create child components.

Then you learned about communicating between parent and child components, followed by a discussion of presentational components. In addition, you were briefly introduced to Angular Pipes and code samples that illustrate how to use them in Angular applications. Finally, you learned how to make HTTP GET requests from an Angular application to retrieve the contents of a JSON file as well as the contents of a CSV file that are in the src/assets subdirectory.

## CHAPTER 3

FORMS AND SERVICES

T his chapter shows you how to create Angular applications that use Angular Forms and Services. The code samples rely on an understanding of the functionality that is discussed in the previous chapter, such as how to make HTTP requests in Angular.

The first section in this chapter contains Angular applications that use Angular Controls and Control Groups. This section also provides an example of an Angular application that contains a form that makes HTTP GET requests.

The second part of this chapter contains code samples that retrieve data from an external endpoint. Specifically, this section shows you how to retrieve GitHub details for a hard-coded user. It also explains how to provide a GitHub user name in a text field, and then search GitHub for additional details regarding that user.

One other point to keep in mind: the focus of the code samples in this book is on Angular-specific features, which means a "no frills" approach to the UI portion of the applications. Hence, the UI portion is minimalistic, but you can enhance the UI by providing your own custom code.

Overview of Angular Forms

An Angular FormControl represents a single input field, a FormGroup consists of multiple logically related fields, and an NgForm component represents a `<form>` element in an HTML Web page. The `ngSubmit` action for submitting a form has this syntax:

```
(ngSubmit)="onSubmit(myForm.value)".
```

Note that `NgForm` provides the `ngSubmit` event, whereas you must define the `onSubmit()` method in the component class. The expression `myForm.value` consists of the key/value pairs in the form. Later in the chapter, you will see examples involving these controls, as well as `FormBuilder`, which supports additional useful functionality.

Angular also supports template-driven forms (with a `FormsModule`) and reactive forms (with a `ReactiveFormsModule`), both of which belong to `@angular/forms`. However, Reactive Forms are synchronous whereas template-driven forms are asynchronous.

Reactive forms

Reactive forms involve the explicit management of the data flowing between a non-UI data model and a UI-oriented form model that retains the states and values of the HTML controls on the screen. Reactive forms offer the ease of using reactive patterns, testing, and validation.

Reactive forms involve the creation of a tree of Angular form control objects in the component class `app.component.ts`, which are also bound to them natively to form control elements in the component template `app.component.html`.

The component class has access to the data model and the form control structure, which enables you to propagate data model values into the form controls and also retrieve user-supplied values in the HTML controls. The component can observe changes in the form control state and react to those changes.

One advantage of working with form control objects directly is that the value and validity updates are always synchronous and under your control. You won't encounter the timing issues that sometimes plague a template-driven form, and reactive forms can be easier to unit test. Since reactive forms are created directly via code, they are always available, which enables you to immediately update values and "drill down" to descendant elements.

Template-driven forms

Template-driven forms involve placing HTML form controls (such as `<input>`, `<select>`, and so forth) in the component template. In addition, the form controls are bound to the data model properties in the component via directives such as ngModel.

Note that Angular directives create Angular form objects based on the information in the provided data bindings. Angular uses ngModel to handle the transfer of data values, and also updates the mutable data model with user changes as they happen. Consequently, the ngModel directive does not belong to the ReactiveFormsModule.

Before delving into the material in this section, look at the Angular application MasterForm that has form-related code on the companion files. Although this code sample does not use an Angular FormGroup, you might find some useful features in the code.

The next section shows you how to use the Angular ngForm component to create a form "the Angular way." You will see an example that shows you how to use an Angular FormGroup in an Angular Application.

An Angular Form Example

This section contains a simple example of creating a form in an Angular application. Now copy the directory NGForm from the companion files into a convenient location. Listing 3.1 displays the content of app.component.ts, which illustrates how to use the <input> elements with an ngModel attribute in an Angular application.

LISTING 3.1 app.component.ts

```
import { Component } from '@angular/core';

@Component({
  selector: 'app-root',
  template: `
    <div>
      <h2>A Sample Form</h2>
      <form #f="ngForm"
            (ngSubmit)="onSubmit(f.value)"
            class="ui form">
        <div class="field">
          <label for="fname">fname</label>
          <input type="text"
                 id="fname"
                 placeholder="fname"
                 name="fname" ngModel>
```

```
            <label for="lname">lname</label>
            <input type="text"
                   id="lname"
                   placeholder="lname"
                   name="lname" ngModel>
        </div>

        <button type="submit">Submit</button>
      </form>
    </div>

  })
  export class AppComponent {
    myForm: any;

    onSubmit(form: any): void {
      console.log('you submitted value:', form);
    }
  }
```

Listing 3.1 defines a `template` property that contains a `<form>` element that contains two `<div>` elements, each of which contains an `<input>` element. The first `<input>` element is for the first name and the second `<input>` element is for the last name of a new user.

Angular provides the `NgModel` directive that enables you to use the instance variable `myForm` in an Angular form. For example, the following code snippet specifies `myForm` as the control group for the given form:

```
<form [ngModel]="myForm"
    (ngSubmit)="onSubmit(myForm.value)"
```

Notice that `onSubmit` specifies `myForm` and that a `Control` is "bound" to the input element.

NOTE *Add the attribute `novalidate` to the `<form>` element to disable browser validation.*

Listing 3.2 displays the content of `app.module.ts`, which imports a `FormsModule` and includes it in the `imports` property.

LISTING 3.2 app.module.ts

```
import { NgModule }      from '@angular/core';
import { FormsModule }   from '@angular/forms';
```

```
import { BrowserModule } from '@angular/platform-browser';
import { AppComponent }  from './app.component';

@NgModule({
  imports:       [ BrowserModule, FormsModule ],
  declarations: [ AppComponent ],
  bootstrap:     [ AppComponent ]
})
export class AppModule { }
```

Listing 3.2 is straightforward: it contains two lines (shown in bold) involving the FormsModule that is required for this code sample.

Launch this application and navigate to localhost:4200 in a browser session, where you will see a simple form with two input fields labeled fname and lname. Enter a pair of values – let's say tom and jones – for these two fields. Open the Inspector for this browser session and you will see the following information displayed:

```
you submitted value: Object { fname: "tom", lname:
"jones" }
you submitted value: Object { fname: "tom", lname:
"jones" }
```

Data Binding and ngModel

Angular supports three types of binding in a form: no binding, one-way binding, and two-way binding. Here are some examples:

```
<!-- no binding -->
<input name="fname" ngModel>

<!-- one-way binding -->
<input name="fname" [ngModel]="fname">

<!-- two-way binding -->
<input name="fname" [ngModel]="fname"
       (ngModelChange)="fname=$event">

<!-- two-way binding -->
<input name="fname" [(ngModel)]="fname">
```

The one-way binding example will look for the fname property in the associated component and initialize the <input> field with the value of the fname property.

The two-way binding example fires the ngModelChange event when users alter the value of the <input> field, which causes an update to the fname property in the component, thereby ensuring that the input value and its associated component value are the same. You can also replace the value of ngModelChange with the output of a function (e.g., capitalizing the text string that users enter in the input field).

The second example of two-way data binding uses the "banana in a box" syntax, which is a shorthand way of achieving the same result as the first two-way data binding example. However, this syntax does not support the use of a function that is possible with the longer syntax for two-way data binding.

The next section in this chapter shows you how to work with forms in the "Angular way."

Angular Forms with FormBuilder

The FormBuilder class and the FormGroup class are built-in Angular classes for creating forms. FormBuilder supports the control() function for creating a FormControl and the group() function for creating a FormGroup.

Copy the directory FormBuilder from the companion files to a convenient location. Listing 3.3 displays the content of app.component.ts, which illustrates how to use an Angular form in an Angular application.

LISTING 3.3 app.component.ts

```
import { Component }   from '@angular/core';
import { FormBuilder } from '@angular/forms';
import { FormGroup }   from '@angular/forms';

@Component({
  selector: 'app-root',
  template: `
    <div>
      <h2>A FormBuilder Form</h2>

      <form [formGroup]="myForm"
            (ngSubmit)="onSubmit(myForm.value)"
            class="ui form">

        <div class="field">
          <label for="fname">fname</label>
```

```
        <input type="text"
               id="fname"
               placeholder="fname"
          [formControl]="myForm.controls['fname']">
      </div>

      <div class="field">
        <label for="lname">lname</label>
        <input type="text"
               id="lname"
               placeholder="lname"
          [formControl]="myForm.controls['lname']">
      </div>

      <button type="submit">Submit</button>
    </form>
  </div>
})
export class AppComponent {
  myForm: FormGroup;

  constructor(fb: FormBuilder) {
    this.myForm = fb.group({
      'fname': ['John'],
      'lname': ['Smith']
    });
  }

  onSubmit(value: string): void {
    console.log('you submitted value:', value);
  }
}
```

Listing 3.3 contains a <form> element with two <div> elements, each of which contains an <input> element. The first <input> element is for the first name and the second <input> element is for the last name of a new user.

In Listing 3.3, FormBuilder is injected into the constructor, which creates an instance of FormBuilder that is assigned to the fb variable in the constructor. Next, myForm is initialized by invoking the group() method that takes an object of the key/value pairs. In this case, fname and lname are keys, and both of them appear as `<input>` elements in the `template` property. The values of these keys are optional initial values.

Launch this application and navigate to `localhost:4200` in a browser session, where you will see a simple form with two input fields labeled `fname` and `lname` that are pre-populated with the values `John` and `Smith`, respectively. Open the Inspector for this browser session and you will see the following information displayed:

```
you submitted value: Object { fname: "John", lname:
"Smith" }
```

Obviously, you can add many other properties inside the `group()` method (such as address-related fields). Moreover, you can add a different form for each new entity. For example, you could create separate forms for a `Customer`, `PurchaseOrder`, and `LineItems`.

Angular Reactive Forms

This section contains a code sample for creating a reactive Angular form, whose purpose will become clear after you see the `Form`-related code in Listing 3.6.

Now copy the directory `ReactiveForm` from the companion files to a convenient location. Listing 3.4 displays the content of `app.component.ts`, which illustrates how to define a reactive Angular form in an Angular application.

LISTING 3.4 app.component.ts

```
import { Component }   from '@angular/core';
import { FormBuilder } from '@angular/forms';
import { FormGroup }   from '@angular/forms';
import { FormControl } from '@angular/forms';

@Component({
  selector:    'app-root',
  templateUrl: './app.component.html',
  styleUrls:   ['./app.component.css']
})
export class AppComponent {
  userForm: FormGroup;
```

```
    disabled:boolean;

    constructor(fb: FormBuilder) {
        this.userForm = fb.group({
            name:     'Jane',
            email:    'jsmith@yahoo.com',
            address: fb.group({
                city: 'San Francisco',
                state: 'California'
            })
        });
    }

    onFormSubmitted(theForm : FormGroup) {
        console.log("name   = "+theForm.controls['name'].
value);
        console.log("email = "+theForm.controls['email'].
value);
        console.log("city  = "+theForm.get('address.city').
value);
        console.log("city  = "+theForm.get('address.state').
value);
    }
}
```

Listing 3.4 contains the usual import statements, and notice how the variable userForm, which has type FormBuilder, is initialized in the constructor. In addition to two text fields, userForm contains the address element, which also has type FormBuilder.

Listing 3.5 displays the contents of app.module.html with an Angular form that contains <input> elements that correspond to the fields in the userForm variable.

LISTING 3.5 app.component.html

```
<form  [formGroup]="userForm"  (ngSubmit)="onFormSubmit-
ted(userForm)">
    <label>
        <span>Name</span>
        <input type="text" formControlName="name" placehold-
er="Name" required>
    </label>
```

```
<div>
  <label>
    <span>Email</span>
    <input type="email" formControlName="email" place-
holder="Email" required>
  </label>
</div>

<div formGroupName="address">
  <div>
    <label>
      <span>City</span>
      <input type="text" formControlName="city" place-
holder="City" required>
    </label>
  </div>
  <label>
    <span>Country</span>
    <input type="text" formControlName="state" place-
holder="State" required>
  </label>
</div>
  <br />
<input type="submit" [disabled]="userForm.invalid">
</form>
```

Listing 3.5 contains very simple HTML markup that enables users to change the default values for each of the input fields.

Listing 3.6 displays the updated contents (shown in bold) of app.module.ts that involve just two code snippets.

LISTING 3.6 app.module.ts

```
import { BrowserModule } from '@angular/platform-browser';
import { NgModule }            from '@angular/core';
import { FormsModule }         from '@angular/forms';
import { ReactiveFormsModule } from '@angular/forms';
import { AppComponent }        from './app.component';
```

```
@NgModule({
  declarations: [
    AppComponent
  ],
  imports: [
    BrowserModule,
    FormsModule,
    ReactiveFormsModule
  ],
  providers: [],
  bootstrap: [AppComponent]
})
export class AppModule { }
```

Listing 3.6 contains one new `import` statement for `ReactiveForms-Module` (which can be combined with the `import` statement for `Forms Module`) that is also referenced in the `imports` property.

Launch this application and navigate to `localhost:4200` in a browser session, where you will see a simple form with several pre-populated input fields. Click the `submit` button. When you open the Inspector for this browser session, you will see the following information displayed:

```
name  = Jane
email = jsmith@yahoo.com
city  = San Francisco
state = California
```

FormGroup versus FormArray

As you now know, a `FormGroup` aggregates the values of `FormControl` elements into one object, where the control name is the key. Angular also supports `FormArray` (a "variation" of `FormGroup`), which aggregates the values of `FormControl` elements into an array.

`FormGroup` data is serialized as an array, whereas `FormArray` data is serialized as an object). If you do not know how many controls are in a given group, consider using a `FormArray` (otherwise use a `FormGroup`). The following link contains an example of using a `FormArray`:

https://alligator.io/angular/reactive-forms-formarray-dynamic-fields/

Other Form Features in Angular

The preceding section gave you a glimpse into the modularized style of Angular forms, and this brief section highlights some additional form-related features in Angular, such as the following:

- form validation
- custom validators
- nested forms
- dynamic forms
- template-driven forms

Validators enable you to perform validation on form fields, such specifying mandatory fields and the minimum and maximum lengths of fields. You can also specify a regular expression that a field must match, which is very useful for zip codes, email addresses, and so forth. Alternatively, you can also specify validators programmatically.

Angular forms also provide event listeners that detect various events pertaining to the state of a form, as shown in the following code snippets:

```
{{myform.form.touched}}
{{myform.form.untouched}}
{{myform.form.pristine}}
{{myform.form.dirty}}
{{myform.form.valid}}
{{myform.form.invalid}}
```

For example, the following `<span>` element is displayed if one or more form fields is invalid:

```
<span *ngIf="!myform.form.valid">The Form is Invalid</span>
```

You can also display error messages using the `*ngIf` directive to display the status of a specific field, as shown here:

```
<label>
  <span>First Name</span>
  <input type="text" formControlName="fname" placeholder="First Name">
    <p *ngIf="userForm.controls.fname.errors">
      This value is invalid
    </p>
</label>
```

An example of a dynamic Angular form is here:

https://angular.io/docs/ts/latest/cookbook/dynamic-form.html

Instead of using plain CSS for styling effects for field-related error messages, consider using something like Bootstrap.

What are Angular Services?

This section contains a brief description of Angular Services, along with a list of some built-in services, followed by an example of defining a custom service in Angular in a subsequent section.

As you probably know, the front-end of Web applications sometimes contain a combination of presentation logic and some business logic. Angular components comprise the presentation tier and services belong to the business-logic tier. Define your Angular services in such a way that they are decoupled from the presentation tier.

Angular services are classes that implement some business logic, and they are designed so that they can be used by components, models, and other services. In other words, services can be providers for other parts of an application.

Because of the "dependency injection" mechanism in Angular, services can be invoked in other sections of an Angular application. Moreover, Angular ensures that services are singletons, which means that each service consumer will access the same instance of the service class.

A sample Angular custom service is shown here:

```
@Injectable()
export class UpperCaseService {
  public upper(message: string): string {
    return message.toUpperCase();
  }
}
```

The preceding class `UpperCaseService` is a service with one method that takes a string as an argument and returns the uppercase version of that string. The `@Injectable()` decorator is required so that this class can be injected as a dependency. Although this decorator is not mandatory in all cases, it's a good idea to mark your services in this manner. Use the `@Injectable` decorator only when a service (or class) "receives" an injection.

An example of the content of `app.component.ts`, which invokes the method in the preceding service, is shown below:

```
import   {UpperCaseService}   from   "./path/to/service/
UpperCaseService";

@Component({
  selector: "convert",
  template: "<button (click)='greet()'>Greet</button>";
})
export class UpperComponent {
  // inject the custom service in the constructor
  constructor(private upperCaseService: UpperCaseService
{
  }

  // invoke the method in the uppercaseService class
  public greet(): void {
    alert(this.upperCaseService.upper("Hello world"));
  }
}
```

The preceding code block imports the `UpperCaseService` class (shown in bold) via an `import` statement and then injects an instance of this class into the constructor of the `UpperComponent` class. Next, the `template` property contains a `<button>` element with a click handler that invokes the `greet()` method defined in the preceding code block. The `greet()` method displays an alert whose contents are the result of invoking the `upper()` method in the custom `UpperCaseService` class.

Built-in Angular services

Angular supports various built-in services that are organized in different modules. For example, the `http` module (in `@angular/common/http`) contains support for HTTP requests that involve typical verbs, such as GET, POST, PUT, and DELETE. In fact, you saw examples of HTTP-based requests in Chapter 2. In addition, the routing module (in `@angular/router`) provides routing support, which includes HTML5 and hash routing. The form module (in `@angular/forms`) provides form-related services. Check the Angular documentation for a complete list of built-in services.

An Angular Service Example

Copy the directory `ServiceExample` from the companion files into a convenient location. Listing 3.7 displays the content of `app.component.ts`, which contains an example of defining a basic custom service in Angular.

LISTING 3.7 app.component.ts

```
import {Component} from '@angular/core';
import {Injectable} from '@angular/core';

@Injectable()
class Service {
  somedata = ["one", "two", "three"];
  constructor() { }

  getData()   { return this.somedata; }
  toString() { return "From toString"; }
}

@Component({
  selector: 'app-root',
  providers: [ Service ],
  template: `Here is the data: {{ service.getData() }}`
})
export class AppComponent {
  constructor(public service: Service) { }
}
```

Listing 3.7 contains a `Service` class that is preceded by the `@Injectable` decorator, which enables us to inject an instance of the `Service` class in the constructor of the `AppComponent` class in Listing 3.7.

Launch this application and navigate to `localhost:4200` in a browser session, where you will see the following information displayed:

```
Data from the service: one,two,three
```

A Service with an EventEmitter

This section contains a code sample that uses EventEmitters for communicating between a component and its child component. Now copy the directory UserServiceEmitter from the companion files to a convenient location. Listing 3.8 displays the content of user.component.ts, which defines a custom component for an individual user.

LISTING 3.8 user.component.ts

```
import {Component} from '@angular/core';

@Component({
  selector: 'user',
  template: '<h2></h>'
})
export class User {
  fname: string;
  lname: string;
  imageUrl: string;

constructor(fname:string,lname:string,imageUrl:string)
{
    this.fname = fname;
    this.lname = lname;
    this.imageUrl = imageUrl;
  }
}
```

Listing 3.8 is straightforward: the custom User class has a constructor with three arguments that represent the first name, last name, and image url, respectively, for a single user.

Listing 3.9 displays the content of user.service.ts, which creates a list of users where each user has a first name, last name, and an associated PNG file.

LISTING 3.9 user.service.ts

```
import {Component} from '@angular/core';
import {User}      from './user.component';
```

```
@Component({
    selector: 'user-comp',
    template: '<h2></h2>'
})
export class UserService {
    userList:User[];

    constructor() {
this.userList = [
        new User('Jane','Smith','assets/sample1.png'),
        new User('John','Stone','assets/sample2.png'),
        new User('Dave','Jones','assets/sample3.png'),
]}

    getUserList() {
        return this.userList;
    }
}
```

Listing 3.9 imports the User custom component (displayed in Listing
3.11), and then defines the UserService custom component that uses
the userList array of User elements in order to keep track of users.
This array is initialized in the constructor, and it contains three new User
instances that are created and populated with data. The getUserList()
method performs the "service" that returns the userList array.

Listing 3.10 displays the contents of app.component.ts that references
the two preceding custom components and renders user-related information in an unordered list.

LISTING 3.10 *app.component.ts*

```
import {Component}      from '@angular/core';
import {EventEmitter}   from '@angular/core';
import {UserService}    from './user.service';
import {User}           from './user.component';

@Component({
    selector: 'app-root',
    providers: [User, UserService],
    template: `
        <div class="ui items">
```

```
          <user-comp
           *ngFor="let user of userList; let i=index"
            [user]="user"
            (mouseover)='mouseEvent(user)'
            [class.chosen]="isSelected(user)">
            USER {{i+1}}: {{user.fname}}-{{user.lname}}
            <img class="user-image" [src]="user.imageUrl"
                (mouseenter)="mouseEnter(user)"
                width="50" height="50">
        </user-comp>
      </div>

})
export class AppComponent {
  user:User;
  currentUser:User;
  userList:User[];
  onUserSelected: EventEmitter<User>;

  mouseEvent(user:User) {
      console.log("current user: "+user.fname+" "+user.
lname);
      this.currentUser = user;
      this.onUserSelected.emit(user);
  }

  mouseEnter(user:User) {
     console.log("image name: "+user.imageUrl);
     alert("Image name: "+user.imageUrl);
  }

  isSelected(user: User): boolean {
    if (!user || !this.currentUser) {
      return false;
    }

    return user.lname === this.currentUser.lname;
//return true;
  }

  constructor(userService:UserService) {
     this.onUserSelected = new EventEmitter();
     this.userList = userService.getUserList();
```

```
    }
}
```

Listing 3.10 contains a `template` property that displays the current list of users (i.e., the three users that are initialized by executing the code in the constructor in Listing 3.10). Notice the syntax to display information about each user in the list of users:

```
USER {{i+1}}: {{user.fname}}-{{user.lname}}
<img class="user-image" [src]="user.imageUrl"
    (mouseenter)="mouseEnter(user)"
    width="50" height="50">
```

Whenever users move their mouse over the displayed list, the `mouseEvent()` method is invoked in order to set `currentUser` to refer to the current user. In addition, when users move their mouse over one of the images, the `mouseEnter()` method is invoked, which displays a message via `console.log()` and also displays an alert.

Listing 3.11 displays the content of `app.module.ts`, which references the custom component and custom service.

LISTING 3.11 app.module.ts

```
import { NgModule }        from '@angular/core';
import {CUSTOM_ELEMENTS_SCHEMA} from '@angular/core';
import { BrowserModule } from '@angular/platform-browser';
import { AppComponent }   from './app.component';
import { UserService }    from './user.service';

@NgModule({
    imports:       [ BrowserModule ],
    providers:     [ UserService ],
    declarations:  [ AppComponent ],
    bootstrap:     [ AppComponent ],
    schemas:       [CUSTOM_ELEMENTS_SCHEMA]
})
export class AppModule { }
```

Listing 3.11 has essentially the same contents as the example in Chapter 2 that contains the `schemas` property. The lines shown in bold are the modifications that are required for the code sample in this section. You can refresh your memory by reading the comments that follow Listing 2.20 that pertain to the code snippets regarding schemas shown in bold in Listing 3.11.

Searching for a GitHub User

This section shows you how to read a GitHub user name from an input field, perform a GitHub search for that user, and then append a subset of the details pertaining to that user in a list.

Copy the directory SearchGithubUsers from the companion files into a convenient location. Listing 3.12 displays the content of app.component.ts, which illustrates how to make an HTTP GET request in order to retrieve information about GitHub users.

LISTING 3.12 *app.component.ts*

```
import { Component }        from '@angular/core';
import { Inject }           from '@angular/core';
import { HttpClient }       from '@angular/common/http';
import { UserComponent }    from './user.component';
import { Observable }       from 'rxjs';

@Component({
  selector: 'app-root',
  template: `
    <div>
      <form>
        <h3>Search GitHub For User:</h3>
        <div class="field">
          <label for="guser">GitHub Id</label>
          <input type="text" #guser>
        </div>

        <button (click)="findGitHubUser(guser)">
          >>> Find User <<<
        </button>
      </form>

    <div id="container">
      <div class="onerow">
        <h3>List of Users:</h3>
```

```
        <ul>
         <li *ngFor="let user of users"
             (mouseover)="currUser(user)">
           {{user.field1}} {{user.field2}}</li>
         </ul>
        </div>
       </div>
      </div>


})
export class AppComponent {
            currentUser:UserComponent       =       new
UserComponent('ABC','DEF','');
  users: UserComponent[];
  GitHubUserInfo : any;
  GitHubUserJSON:JSON;
  user:UserComponent;
  userStr:string = "";
  guserStr:string = "";

   constructor(@Inject(HttpClient) public http:HttpCli-
ent) {
     this.users = [
       new UserComponent('Jane', 'jsmith', ''),
       new UserComponent('John', 'jstone', ''),
     ];
   }

   currUser(user) {
      console.log("fname: "+user.field1+" lname: "+user.
field2);
      this.currentUser = new UserComponent(user.field1,
                                   user.field2,
                                   user.field3);

   }

  findGitHubUser(guser: HTMLInputElement): boolean {
    if((guser.value == undefined) || (guser.value == ""))
{
       alert("Please enter a user name");
       return;
     }
```

```
       // guser.value is not available in the 'subscribe'
method
       this.guserStr = guser.value;

     this.http.get('https://api.GitHub.com/users/'+guser.
value)
         .subscribe(data => {
           this.GitHubUserInfo = data;
         //console.log("GitHub info = "+JSON.stringify(data));

         // create a new User instance:
         this.user = new UserComponent(this.GitHubUserInfo.
name,
                                       this.guserStr,
                                       this.GitHubUserInfo.
created_at);

         // append new User instance to list of users:
         this.users.push(this.user); },
       err => {
         console.log("Lookup error: "+err);
         alert("Lookup error: "+err);
       }
     );

     // reset the input field to an empty string
     guser.value = "";

     // prevent a page reload:
     return false;
   }
}
```

Listing 3.12 contains the usual import statements, followed by an @ Component decorator that contains the usual selector property and an extensive code block for the template property.

The template property consists of a top-level <div> element that contains a <form> element and another <div> element. The <form> element contains an <input> element where users can enter a GitHub username, whereas the <div> element contains a <ul> element that in turn renders the list of current users. Notice that each <li> element in the <ul> element handles a mouseover event by setting the current user to the element that users have highlighted with their mouse.

The next portion of Listing 3.12 defines the exported class `AppComponent` that initializes some instance variables, followed by a constructor that initializes the `users` array with two hard-coded users. Next, the `currUser()` method "points" to the user that users have highlighted with their mouse. This functionality is not essential, but it's available in case you need to keep track of the user that is currently highlighted.

The `findGitHubUser()` method displays an alert if the `<input>` element is empty (which prevents a redundant invocation of the `http()` method). If a user is specified in the `<input>` element, the code invokes an HTTP GET request from the `GitHub` website and appends the new user (as an instance of the `UserComponent` class) to the `users` array. In addition, an alert is displayed if there is no `GitHub` user account that matches the input string.

Another small but important detail is the following code snippet that keeps track of the user-specified input string:

```
this.guserStr = guser.value;
```

The preceding snippet is required because of the context change that occurs inside the invocation of the `get()` method, which loses the reference to the `guser` argument.

Listing 3.13 displays the content of `user.component.ts`, which contains three strings for keeping track of three user-related fields.

LISTING 3.13 user.component.ts

```
import {Component} from '@angular/core';

@Component({
  selector: 'current-user',
  template: '<h1></h1>'
})
export class UserComponent {
  field1:string = "";
  field2:string = "";
  field3:string = "";

  constructor(field1:string, field2:string, field3:string)
  {
      this.field1 = field1;
      this.field2 = field2;
```

```
        this.field3 = field3;
    }
}
```

Listing 3.13 contains the string properties field1, field2, and field3 for keeping track of three attributes from the JSON-based string of information for a GitHub user. The property names in the UserComponent class are generic so that you can store different properties from the JSON string, such as followers, following, and created_at.

You now have a starting point for displaying additional details regarding a user, and you can improve the styling of the output by using Bootstrap or some other toolkit for UI-related layouts.

Figure 3.1 displays the output from launching this Angular application and adding information about GitHub users. One thing to notice is that duplicates are allowed in the current sample (the code for preventing duplicates is an exercise for you).

Search Github For User:

Github Id ocampesato

>>> Find User <<<

List of Users:

- Jane jsmith
- John jstone

FIGURE 3.1 Search and Display GitHub Users in a List

Other Service-Related Use Cases

As you saw in the previous section, services are useful for retrieving external data. In addition, there are other situations that involve sharing data and services in an Angular application. In particular, one Angular application might need multiple instances of a service class, whereas another Angular application might need to enforce a single instance of a service class. Yet another situation involves sharing data between components in an Angular application.

These three scenarios are discussed briefly in the following subsections, and they are based on a very simple UserService class that is defined as follows:

```
export class UserService {
    private users: string[];
```

```
adduser(user: string) {
    this.users.push(user);
}

getUsers() {
    return this.users;
}
}
```

Multiple Service Instances

Suppose that UserService, MyComponent1, and MyComponent2 are defined in the TypeScript files user.service.ts, component1.ts, and component2.ts, respectively. If you need a different instance of the UserService class in each component, inject this class in their constructors, as shown here:

```
// component1.ts
export class MyComponent1 {
    constructor(private userService: UserService) {
    }
}

// component2.ts
export class MyComponent2 {
    constructor(private userService: UserService) {
    }
}
```

In the preceding code block, the instance of the UserService class in MyComponent1 is different from the instance of the UserService class in MyComponent2.

Single Service Instance

Consider the situation in which two Angular components must share the same instance of the UserService class. For simplicity, let's assume that the two components are children of the root component. In this scenario, perform the following sequence of steps:

1) Create a new service component (ng g s service).
2) Include UserService in the providers array in app.module.ts.
3) Import MyComponent1 and MyComponent2 in service.component.ts.

4) Remove the `UserService` class from the `providers` array in `MyComponent1`.

5) Remove the `UserService` class from the `providers` array in `MyComponent2`.

Step #2 ensures that the `UserService` class is available to all components in this Angular application, and there is only one instance of the `UserService` class throughout the application.

Services and Inter-Component Communication

There are three steps required in order to send a new user from `MyComponent1` to `MyComponent2`.

Step #1: Define a variable `sendUser` that is an instance of `EventEmitter` and a `sendNewUser()` method in `UserService`:

```
export class UserService {
    sendUser = new EventEmitter<string>();
    ...
    sendNewUser(user:string) {
       this.sendUser.emit(user);
    }
}
```

Step #2: Define an `onSend()` method in `MyComponent1` in order to send a new user to `MyComponent2`:

```
onSend(user:string) {
    this.userService.sendNewUser(user);
}
```

Step #3: Define an `Observable` in `MyComponent2` in order to "listen" for data that is emitted from `MyComponent1`:

```
ngOnInit() {
   this.userService.subscribe(...);
}
```

Another way to summarize the logical flow in the preceding code blocks is shown here:

- Users click a button to add a new user.
- The `UserService` instance sends the data to `Component1`.
- The `Component1` instance "emits" the new user.
- The `Component2` instance "listens" for the new user via an `Observable`.

Injecting Services into Services

You have seen how to use DI to inject a service into a component via its constructor. In addition, you can inject services into other services. In order to do so, use the @Injectable decorator in the "injected service:"

```
@Injectable
@Component({
})
export MyService(...)
```

DI in Angular only works in classes that have a suitable decorator as part of the class definition.

Flickr Image Search Using jQuery and Angular

The code sample in this section shows you how to use jQuery in an Angular application, which is relevant for existing HTML Web pages that perform HTTP GET requests via jQuery.

Copy the directory SearchFlickr from the companion files into a convenient location. Now type "cd" inside this application and install jQuery as shown here:

```
npm install jquery --save
```

Listing 3.14 displays the content of app.component.ts, which illustrates how to make an HTTP GET request to retrieve images from Flickr that are based on text string that users enter in a search box.

LISTING 3.14 app.component.ts

```
import {Component} from '@angular/core';

// remember: npm install jquery --save
import * as $ from "jquery";

@Component({
    selector: 'app-root',
    template: `
        Enter a word and search for related images:
        <br />
        <input id="searchterm" />
        <button (click)="httpRequest()">Search</button>
        <div id="images"></div>
```

```
})
export class AppComponent {
  imageCount = 4;
  url = "http://api.flickr.com/services/feeds/photos_pub-
lic.gne?jsoncallback=?";

  constructor() {}

  httpRequest() {
    $.getJSON(this.url,
    {
      tags: $("#searchterm").val(),
      tagmode: "any",
      format: "json"
    },
    function(data) {
      $.each(data.items, function(i,item){
                $("<img/>").attr("src",  item.media.m).
prependTo("#images");
      //if ( i == this.imageCount ) return false;
      });
    });
  }
}
```

Listing 3.14 contains a standard `import` statement, followed by this code snippet:

```
import * as $ from "jquery";
```

The preceding snippet is necessary for TypeScript to "find" jQuery, which is possible after you have installed it via the `npm` command. However, keep in mind that if you remove the preceding code snippet, you will see the following error (or something similar):

```
ERROR ReferenceError: "$ is not defined"
```

NOTE
The code in this section works for Angular 6 onward, whereas the code for Angular 4 requires a different syntax.

The next portion of Listing 3.14 is the `@Component` decorator, whose `template` property contains `<input>`, `<button>`, and `<div>` elements to capture users' search string, perform a search with that string, and display the results of the search, respectively.

The next portion of Listing 3.14 is the exported class `@AppComponent` that defines the `url` variable that is initialized with a hard-coded string value that "points" to the Flickr website.

Next, an empty constructor is defined, followed by the `httpRequest()` method that is invoked when users click on the `<button>` element. This method invokes the jQuery `getJSON()` method that performs a Flickr image search based on the text string entered in the `<input>` element because of this code snippet:

```
tags: $("#searchterm").val()
```

When the matching images are retrieved, they are available via `data.items`, and the jQuery `each()` method iterates through the list of images. Each image is dynamically inserted in the `<images>` element via this snippet:

```
$("<img/>").attr("src",                    item.media.m).
prependTo("#images");
```

Take a minute to absorb the compact manner in which jQuery achieves the desired result.

Figure 3.2 displays the output from launching this Angular application and searching Flickr with the keyword `pasta`.

FIGURE 3.2 A Partial List of Figures with Pasta

HTTP GET Requests with a Simple Server

This section shows you how to work with the command line utility json-server that can serve JSON-based data. This utility performs the function of a very simple server: clients can make GET requests to retrieve JSON data from a server. Moreover, a simple command in the console where json-server was launched enables you to save the in-memory data to a file.

Although json-server does not perform the functions of a Node-based application that contains Express and MongoDB, json-server is a convenient program that helps you learn how an Angular application can interact with a file server.

You need to perform the following steps before you launch the Angular application in this section:

- Step 1: Install json-server.
- Step 2: Launch json-server.
- Step 3: Launch the Angular application.

Install json-server via the following command:
```
[sudo] npm install -g json-server
```

Navigate to the src/assets directory that contains the JSON file posts.json and invoke this command:

```
json-server posts.json
```

The preceding command launches a file server at port 3000 and reads the contents of posts.json into the memory, making that data available to HTTP GET requests.

Now copy the directory JSONServerGET from the companion files into a convenient location. Listing 3.15 displays the content of app.component.ts, which illustrates how to make an HTTP GET request to retrieve data from a file server.

LISTING 3.15 app.component.ts

```
import {Component}      from '@angular/core';
import {Inject}         from '@angular/core';
import {HttpClient}     from '@angular/common/http';
import {HTTP_BINDINGS}  from '@angular/common/http';

@Component({
    selector: 'app-root',
```

```
    template: `
      <button (click)="httpRequest()">Get Information</
button>
      <div>
        <li *ngFor="let post of postData">
          {{post.author}}
          {{post.title}}
        </li>
      </div>

})
export class AppComponent {
  postData = "";

  constructor(@Inject(HttpClient) public http:HttpCli-
ent) {
  }

  httpRequest() {
    this.http.get('http://localhost:3000/posts')
      .subscribe(
        data => this.postData = JSON.stringify(data),
        err => console.log('error'),
        () => this.postInfo()
      );
  }

  postInfo() {
    //-----------------------------------------------
    // the 'eval' statement is required in order to
    // convert the data retrieved from json-server
    // to an array of JSON objects (else an error)
    //-----------------------------------------------
    var myObject = eval('(' + this.postData + ')');
    console.log("myObject = "+JSON.stringify(myObject));
    this.postData = myObject;
  }
}
```

Listing 3.15 contains code that is similar to earlier code samples. The first difference involves the details of the unordered list that is displayed in the template property.

The second difference is the endpoint `http://localhost:3000/posts` in the `HTTP GET` request. This endpoint provides JSON data via the `json-server` that is listening on port 3000.

Listing 3.16 displays the contents of `posts.json` retrieved during the `HTTP GET` request in Listing 3.15.

LISTING 3.16 posts.json

```
{
  "posts": [
        {"id":    100,"title":   "json-server","author":
"smartguy"},
    {"id": 200,"title": "pizza-maker","author": "chicago"},
    {"id": 300,"title": "good-beer",  "author": "escondido"}
    ]
}
```

The next section shows you how to make an `HTTP POST` request to a local file server in an Angular application.

HTTP POST Requests with a Simple Server

The Angular application in this section makes an `HTTP POST` request with the utility `json-server` that can serve JSON-based data. Keep in mind that the server in this code sample only handles basic data requests: "universal" JavaScript (sometimes also called "isomorphic" JavaScript) is not covered in this chapter.

Please note that this application is not production-ready code, specifically because the id value is based on a randomly generated integer.

Now copy the directory `JSONServerPOST` from the companion files into a convenient location. Navigate to the `src/assets` subdirectory, which contains the JSON file `authors.json`, and launch this command:

```
json-server authors.json
```

The preceding command launches a file server at port 3000 and reads the contents of `authors.json` into the memory, making that data available to `HTTP GET` requests.

NOTE *You must launch* `json-server` *before you launch the Angular application in this section.*

Listing 3.17 displays the content of `app.component.ts`, which illustrates how to make an HTTP POST request to a local file server.

LISTING 3.17 app.component.ts

```
import { Component } from '@angular/core';
import {Inject}       from '@angular/core';
import {HttpClient}   from '@angular/common/http';

// remember: npm install jquery --save
import * as $ from "jquery";

@Component({
   selector: 'app-root',
   template: `
      <button (click)="getEmpData()">Click to Display
Author Info</button>
    <div>
      <table>
        <thead *ngIf="foundData">
          <th>AUTHORID</th>
          <th>Title</th>
          <th>Author</th>
        </thead>
        <tbody>
          <tr *ngFor="let author of authorData">
            <td>{{author.id}}</td>
            <td>{{author.title}}</td>
            <td>{{author.author}}</td>
          </tr>
        </tbody>
      </table>
      <button (click)="postAuthorData()">Click to Add
New Author Info</button>
    </div>

})
export class AppComponent {
  foundData   = false;
  authorData  : any;
  currData    = {};
  idIncr      = 100;
```

```
  newAuthorId = 0;
  newTitle    = "";
  newAuthor   = "";
  largestId   = 0;

    constructor(@Inject(HttpClient) public http:HttpCli-
ent) {}
  postAuthorData() {
    this.newAuthorId = 0+this.largestId+this.idIncr;
    this.newTitle    = "The Book of "+this.newAuthorId;
    this.newAuthor   = "My New Title"+this.newAuthorId;

    var postNewAuthor = {id:this.newAuthorId,
                         title:this.newTitle,
                         author:this.newAuthor};
//console.log("postNewAuthor:"+JSON.stringify(post-
NewAuthor));

    $.post("http://localhost:3000/authors",
        postNewAuthor,
        function(result, textStatus, jqXHR) {
          //console.log("2returned    result:    "+JSON.
stringify(result));
            this.authorData.push(postNewAuthor);
        }.bind(this),"json")
         .fail(function(jqXHR, textStatus, errorThrown) {
      console.log("error:   "+errorThrown+"   textStatus:
"+textStatus);
        });
  }

  getAuthorData() {
    this.http.get('http://localhost:3000/authors')
      .subscribe(
        data => this.authorData = data,
        err => console.log('error'),
        () => this.authorInfo()
      );
  }

  authorInfo() {
    this.largestId =
```

```
            parseInt(this.authorData[this.authorData.
length-1].id,10);

    //console.log("largestId   = "+ this.largestId);
    //console.log("authorData1 = "+ JSON.stringify(this.
authorData));
        this.foundData = true;
  }
}
```

Listing 3.17 contains the usual import statements, followed by a template property that displays a table of author-based data. When users click on the <button> element, the postAuthorData() adds a hard-coded new author to the list of authors. This method performs a standard jQuery POST request instead of using an Observable. Note that this method increments the value of the id property of each author so that they are treated as distinct authors (even though the names of the new users are almost the same).

On the other hand, the getAuthorData() method does involve an Observable for retrieving author-related data (shown in Listing 3.18) from the file server that is running on port 3000.

One other point: the browser is reloaded after each invocation of the postAuthorData() method, so you need to click the "Author Info" button to see the newly added author. However, you can prevent a page reload by issuing either of the following commands from the command line:

```
ng serve --live-reload false OR
ng serve --no-live-reload
```

Listing 3.18 displays a portion of the contents of authors.json, whose contents are displayed in this Angular application.

LISTING 3.18 authors.json

```
{
  "authors": [
    {
      "id": 100,
      "title": "json-server",
      "author": "typicode"
    },
```

```
    {
        "id": 200,
        "title": "pizza-maker",
        "author": "chicago"
    },
// sections omitted for brevity
    {
        "id": "900",
        "title": "The Book of 900",
        "author": "My New Title900"
    }
]
}
```

As you can see, Listing 3.18 is a very simple collection of JSON-based data items, where each item contains the elements id, title, and author.

An SVG Line Plot from Simulated Data in Angular (optional)

The Angular application in this section reads the contents of a CSV file (located in the src/assets subdirectory) and then uses that data to display an SVG-based line graph. However, if you are not interested in generating SVG-based line graphs, then you can skip this section with no loss of continuity.

Now copy the directory ReadDataCSVLRPlot from the companion files into a convenient location. Listing 3.19 displays the content of app. component.ts, which illustrates how to read the contents of assets/ wine.csv and then display the data in tabular form.

LISTING 3.19 app.component.ts

```
import { Component }  from '@angular/core';
import { Inject }     from '@angular/core';
import { Observable } from 'rxjs';
import { HttpClient } from '@angular/common/http';

@Component({
  selector: 'app-root',
  styleUrls: ['./app.component.css'],
  template: `
```

```
    <svg width="600" height="200">
      <rect x="0" y="0" width="600" height="200"
          stroke="black" stroke-width="4" fill="white" />
      <polyline [attr.points]="polyPts"
                    style="fill:none;stroke:red;stroke-wi
dth:4" />
    </svg>
    <table>
      <tbody>
        <p>Data points for this line graph:</p>
        <tr *ngFor="let record of records;let i = index;">
          <td> <span>{{record[0]}}</span> </td>
          <td> <span>{{record[1]}}</span> </td>
        </tr>
      </tbody>
    </table>
  `,
})
export class AppComponent {
  public xValue:number    = 0;
  public yValue:number    = 0;

  // points for an SVG polyline
  public polyPts : any = "";

  // populate an array with CSV data
  public records : any = [];
  public csvUrl  = 'assets/rand20.csv';
  public allTextLines:any = "";

   constructor(@Inject(HttpClient) public http:HttpCli-
ent) {
      this.readCsvData ();
  }

  readCsvData () {
    this.http.get(this.csvUrl, {responseType: 'text'})
      .subscribe(
        data => { this.extractData(data) },
        err => { console.log(err) }
      );
  }
```

```
//----------------------------------------------------
// After the readCsvData reads the CSV file in the
// assets directory, the extractData method is invoked
// in order to populate an array with that CSV data.
// This method also invokes constructLineGraph that
// constructs a line graph of the set of datapoints
//----------------------------------------------------
private extractData(res: any) {
  let csvData = res || '';
  this.allTextLines = csvData.split(/\r\n|\n/);

  let lines = [];
  let onerow = this.allTextLines[0].split(',');
  let columnCount = onerow.length;

  for (let i=0; i<this.allTextLines.length-1; i++)
  {
     // split content based on comma
     let data = this.allTextLines[i].split(',');

     let tarr = [];
     for ( let j = 0; j < columnCount; j++) {
        tarr.push(data[j]);
     }
     lines.push(tarr);
  }
  this.records = lines;

  this.constructLineGraph();
}

private constructLineGraph() {
  // construct a line graph
  for ( let i = 0; i < this.records.length; i++) {
   //console.log("this.xValue:",  this.records[i][0]);
   //console.log("this.yValue:",  this.records[i][1]);

     // append current point to the SVG polyline:
     this.polyPts += this.xValue.toString() + "," +
                     this.yValue.toString() + " ";

     this.xValue += +this.records[i][0];
     this.yValue = +this.records[i][1];
```

```
      }
   }
}
```

Listing 3.19 starts with the usual `import` statements, followed by the `template` property that contains two main parts. The first part consists of an SVG `<svg>` element, as shown here:

```
<svg width="600" height="200">
   <rect x="0" y="0" width="600" height="200"
         stroke="black" stroke-width="4" fill="white" />
   <polyline [attr.points]="polyPts"
             style="fill:none;stroke:red;stroke-width:4" />
</svg>
```

As you can see, the SVG `<svg>` element in the preceding code block has a width of 600 pixels and a height of 200 pixels, both of which you can adjust if you need to do so. In addition, the SVG `<svg>` element contains an SVG `<rect>` element that is essentially just an outer border, followed by an SVG `<polyline>` element that represents a line graph.

The second portion of the `<template>` property displays the header information about the data in the CSV file, followed by an `ngFor` code block that displays the contents of the CSV file.

Next, the constructor invokes the `readCsvData()` method, which in turn involves an `Observable` that reads the contents of the CSV file `rand20.csv`, which is in the `src/assets` subdirectory.

After the data is successfully read from the CSV file, the `extractData()` method is invoked to populate the `records` variable with an array of values from the retrieved data. This step is necessary because the data that is retrieved in the `readCsvData()` is simply a collection of strings, each of which contains a comma-separated value. Keep in mind that each row in the `records` array consists of a pair of numbers that is treated as an (x,y) point in the plane.

The final code snippet in the `readCsvData()` method invokes the method `constructLineGraph()` that appends each row in the `records` array to the variable `polyPts`, which constructs a contiguous set of line segments that is rendered as a line graph. This technique works because the values in `rand20.csv` are sorted in increasing order, based on the values in the first column.

Listing 3.20 displays a portion of the contents of rand20.csv, which is located in the src/assets subdirectory.

LISTING 3.20 *rand20.csv*

```
46,8
46,13
70,40
92,55
174,74
// details omitted for brevity
536,204
543,208
553,220
572,246
596,247
```

Figure 3.3 displays the output from launching the Angular application in this section.

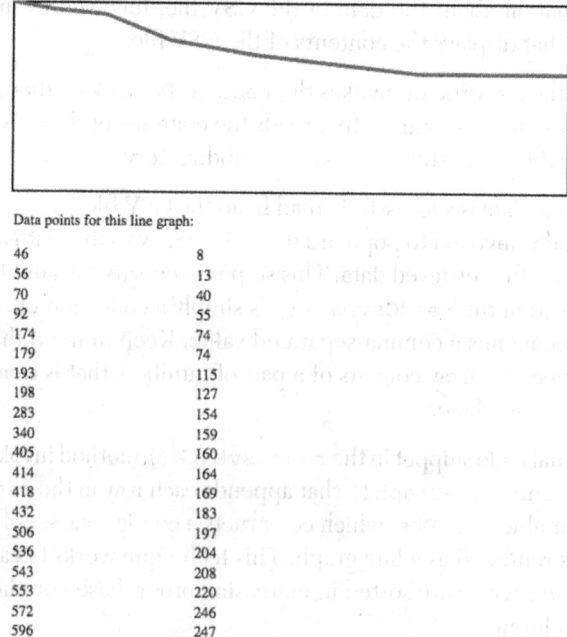

Data points for this line graph:

46	8
56	13
70	40
92	55
174	74
179	74
193	115
198	127
283	154
340	159
405	160
414	164
418	169
432	183
506	197
536	204
543	208
553	220
572	246
596	247

FIGURE 3.3 A Line Graph from a List of Numbers

Summary

This chapter showed you how to create Angular applications with HTML5 `Forms` as well as `Forms` that contain Angular `Controls` and `FormGroups`. You also saw how to save form-based data in local storage. Next, you learned about Angular `Pipes`, along with an example that showed you how to implement this functionality.

You also learned about Angular `Services` and an example that illustrated how to use `Services`. Next, you saw an example of the `http()` method (which returns an `Observable`) of the `Http` class to retrieve data for any `GitHub` user and display portions of that data in a list of users. Finally, you saw how to read a CSV file with numeric data that was used to generate and display an SVG line graph.

## CHAPTER 4

INTRO TO MACHINE LEARNING

This chapter introduces numerous concepts in machine learning, such as feature selection, feature engineering, data cleaning, training sets, and linear regression.

The first part of this chapter briefly discusses machine learning and the sequence of steps typically required to prepare a dataset. These steps include "feature selection" or "feature extraction" that can be performed using various algorithms.

The second section describes the types of data that you can encounter, issues that can arise with the data in datasets, and how to rectify them. You will also learn about the difference between "hold out" and "k-fold" when you perform the training step.

The third part of this chapter briefly discusses the basic concepts involved in linear regression. Although linear regression was developed more than 200 years ago, this technique is still one of the "core" techniques for solving (albeit simple) problems in statistics and machine learning. In fact, the technique known as the "Mean Squared Error" (MSE) for finding a best-fitting line for data points in a 2D plane (or a hyperplane for higher dimensions) is implemented in Python and Keras to minimize so-called "loss" functions that are discussed later.

The fourth section in this chapter contains additional code samples involving linear regression tasks using standard techniques in NumPy. Hence, if you are comfortable with this topic, you can probably skim quickly through the first two sections of this chapter. The third section shows you how to solve a linear regression using Keras.

One point to keep in mind is that some algorithms are mentioned without delving into the details about them. For instance, the section pertaining to supervised learning contains a list of algorithms that appear later in the chapter in the section that pertains to classification algorithms. The algorithms that are displayed in bold in a list are the algorithms that are of greater interest for this book. In some cases, the algorithms are discussed in greater detail in the next chapter; otherwise, you can perform an online search for additional information about the algorithms that are not discussed in detail in this book.

What is Machine Learning?

In high level terms, machine learning is a subset of AI that can solve tasks that are infeasible or too cumbersome with "traditional" programming languages. A spam filter for email is an early example of machine learning. Machine learning generally supersedes the accuracy of older algorithms.

Despite the variety of machine learning algorithms, the data is arguably more important than the selected algorithm. Many issues can arise with data: insufficient data, poor data quality, incorrect data, missing data, irrelevant data, duplicate data values, and so forth. Later in this chapter, you will see techniques that address many of these data-related issues.

If you are unfamiliar with machine learning terminology, a dataset is a collection of data values, which can be in the form of a CSV file or a spreadsheet. Each column is called a feature, and each row is a datapoint that contains a set of specific values for each feature. If a dataset contains information about customers, then each row pertains to a specific customer.

Types of Machine Learning

Here are the main types of machine learning (combinations of these are also possible) that you will encounter:

- supervised learning
- unsupervised learning
- semi-supervised learning
- reinforcement learning

Supervised learning means that the datapoints in a dataset have a label that identifies its contents. For example, the MNIST dataset contains

28x28 PNG files, each of which contains a single hand-drawn digit (i.e., 0 through 9 inclusive). Every image with the digit 0 has the label 0; every image with the digit 1 has the label 1; all other images are labeled according to the digit that is displayed in those images.

As another example, the columns in the Titanic dataset are features about passengers, such as their gender, the cabin class, the price of their ticket, whether the passenger survived, and so forth. Each row contains information about a single passenger, including the value 1 if the passenger survived. The MNIST dataset and the Titanic dataset involve a *classification* task: the goal is to train a model based on a training dataset and then predict the class of each row (which is an image in the MNIST dataset and a passenger in the Titanic dataset) in a test dataset.

In general, the datasets for classification tasks have a small number of possible values: one of nine digits in the range of 0 through 9, one of four animals (dog, cat, horse, giraffe), or one of two values (survived versus perished, purchased versus not purchased). As a rule of thumb, if the number of outcomes can be displayed reasonably well in a drop-down list, then it's probably a classification task.

By contrast, a dataset for real estate data contains multiple rows of data, where each row contains information about a specific house, such as the number of bedrooms, the square feet of the house, the number of bathrooms, the price of the house, and so forth. In this dataset, the price of the house is the label for each row. Notice that the range of possible prices is too large to fit reasonably well in a drop-down list. A real estate dataset involves a *regression* task: the goal is to train a model based on a training dataset and then predict the price of each house in a test dataset.

Unsupervised learning involves unlabeled data, which is typically the case for clustering algorithms (discussed later). Some important unsupervised learning algorithms that involve *clustering* are listed below:

- k-Means
- Hierarchical Cluster Analysis (HCA)
- expectation maximization

Some important unsupervised learning algorithms that involve *dimensionality reduction* (discussed in more detail later) are listed below:

- PCA (Principal Component Analysis)
- Kernel PCA
- LLE (Locally Linear Embedding)

■ t-SNE (t-distributed Stochastic Neighbor Embedding)

There is one more very important unsupervised task called anomaly detection. This task is relevant for fraud detection and detecting outliers (discussed later in more detail).

Semi-supervised learning is a combination of supervised and unsupervised learning: some datapoints are labeled and some are unlabeled. One technique involves using the labeled data to classify (i.e., label) the unlabeled data, after which you can apply a classification algorithm.

Reinforcement learning pertains to maximizing a reward, and this type of learning is beyond the scope of this book.

Types of Machine Learning Algorithms

There are three main types of machine learning algorithms:

■ regression (ex: linear regression)
■ classification (ex: k-Nearest-Neighbor)
■ clustering (ex: k-Means)

Regression is a supervised learning technique to predict numerical quantities. An example of a regression task is predicting the value of a particular stock. Note that this task is different from predicting whether the value of a particular stock will increase or decrease tomorrow (or some other future time period). Another example of a regression task involves predicting the cost of a house in a real estate dataset. Both of these tasks are examples of a regression task.

Regression algorithms in machine learning include linear regression and generalized linear regression (also called "multivariate analysis" in traditional statistics).

Classification is also a supervised learning technique, but it's for predicting categorical quantities. An example of a classification task is detecting the occurrence of spam, fraud, or determining the digit in a PNG file (such as the MNIST dataset). In this case, the data is already labeled, so you can compare the prediction with the label that was assigned to the given PNG.

Classification algorithms in machine learning include the following list of algorithms (they are discussed in greater detail in the next chapter):

■ decision trees (a single tree)
■ random forests (multiple trees)

- kNN (k Nearest Neighbor)
- logistic regression (despite its name)
- Naïve Bayes
- SVM (Support Vector Machines)

Some machine learning algorithms (such as SVMs, random forests, and kNN) support regression as well as classification. In the case of SVMs, the scikit-learn implementation of this algorithm provides two APIs: SVC for classification and SVR for regression.

Each of the preceding algorithms involves a model that is trained on a dataset, after which the model is used to make a prediction. By contrast, a random forest consists of *multiple* independent trees (the number is specified by you), and each tree makes a prediction regarding the value of a feature. If the feature is numeric, take the mean or the mode (or perform some other calculation) to determine the "final" prediction. If the feature is categorical, use the mode (i.e., the most frequently occurring class) as the result; in the case of a tie, you can select one of them in a random fashion.

Incidentally, the following link contains more information regarding the kNN algorithm for classification as well as regression:

http://saedsayad.com/k_nearest_neighbors_reg.htm

Clustering is an unsupervised learning technique for grouping similar data together. Clustering algorithms put data points in different clusters without knowing the nature of the data points. After the data has been separated into different clusters, you can use the SVM (Support Vector Machine) algorithm to perform classification.

Clustering algorithms in machine learning include the following (some of which are variations of each other):

- k-Means
- meanshift
- Hierarchical Cluster Analysis (HCA)
- expectation maximization

Keep in mind the following points. First, the value of k in k-Means is a hyper parameter, and it's usually an odd number to avoid ties between two classes. Next, the meanshift algorithm is a variation of the k-Means algorithm that does *not* require you to specify a value for k. In fact, the meanshift algorithm determines the optimal number of clusters. However, this algorithm does not scale well for large datasets.

Machine Learning Tasks

Unless you have a dataset that has already been sanitized, you need to examine the data in a dataset to make sure that it's in a suitable condition. The data preparation phase involves 1) examining the rows ("data cleaning") to ensure that they contain valid data (which might require domain-specific knowledge), and 2) examining the columns (feature selection or feature extraction) to determine if you can retain only the most important columns.

A high level list of the sequence of machine learning tasks (some of which might not be required) is shown below:

- obtain a dataset
- data cleaning
- feature selection
- dimensionality reduction
- algorithm selection
- train-versus-test data
- training a model
- testing a model
- fine-tuning a model
- obtain metrics for the model

First, you obviously need to obtain a dataset for your task. In the ideal scenario, this dataset already exists; otherwise, you need to cull the data from one or more data sources (e.g., a CSV file, a relational database, a NoSQL database, a Web service, and so forth).

Second, you need to perform *data cleaning*, which you can do via the following techniques:

- Missing Value Ratio
- Low Variance Filter
- High Correlation Filter

In general, data cleaning involves checking the data values in a dataset in order to resolve one or more of the following:

- Fix incorrect values.
- Resolve duplicate values.
- Resolve missing values.
- Decide what to do with outliers.

Use the Missing Value Ratio technique if the dataset has too many missing values. In extreme cases, you might be able to drop features with a large number of missing values. Use the Low Variance filter technique to identify and drop features with constant values from the dataset. Use the High Correlation filter technique to find highly correlated features, which increase multicollinearity in the dataset. Such features can be removed from a dataset (but check with your domain expert before doing so).

Depending on your background and the nature of the dataset, you might need to work with a domain expert, who is a person with a deep understanding of the contents of the dataset.

For example, you can use a statistical value (mean, mode, and so forth) to replace incorrect values with suitable values. Duplicate values can be handled in a similar fashion. You can replace missing numeric values with zero, the minimum, the mean, the mode, or the maximum value in a numeric column. You can replace missing categorical values with the mode of the categorical column.

If a row in a dataset contains a value that is an outlier, you have three choices:

- Delete the row.
- Keep the row.
- Replace the outlier with some other value (mean?).

When a dataset contains an outlier, you need to make a decision based on domain knowledge that is specific to the given dataset. Suppose that a dataset contains stock-related information. As you know, there was a stock market crash in 1929, which you can view as an outlier. Such an occurrence is rare, but it can contain meaningful information. Incidentally, the source of wealth for some families in the 20th century was based on buying massive amounts of stock at very low prices during the Great Depression.

Feature Engineering, Selection, and Extraction

In addition to creating a dataset and "cleaning" its values, you also need to examine the features in that dataset to determine whether you can reduce the dimensionality (i.e., the number of columns) of the dataset. The process for doing so involves three main techniques:

- feature engineering
- feature selection
- feature extraction (aka feature projection)

Feature engineering is the process of determining a new set of features that are based on a combination of existing features in order to create a meaningful dataset for a given task. Domain expertise is often required for this process, even in cases of relatively simple datasets. Feature engineering can be tedious and expensive, and in some cases, you might consider using automated feature learning. After you have created a dataset, it's a good idea to perform feature selection or feature extraction (or both) to ensure that you have a high quality dataset.

Feature selection is also called variable selection, attribute selection, or variable subset selection. Feature selection involves selecting the subset of relevant features in a dataset. In essence, feature selection involves selecting the most important features in a dataset, which provides these advantages:

- reduced training time
- simpler models that are easier to interpret
- avoidance of the curse of dimensionality
- better generalization due to a reduction in overfitting ("reduction of variance")

Feature selection techniques are often used in domains where there are many features and comparatively few samples (or data points). Keep in mind that a low-value feature can be redundant or irrelevant, which are two different concepts. For instance, a relevant feature might be redundant when it's combined with another strongly correlated feature.

Feature selection can use three strategies: the filter strategy (e.g. information gain), the wrapper strategy (e.g. search guided by accuracy), and the embedded strategy (prediction errors are used to determine whether the features are included or excluded while developing a model). Another interesting point is that feature selection can also be useful for regression as well as classification tasks.

Feature extraction creates new features from functions that produce combinations of the original features. By contrast, feature selection involves determining a subset of the existing features.

Feature selection and feature extraction both result in the *dimensionality reduction* for a given dataset, which is the topic of the next section.

Dimensionality Reduction

Dimensionality reduction refers to algorithms that reduce the number of features in a dataset. As you will see, there are many techniques available, and they involve either feature selection or feature extraction.

Algorithms that use feature selection to perform dimensionality reduction are listed here:

- Backward Feature Elimination
- Forward Feature Selection
- Factor Analysis
- Independent Component Analysis

Algorithms that use feature extraction to perform dimensionality reduction are listed here:

- principal component analysis (PCA)
- non-negative matrix factorization (NMF)
- kernel PCA
- graph-based kernel PCA
- linear discriminant analysis (LDA)
- generalized discriminant analysis (GDA)
- autoencoder

The following algorithms combine feature extraction and dimensionality reduction:

- principal component analysis (PCA)
- linear discriminant analysis (LDA)
- canonical correlation analysis (CCA)
- non-negative matrix factorization (NMF)

These algorithms can be used during a pre-processing step before using clustering or some other algorithm (such as kNN) on a dataset.

Another group of algorithms involves methods based on projections, which includes t-Distributed Stochastic Neighbor Embedding (t-SNE) as well as UMAP.

This chapter discusses PCA, and you can perform an online search to find more information about the other algorithms.

PCA

Principal components are new components that are linear combinations of the initial variables in a dataset. In addition, these components are uncorrelated, and the most meaningful or important information is contained in these new components.

There are two advantages to PCA: 1) reduced computation time due to far fewer features and 2) the ability to graph the components when there are, at most, three components. If you have four or five components, you won't be able to display them visually, but you could select subsets of the three components for visualization, and perhaps gain some additional insight into the dataset.

PCA uses the variance as a measure of information: the higher the variance, the more important the component. In fact, PCA determines the eigenvalues and eigenvectors of a covariance matrix (discussed later), and constructs a new matrix whose columns are eigenvectors, ordered from left-to-right based on the maximum eigenvalue in the left-most column, decreasing until the right-most eigenvector also has the smallest eigenvalue.

Covariance Matrix

As a reminder, the statistical quantity called the variance of a random variable x is defined as follows:

```
variance(x) = [SUM (x - xbar)*(x-xbar)]/n
```

A covariance matrix C is an nxn matrix whose values on the main diagonal are the variance of the variables $X1, X2, \ldots, Xn$. The other values of C are the covariance values of each pair of variables Xi and Xj.

The formula for the covariance of the variables X and Y is a generalization of the variance of a variable, and the formula is shown here:

```
covariance(X, Y) = [SUM (x - xbar)*(y-ybar)]/n
```

Notice that you can reverse the order of the product of the terms (multiplication is commutative), and therefore the covariance matrix C is a symmetric matrix:

```
covariance(X, Y) = covariance(Y,X)
```

PCA calculates the eigenvalues and the eigenvectors of the covariance matrix A.

Working with Datasets

In addition to data cleaning, there are several other steps that you need to perform, such as selecting training data versus test data, and deciding whether to use "hold out" or cross-validation during the training process. More details are provided in the subsequent sections.

Training Data versus Test Data

After you have performed the tasks described earlier in this chapter (i.e., data cleaning and perhaps dimensionality reduction), you are ready to split the dataset into two parts. The first part is the *training set*, which is used to train a model, and the second part is the *test set*, which is used for "inferencing" (another term for making predictions). Make sure that you conform to the following guidelines for your test sets:

1) The set is large enough to yield statistically meaningful results.
2) It's representative of the data set as a whole.
3) Never train on test data.
4) Never test on training data.

What is Cross-validation?

The purpose of cross-validation is to test a model with non- overlapping test sets, which is performed in the following manner:

Step 1) Split the data into k subsets of equal size.
Step 2) Select one subset for testing and the others for training.
Step 3) Repeat Step 2) for the other k-1 subsets.

This process is called *k-fold cross-validation*, and the overall error estimate is the average of the error estimates. A standard method for evaluation involves ten-fold cross-validation. Extensive experiments have shown that ten subsets are the best choice to obtain an accurate estimate. In fact, you can repeat ten-fold cross-validation ten times and compute the average of the results, which helps to reduce the variance.

The next section discusses regularization, which is an important yet optional topic if you are primarily interested in Angular code. If you plan to become proficient in machine learning, you will need to learn about regularization.

What is Regularization?

Regularization helps to solve the overfitting problem, which occurs when a model performs well on training data but poorly on validation or test data.

Regularization solves this problem by adding a penalty term to the loss function, thereby controlling the model complexity with this penalty term. Regularization is generally useful for:

1) a large number of variables
2) a low ratio of (# observations)/(# of variables)
3) high multi-collinearity

There are two main types of regularization: L1 Regularization (which is related to the MAE, or the absolute value of differences) and L2 Regularization (which is related to the MSE, or the square of differences). In general, L2 performs better than L1, and L2 is also efficient in terms of computation.

ML and Feature Scaling

Feature scaling standardizes the range of the features of the data. This step is performed during the data preprocessing step, in part because the gradient descent benefits from feature scaling.

The assumption is that the data conforms to a standard normal distribution, and standardization involves subtracting the mean and dividing by the standard deviation for every data point, which results in the N(0,1) normal distribution.

Data Normalization versus Standardization

Data normalization is a linear scaling technique. Let's assume that a dataset has the values {X1, X2, . . . , Xn} along with the following terms:

```
Minx = minimum of Xi values
```

```
Maxx = maximum of Xi values
```

Now calculate a set of new Xi values as follows:

```
Xi = (Xi - Minx)/[Maxx - Minx]
```

The new Xi values are now scaled so that they are between 0 and 1.

The Bias-Variance Tradeoff

Bias in machine learning can be due to an error from wrong assumptions in a learning algorithm. High bias might cause an algorithm to miss relevant relations between features and target outputs (underfitting). Prediction bias can occur because of "noisy" data, an incomplete feature set, or a biased training sample.

Error due to bias is the difference between the expected (or average) prediction of your model and the correct value that you want to predict. Repeat the model building process multiple times, gather new data each time, and perform an analysis to produce a new model. The resulting models have a range of predictions because the underlying data sets have a degree of randomness. Bias measures the extent from the predictions to the correct value for these models.

Variance in machine learning is the expected value of the squared deviation from the mean. A high variance can/might cause an algorithm to model the random noise in the training data, rather than the intended outputs (a.k.a., overfitting)

Adding parameters to a model increases its complexity, increases the variance, and decreases the bias. Dealing with bias and variance is dealing with underfitting and overfitting.

Error due to variance is the variability of a model prediction for a given data point. As before, repeat the entire model building process, and the variance is the extent to which the predictions for a given point vary among different "instances" of the model.

Metrics for Measuring Models

One of the most frequently used metrics is R-squared, which measures how close the data is to the fitted regression line (regression coefficient). The R-squared value is always a percentage between 0 and 100%. The value 0% indicates that the model explains none of the variability of the response data around its mean. The value 100% indicates that the model explains all the variability of the response data around its mean. In general, a higher R-squared value indicates a better model.

Limitations of R-Squared

Although high R-squared values are preferred, they are not necessarily always good values. Similarly, low R-squared values are not always bad. For example, an R-squared value for predicting human behavior is often less than 50%. Moreover, R-squared cannot determine whether the coefficient estimates and predictions are biased. In addition, an R-squared value does not indicate whether a regression model is adequate. Thus, it's possible to have a low R-squared value for a good model, or a high

R-squared value for a poorly fitting model. Evaluate R-squared values in conjunction with residual plots, other model statistics, and subject area knowledge.

Confusion Matrix

In its simplest form, a confusion matrix (also called an error matrix) is a type of contingency table with two rows and two columns that contains the number of false positives, false negatives, true positives, and true negatives. The four entries in a 2x2 confusion matrix can be labeled as follows:

```
TP: True Positive
FP: False Positive
TN: True Negative
FN: False Negative
```

The diagonal values of the confusion matrix are correct, whereas the off-diagonal values are incorrect predictions. In general, a lower FP value is better than a FN value. For example, FP indicates that a healthy person was incorrectly diagnosed with a disease, whereas FN indicates that an unhealthy person was incorrectly diagnosed as healthy.

Accuracy versus Precision versus Recall

A 2x2 confusion matrix has four entries that represent the various combinations of correct and incorrect classifications. Given the definitions in the preceding section, the definitions of precision, accuracy, and recall are given by the following formulas:

```
precision = TP/(TN + FP)
accuracy  = (TP + TN)/[P + N]
recall    = TP/[TP + FN]
```

Accuracy can be an unreliable metric because it yields misleading results in unbalanced data sets. When the number of observations in different classes are substantially different, that gives equal importance to both false positive and false negative classifications. For example, declaring cancer as benign is worse than incorrectly informing patients that they are suffering from cancer. Unfortunately, accuracy won't differentiate between these two cases.

Keep in mind that the confusion matrix can be an n×n matrix and not just a 2×2 matrix. For example, if a class has five possible values, then the confusion matrix is a 5×5 matrix, and the numbers on the main diagonal are the "true positive" results.

The ROC Curve

The ROC (receiver operating characteristic) curve is a curve that plots the TPR, which is the true positive rate (i.e., the recall) against the FPR, which is the false positive rate). Note that the TNR (the true negative rate) is also called the specificity.

The following link contains a Python code sample using SKLearn and the Iris dataset, and also code for plotting the ROC:

https://scikit-learn.org/stable/auto_examples/model_selection/plot_roc.html

The following link contains an assortment of Python code samples for plotting the ROC:

https://stackoverflow.com/questions/25009284/how-to-plot-roc-curve-in-python

Other Useful Statistical Terms

Machine learning relies on a number of statistical quantities in order to assess the validity of a model, some of which are listed here:

- RSS
- TSS
- R^2
- F1 score
- p-value

The definitions of RSS, TSS, and R^2 are shown below, where y^ is the y-coordinate of a point on a best-fitting line and y_ is the mean of the y-values of the points in the dataset:

RSS = sum of the squares of the residuals `(y - y^)**2`
TSS = total sum of the squares `(y - y_)**2`
R^2 = 1 - RSS/TSS

What is an F1 score?

The F1 score is a measure of the accuracy of a test, and it's defined as the harmonic mean of the precision and recall. Here are the relevant formulas, where p is the precision and r is the recall:

```
p = (# of correct positive results)/(# of all positive
results)
```

```
r = (# of correct positive results)/(# of all relevant
samples)

F1-score  = 1/[((1/r) + (1/p))/2]
          = 2*[p*r]/[p+r]
```

The best value of an F1 score is 1 and the worse value is 0. Keep in mind that an F1 score tends to be used for categorical classification problems, whereas the R^2 value is typically used for regression tasks (such as linear regression).

What is a p-value?

The p-value is used to reject the null hypothesis if the p-value is small enough (< 0.005), which indicates a higher significance. Recall that the null hypothesis states that there is no correlation between a dependent variable (such as y) and an independent variable (such as x). The threshold value for p is typically 1% or 5%.

There is no straightforward formula for calculating p-values, which are values that are always between 0 and 1. In fact, p-values are statistical quantities to evaluate the so-called "null hypothesis," and they are calculated by means of p-value tables or via spreadsheet/statistical software.

What is Linear Regression?

The goal of linear regression is to find the best fitting line that "represents" a dataset. Keep in mind two key points. First, the best fitting line does not necessarily pass through all (or even most of) the points in the dataset. The purpose of a best fitting line is to minimize the vertical distance of that line from the points in the dataset. Second, linear regression does not determine the best-fitting polynomial. The latter involves finding a higher-degree polynomial that passes through many of the points in a dataset.

Moreover, a dataset in the plane can contain two or more points that lie on the same *vertical* line, which is to say that those points have the same x value. However, a function *cannot* pass through such a pair of points: if two points (x1,y1) and (x2,y2) have the same x value, then they must have the same y value (i.e., y1=y2). On the other hand, a function can have two or more points that lie on the same *horizontal* line.

Now consider a scatter plot with many points in the plane that are sort of clustered in an elongated cloud-like shape: a best-fitting line will probably intersect only limited number of points (in fact, a best-fitting line might not intersect *any* of the points).

One other scenario to keep in mind: suppose a dataset contains a set of points that lie on the same line. For instance, let's say the x values are in the set {1,2,3,...,10} and the y values are in the set {2,4,6,...,20}. Then the equation of the best-fitting line is y=2*x+0. In this scenario, all the points are *collinear*, which is to say that they lie on the same line.

Linear Regression versus Curve-Fitting

Suppose a dataset consists of n data points of the form (x, y), and no two of those data points have the same x value. Then, according to a well-known result in mathematics, there is a polynomial of degree less than or equal to n-1 that passes through those n points (if you are really interested, you can find a mathematical proof of this statement online). For example, a line is a polynomial of degree one, and it can intersect any pair of non-vertical points in the plane. For any triple of points (that are not all on the same line) in the plane, there is a quadratic equation that passes through those points.

In addition, sometimes a lower degree polynomial is available. For instance, consider the set of 100 points in which the x value equals the y value: in this case, the line y = x (which is a polynomial of degree one) passes through all 100 points.

However, keep in mind that the extent to which a line "represents" a set of points in the plane depends on how closely those points can be approximated by a line, which is measured by the *variance* of the points (the variance is a statistical quantity). The more collinear the points, the smaller the variance; conversely, the more "spread out" the points are, the larger the variance.

When are Solutions Exact Values?

Statistics-based solutions provide closed-form solutions for linear regression, whereas neural networks provide *approximate* solutions. This is due to the fact that machine learning algorithms for linear regression involve a sequence of approximations that converges to optimal values, which means that machine learning algorithms produce estimates of the exact values. For example, the slope m and y-intercept b of a best-fitting line for a set of points a 2D plane have a closed-form solution in statistics, but they can only be approximated via machine learning algorithms (exceptions do exist, but they are rare situations).

Keep in mind that even though a closed-form solution for "traditional" linear regression provides an exact value for both m and b, sometimes you can only use an approximation of the exact value. For instance, suppose that the slope m of a best-fitting line equals the square root of 3 and the y-intercept b is the square root of 2. If you plan to use these values in source code, you can only work with an approximation of these two numbers. In the same scenario, a neural network computes approximations for m and b, regardless of whether or not the exact values for m and b are irrational, rational, or integer values. However, machine learning algorithms are better suited for complex, non-linear, multi-dimensional datasets, which is beyond the capacity of linear regression.

As a simple example, suppose that the closed form solution for a linear regression problem produces integer or rational values for both m and b. Specifically, let's suppose that a closed form solution yields the values 2.0 and 1.0 for the slope and y-intercept, respectively, of a best-fitting line. The equation of the line looks like this:

```
y = 2.0 * x + 1.0
```

However, the corresponding solution from training a neural network might produce the values 2.0001 and 0.9997 for the slope m and the y-intercept b, respectively, as the values of m and b for a best-fitting line. Always keep this point in mind, especially when you are training a neural network.

What is Multivariate Analysis?

Multivariate analysis generalizes the equation of a line in the Euclidean plane to higher dimensions, and it's called a *hyper plane* instead of a line. The generalized equation has the following form:

```
y = w1*x1 + w2*x2 + . . . + wn*xn + b
```

In the case of 2D linear regression, you only need to find the value of the slope (m) and the y-intercept (b), whereas in multivariate analysis, you need to find the values for `w1, w2, . . ., wn`. Note that multivariate analysis is a term from statistics, and in machine learning it's often referred to as "generalized linear regression."

Keep in mind that most of the code samples in this book that pertain to linear regression involve 2D points in the Euclidean plane.

Other Types of Regression

Linear regression finds the best fitting line that "represents" a dataset, but what happens if a line in the plane is not a good fit for the dataset? This is a relevant question when you work with datasets.

Some alternatives to linear regression include quadratic equations, cubic equations, or higher-degree polynomials. However, these alternatives involve trade-offs, as we'll discuss later.

Another possibility is a sort of hybrid approach that involves piece-wise linear functions, which comprises a set of line segments. If contiguous line segments are connected, then it's a piece-wise linear continuous function; otherwise it's a piece-wise linear discontinuous function.

Thus, given a set of points in the plane, regression involves addressing the following questions:

1) What type of curve fits the data well? How do we know?
2) Does another type of curve fit the data better?
3) What does "best fit" mean?

One way to check if a line fits the data involves a visual check, but this approach does not work for data points that are higher than two dimensions. Moreover, this is a subjective decision, and some sample datasets are displayed later in this chapter. By a visual inspection of a dataset, you might decide that a quadratic or cubic (or even higher degree) polynomial has the potential of being a better fit for the data. However, visual inspection is probably limited to points in a 2D plane or in three dimensions.

Let's defer the non-linear scenario, and let's make the assumption that a line would be a good fit for the data. There is a well-known technique for finding the "best fitting" line for such a dataset that involves minimizing the Mean Squared Error (MSE) that we'll discuss later in this chapter.

The next section provides a quick review of linear equations in the plane, along with some images that illustrate examples of linear equations.

Working with Lines in the Plane (optional)

This section contains a short review of lines in the Euclidean plane, so you can skip this section if you are comfortable with this topic. A minor point that's often overlooked is that lines in the Euclidean plane have infinite length. If you select two distinct points of a line, then all the points between those two selected points is a *line segment*. A *ray* is a "half infinite" line: when you select one point as an endpoint, then all the points on one side of the line constitutes a ray.

For example, the points in the plane whose y-coordinate is 0 is a horizontal line and also the x-axis, whereas the points between (0,0) and (1,0) on the x-axis form a line segment. In addition, the points on the x-axis that are to the right of (0,0) form a ray, and the points on the x-axis that are to the left of (0,0) also form a ray.

For simplicity and convenience, in this book we'll use the terms "line" and "line segment" interchangeably. Now let's delve into the details of lines in the Euclidean plane. Just in case you're a bit fuzzy on the details, here is the equation of a (non-vertical) line in the Euclidean plane:

```
y = m*x + b
```

The value of m is the slope of the line and the value of b is the y-intercept (i.e., the place where the line intersects the y-axis).

If need be, you can use a more general equation that can also represent vertical lines, as shown here:

```
a*x + b*y + c = 0
```

However, we won't be working with vertical lines, so we'll stick with the first formula.

Figure 4.1 displays three horizontal lines whose equations (from top to bottom) are y = 3, y = 0, and y = -3.

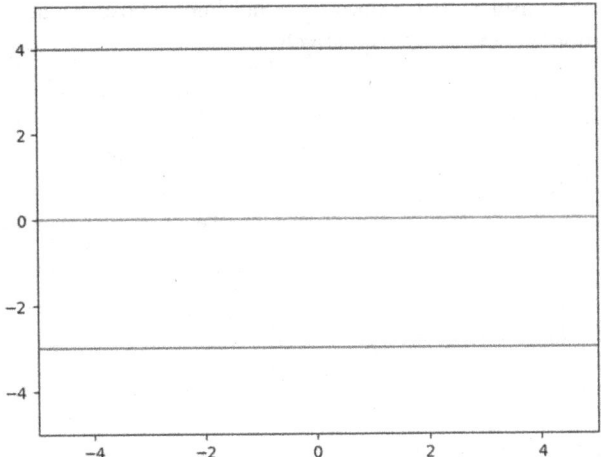

FIGURE 4.1 A Graph of Three Horizontal Line Segments

Figure 4.2 displays two slanted lines whose equations are $y = x$ and $y = -x$, respectively.

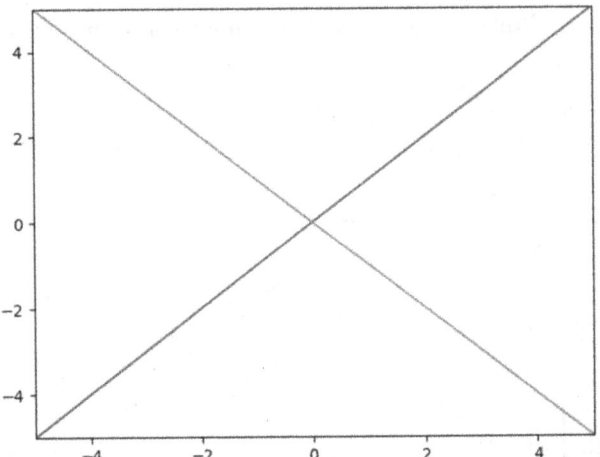

FIGURE 4.2 A Graph of Two Diagonal Line Segments

Figure 4.3 displays two slanted parallel lines whose equations are $y = 2*x$ and $y = 2*x + 3$, respectively.

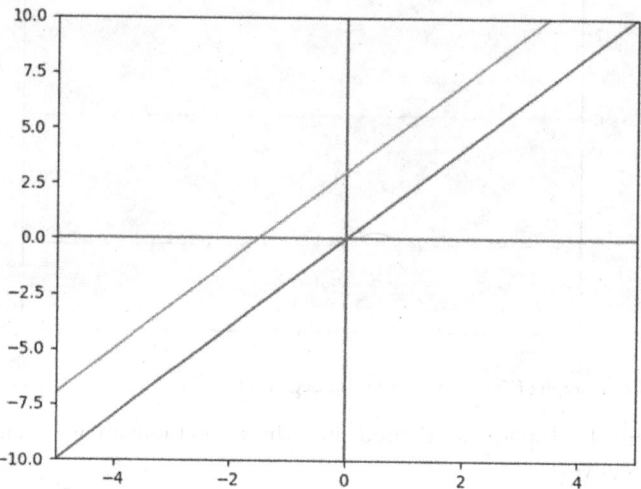

FIGURE 4.3 A Graph of Two Slanted Parallel Line Segments

Figure 4.4 displays a piece-wise linear graph consisting of connected line segments.

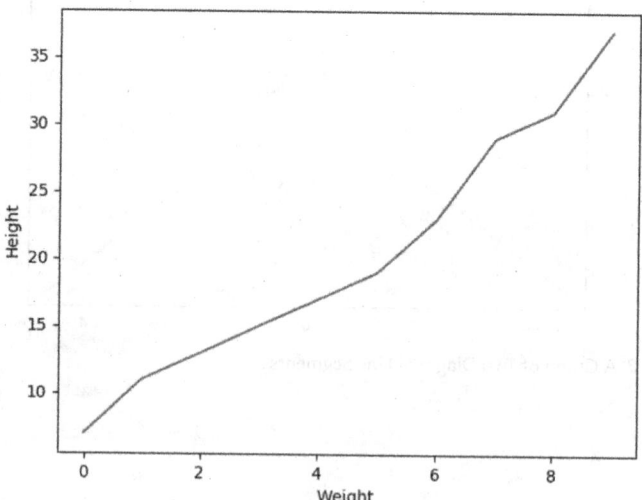

FIGURE 4.4 A Piece-wise Linear Graph of Line Segments

Now let's turn our attention to generating quasi-random data using a NumPy API, and then we'll plot the data using Matplotlib.

Scatter Plots with NumPy and Matplotlib (1)

Listing 4.1 displays the content of np_plot1.py, which illustrates how to use the NumPy randn() API to generate a dataset and then the scatter() API in Matplotlib to plot the points in the dataset.

One detail to note is that all the adjacent horizontal values are equally spaced, whereas the vertical values are based on a linear equation plus a "perturbation" value. This "perturbation technique" (which is not a standard term) is used in other code samples in this chapter in order to add a slightly randomized effect when the points are plotted. The advantage of this technique is that the best-fitting values for m and b are known in advance, and therefore we do not need to guess their values.

LISTING 4.1 np_plot1.py

```
import numpy as np
import matplotlib.pyplot as plt

x = np.random.randn(15,1)
y = 2.5*x + 5 + 0.2*np.random.randn(15,1)

print("x:",x)
print("y:",y)

plt.scatter(x,y)
plt.show()
```

Listing 4.1 contains two import statements, and then initializes the array variable x with 15 random numbers between 0 and 1.

Next, the array variable y is defined in two parts: the first part is a linear equation 2.5*x + 5 and the second part is a perturbation value that is based on a random number. Thus, the array variable y simulates a set of values that closely approximate a line segment.

This technique is used in code samples that simulate a line segment, and then the training portion approximates the values of m and b for the best-fitting line. Obviously, we already *know* the equation of the best fitting-line: the purpose of this technique is to compare the trained values for the slope m and y-intercept b with the known values (which in this case are 2.5 and 5).

A partial output from Listing 4.1 is here:

```
x: [[-1.42736308]
 [ 0.09482338]
 [-0.45071331]
 [ 0.19536304]
 [-0.22295205]
 // values omitted for brevity
y: [[1.12530514]
 [5.05168677]
 [3.93320782]
 [5.49760999]
 [4.46994978]
 // values omitted for brevity
```

Figure 4.5 displays a scatter plot of points based on the values of x and y.

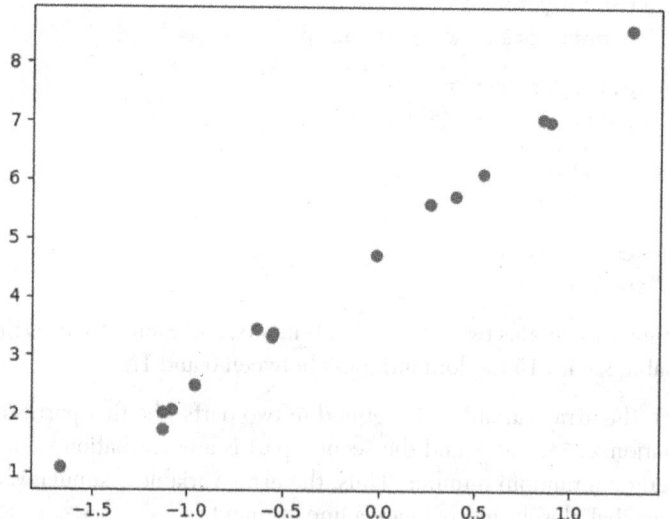

FIGURE 4.5 A Scatter Plot of Points for a Line Segment

Why the Perturbation Technique is Useful

You already saw how to use the perturbation technique. By way of comparison, consider a dataset with the following points that are defined in the Python array variables X and Y:

```
X = [0,0.12,0.25,0.27,0.38,0.42,0.44,0.55,0.92,1.0]

Y = [0,0.15,0.54,0.51, 0.34,0.1,0.19,0.53,1.0,0.58]
```

If you need to find the best fitting line for the preceding dataset, how would you guess the values for the slope m and the y-intercept b? In most cases, you probably cannot guess their values. On the other hand, the perturbation technique enables you to "jiggle" the points on a line whose value for the slope m (and, optionally, the value for the y-intercept b) is specified in advance.

Keep in mind that the perturbation technique only works when you introduce small random values that do not result in different values for m and b.

Scatter Plots with NumPy and Matplotlib (2)

The code in Listing 4.1 assigned random values to the variable x, whereas a hard-coded value is assigned to the slope m. The y values are a hard-coded multiple of the x values, plus a random value that is calculated via the perturbation technique. Hence, we do not know the value of the y-intercept b.

In this section, the values for trainX are based on the np.linspace() API, and the values for trainY involve the perturbation technique that is described in the previous section.

The code in this example simply prints the values for trainX and trainY, which correspond to data points in the Euclidean plane. Listing 4.2 displays the content of np_plot2.py, which illustrates how to simulate a linear dataset in NumPy.

LISTING 4.2 np_plot2.py

```
import numpy as np

trainX = np.linspace(-1, 1, 11)
trainY = 4*trainX + np.random.randn(*trainX.shape)*0.5

print("trainX: ",trainX)
print("trainY: ",trainY)
```

Listing 4.6 initializes the NumPy array variable trainX via the NumPy linspace() API, followed by the array variable trainY that is defined in two parts. The first part is the linear term 4*trainX and the second part involves the perturbation technique that is a randomly generated number. The output from Listing 4.6 is here:

```
trainX:   [-1.   -0.8 -0.6 -0.4 -0.2   0.    0.2  0.4   0.6
0.8   1. ]
trainY:   [-3.60147459 -2.66593108 -2.26491189 -1.65121314
-0.56454605 0.22746004 0.86830728 1.60673482 2.51151543
3.59573877   3.05506056]
```

The next section contains an example that is similar to Listing 4.2, using the same perturbation technique to generate a set of points that approximate a quadratic equation instead of a line segment.

A Quadratic Scatterplot with NumPy and Matplotlib

Listing 4.3 displays the content of np_plot_quadratic.py, which illustrates how to plot a quadratic function in the plane.

LISTING 4.3 np_plot_quadratic.py

```
import numpy as np
import matplotlib.pyplot as plt

#see what happens with this set of values:
#x = np.linspace(-5,5,num=100)

x = np.linspace(-5,5,num=100)[:,None]
y = -0.5 + 2.2*x +0.3*x**2 + 2*np.random.randn(100,1)
print("x:",x)

plt.plot(x,y)
plt.show()
```

Listing 4.3 initializes the array variable x with the values that are generated via the np.linspace() API, which in this case is a set of 100 equally spaced decimal numbers between –5 and 5. Notice the snippet [:,None] in the initialization of x, which results in an array of elements, each of which is an array consisting of a single number.

The array variable y is defined in two parts: the first part is a quadratic equation -0.5 + 2.2*x +0.3*x**2 and the second part is a perturbation value that is based on a random number (similar to the code in Listing 4.1). Thus, the array variable y simulates a set of values that approximates a quadratic equation. The output from Listing 4.3 is here:

```
x:
[[-5.         ]
```

```
[-4.8989899 ]
[-4.7979798 ]
[-4.6969697 ]
[-4.5959596 ]
[-4.49494949]
// values omitted for brevity
[ 4.8989899 ]
[ 5.       ]]
```

Figure 4.6 displays a scatter plot of points based on the values of x and y, which have an approximate shape of a quadratic equation.

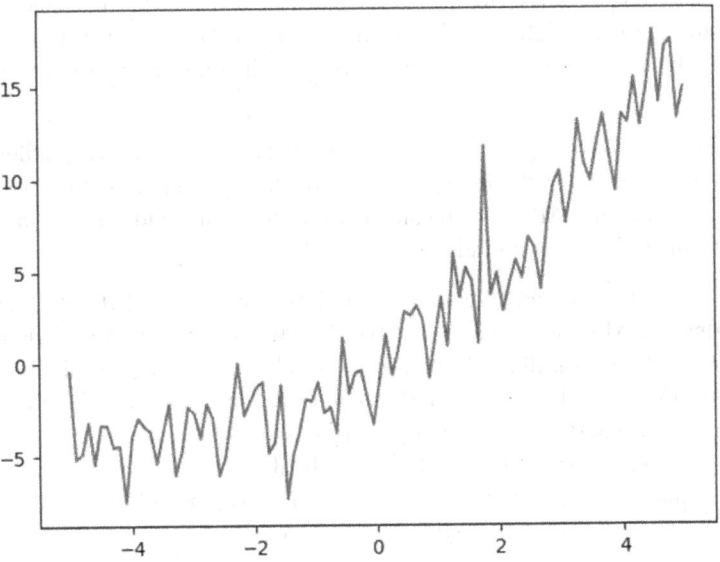

FIGURE 4.6 A Scatter Plot of Points for a Quadratic Equation

The Mean Squared Error (MSE) Formula

The MSE is the sum of the squares of the difference between an actual y value and the predicted y value, divided by the number of points. Notice that the predicted y value is the y value that each point would have if that point were actually on the best-fitting line.

Although the MSE is popular for linear regression, there are other error types available, some of which are discussed briefly in the next section.

A List of Error Types

Although we will only discuss MSE for linear regression in this book, there are other types of formulas that you can use for linear regression, some of which are listed here:

- MSE
- RMSE
- RMSPROP
- MAE

The MSE is the basis for the preceding error types. For example, RMSE is the "Root Mean Squared Error," which is the square root of the MSE.

On the other hand, the MAE is the "Mean Absolute Error," which is the sum of the absolute value of the differences of the y terms (not the square of the differences of the y terms), which is then divided by the number of terms.

The RMSProp optimizer utilizes the magnitude of recent gradients to normalize the gradients. Specifically, RMSProp maintains a moving average over the RMS (root mean squared) gradients, and then divides that term by the current gradient.

Although it's easier to compute the derivative of the MSE, it's also true that the MSE is more susceptible to outliers, whereas the MAE is less susceptible to outliers. The reason is simple: a squared term can be significantly larger than the absolute value of a term. For example, if a difference term is 10, then a squared term of 100 is added to the MSE, whereas only 10 is added to the MAE. Similarly, if a difference term is -20, then a squared term 400 is added to the MSE, whereas only 20 (which is the absolute value of –20) is added to the MAE.

Non-linear Least Squares

When predicting housing prices, where the dataset contains a wide range of values, techniques such as linear regression or random forests can cause the model to overfit the samples with the highest values in order to reduce quantities such as the mean absolute error.

In this scenario, you probably want an error metric, such as relative error, that reduces the importance of fitting the samples with the largest values. This technique is called *non-linear least squares*, which may use a log-based transformation of labels and predicted values.

The next section contains several code samples, the first of which involves calculating the MSE manually, followed by an example that uses NumPy formulas to perform the calculations. Finally, we'll look at a Keras-based example for calculating the MSE.

Calculating the MSE Manually

This section contains two line graphs, both of which contain a line that approximates a set of points in a scatter plot.

Figure 4.7 displays a line segment that approximates a scatter plot of points (some of which intersect the line segment). The MSE for the line in Figure 4.7 is computed as follows:

```
MSE = (1*1 + (-1)*(-1) + (-1)*(-1) + 1*1)/7 = 4/7
```

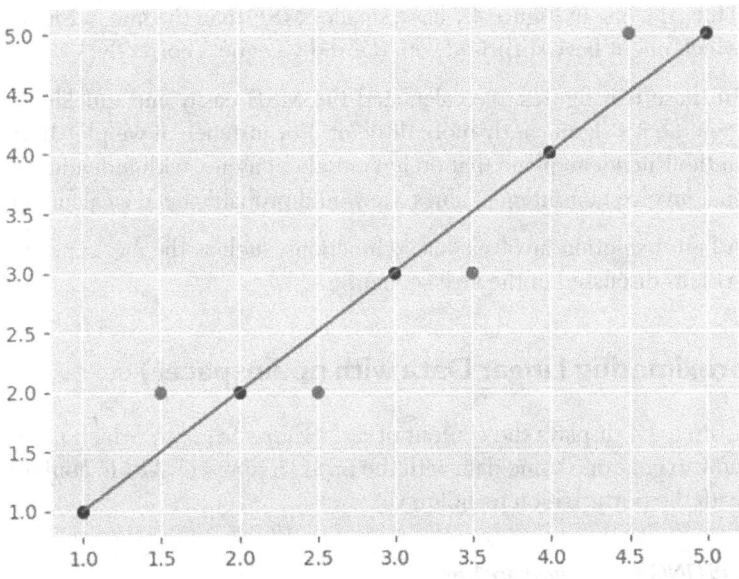

FIGURE 4.7 A Line Graph that Approximates Points of a Scatter Plot

Figure 4.8 displays a set of points and a line that is a potential candidate for the best-fitting line for the data. The MSE for the line in Figure 4.8 is computed as follows:

```
MSE = ((-2)*(-2) + 2*2)/7 = 8/7
```

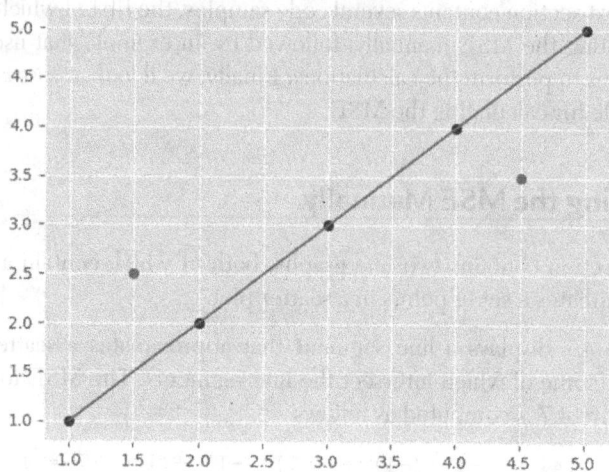

FIGURE 4.8 A Line Graph that Approximates Points of a Scatter Plot

Thus, the line in Figure 4.7 has a smaller MSE than the line in Figure 4.8, which might have surprised you. (Or did you guess correctly?)

In these two figures, we calculated the MSE easily and quickly, but in general, it's significantly more difficult. For instance, if we plot 10 points in the Euclidean plane that do not closely fit a line, with individual terms that involve non-integer values, we would probably need a calculator.

A better solution involves NumPy functions, such as the np.linspace() API, as discussed in the next section.

Approximating Linear Data with np.linspace()

Listing 4.4 displays the content of np_linspace1.py, which illustrates how to generate some data with the np.linspace() API in conjunction with the perturbation technique.

LISTING 4.4 np_linspace1.py

```
import numpy as np

trainX = np.linspace(-1, 1, 6)
trainY = 3*trainX+ np.random.randn(*trainX.shape)*0.5

print("trainX: ", trainX)
print("trainY: ", trainY)
```

The purpose of this code sample is merely to generate and display a set of randomly generated numbers. Later in this chapter, we will use this code as a starting point for an actual linear regression task.

Listing 4.4 starts with the definition of the array variable `trainX` that is initialized via the `np.linspace()` API. Next, the array variable `trainY` is defined via the perturbation technique that you have seen in previous code samples. The output from Listing 4.4 is here:

```
trainX:  [-1.  -0.6 -0.2  0.2  0.6  1. ]
trainY:  [-2.9008553  -2.26684745 -0.59516253  0.66452207
1.82669051  2.30549295]
trainX:  [-1.  -0.6 -0.2  0.2  0.6  1. ]
trainY:  [-2.9008553  -2.26684745 -0.59516253  0.66452207
1.82669051  2.30549295]
```

Now that we know how to generate `(x, y)` values for a linear equation, let's learn how to calculate the MSE, which is discussed in the next section.

The next example generates a set of data values using the `np.linspace()` method and the `np.random.randn()` method in order to introduce some randomness in the data points.

Calculating MSE with np.linspace() API

The code sample in this section differs from many of the earlier code samples in this chapter: it uses a hard-coded array of values for X and also for Y instead of the perturbation technique. Hence, you will *not* know the correct value for the slope and y-intercept (and you probably will not be able to guess their correct values). Listing 4.5 displays the content of `plain_linreg1.py`, which illustrates how to compute the MSE with simulated data.

LISTING 4.5 plain_linreg1.py

```
import numpy as np
import matplotlib.pyplot as plt

X = [0,0.12,0.25,0.27,0.38,0.42,0.44,0.55,0.92,1.0]
Y = [0,0.15,0.54,0.51, 0.34,0.1,0.19,0.53,1.0,0.58]

costs = []
#Step 1: Parameter initialization
```

```
W = 0.45
b = 0.75

for i in range(1, 100):
  #Step 2: Calculate Cost
  Y_pred = np.multiply(W, X) + b
  Loss_error = 0.5 * (Y_pred - Y)**2
  cost = np.sum(Loss_error)/10

  #Step 3: Calculate dW and db
  db = np.sum((Y_pred - Y))
  dw = np.dot((Y_pred - Y), X)
  costs.append(cost)

  #Step 4: Update parameters:
  W = W - 0.01*dw
  b = b - 0.01*db

  if i%10 == 0:
    print("Cost at", i,"iteration = ", cost)
#Step 5: Repeat via a for loop with 1000 iterations

#Plot cost versus # of iterations
print("W = ", W,"& b = ",  b)
plt.plot(costs)
plt.ylabel('cost')
plt.xlabel('iterations (per tens)')
plt.show()
```

Listing 4.5 initializes the array variables X and Y with hard-coded values, and then initializes the scalar variables W and b. The next portion of Listing 4.5 contains a for loop that iterates 100 times. After each iteration of the loop, the variables Y_pred, Loss_error, and cost are calculated. Next, the values for dw and db are calculated, based on the sum of the terms in the array Y_pred-Y, and the inner product of Y_pred-y and X, respectively.

Notice how W and b are updated: their values are decremented by the terms 0.01*dw and 0.01*db, respectively. This calculation ought to look somewhat familiar: the code is programmatically calculating an approximate value of the gradient for W and b, both of which are multiplied by the learning rate (the hard-coded value 0.01). The resulting term is decremented from the current values of W and b in order to produce a new approximation for W and b. Although this technique is very simple, it does calculate reasonable values for W and b.

The final block of code in Listing 4.5 displays the intermediate approximations for W and b, along with a plot of the cost (vertical axis) versus the number of iterations (horizontal axis). The output from Listing 4.5 is here:

```
Cost at 10 iteration =  0.04114630674619492
Cost at 20 iteration =  0.026706242729839392
Cost at 30 iteration =  0.024738889446900423
Cost at 40 iteration =  0.023850565034634254
Cost at 50 iteration =  0.0231499048706651
Cost at 60 iteration =  0.02255361434242207
Cost at 70 iteration =  0.0220425055291673
Cost at 80 iteration =  0.021604128492245713
Cost at 90 iteration =  0.021228111750568435
W =  0.47256473531193927 & b =  0.19578262688662174
```

Figure 4.9 displays a scatter plot of points generated by the code in Listing 4.5.

The code sample plain-linreg2.py is similar to the code in Listing 4.5: the difference is that instead of a single loop with 100 iterations, there is an outer loop that is exe-

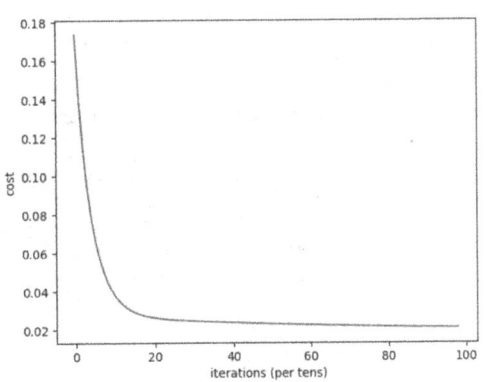

FIGURE 4.9 MSE Values with Linear Regression

cuted 100 times. During each iteration of the outer loop, the inner loop also is executed 100 times.

Linear Regression with Keras

The code sample in this section contains primarily Keras code in order to perform the linear regression. If you have read the previous examples in this chapter, this section will be easier for you to understand because the steps for linear regression are the same.

Before you proceed to the code sample, please make sure that you have Python 3.x installed (downloadable from *https://www.python.org/*

downloads) and then install TensorFlow 2 by invoking the following command:

```
pip3 install tensorflow==2
```

If necessary, you can install `pip3` by following the instructions here:

https://pip.pypa.io/en/stable/installing/

Listing 4.6 displays the content of `keras_linear_regression.py`, which illustrates how to perform a linear regression in `Keras`.

LISTING 4.6 keras_linear_regression.py

```
##########################################################
#Keep in mind the following important points:
#1) Always standardize both the input features and target
variable:
#doing so only on input features produces incorrect
predictions
#2) Data might not be normally distributed: check the
data and
#based on the distribution apply StandardScaler,
MinMaxScaler,
#Normalizer, or RobustScaler
##########################################################

import tensorflow as tf
import numpy as np
import pandas as pd
import seaborn as sns
import matplotlib.pyplot as plt
from sklearn.preprocessing import MinMaxScaler
from sklearn.model_selection import train_test_split

df = pd.read_csv('housing.csv')
X  = df.iloc[:,0:13]
y  = df.iloc[:,13].values

mmsc = MinMaxScaler()
X  = mmsc.fit_transform(X)
y  = y.reshape(-1,1)
y  = mmsc.fit_transform(y)

X_train, X_test, y_train, y_test = train_test_split(X,
y, test_size=0.3)
```

```python
# this Python method creates a Keras model
def build_keras_model():
  model = tf.keras.models.Sequential()
  model.add(tf.keras.layers.Dense(units=13,
  input_dim=13))
  model.add(tf.keras.layers.Dense(units=1))
  model.compile(optimizer='adam',loss='mean_squared_
  error',metrics=['mae','accuracy'])
  return model

batch_size=32
epochs = 40

# specify the Python method 'build_keras_model' to cre-
ate a Keras model
# using the implementation of the scikit-learn regressor
API for Keras
model       =       tf.keras.wrappers.scikit_learn.
KerasRegressor(build_fn=build_keras_model,
batch_size=batch_size,epochs=epochs)

# train ('fit') the model and then make predictions:
model.fit(X_train, y_train)
y_pred = model.predict(X_test)
#print("y_test:",y_test)
#print("y_pred:",y_pred)

# scatter plot of test values-vs-predictions
fig, ax = plt.subplots()
ax.scatter(y_test, y_pred)
ax.plot([y_test.min(), y_test.max()], [y_test.min(), y_
test.max()], 'r*--')
ax.set_xlabel('Calculated')
ax.set_ylabel('Predictions')
plt.show()
```

Listing 4.6 starts with multiple import statements and then initializes the dataframe df with the contents of the CSV file housing.csv (a portion of which is shown in Listing 4.7). Notice that the training set X is initialized with the contents of the first 13 columns of the dataset housing.csv, and the variable y contains the rightmost column of the dataset housing.csv.

The next section in Listing 4.6 uses the MinMaxScaler class to calculate the mean and standard deviation, and then invokes the fit_transform()

method in order to update the x values and the y values so that they have a mean of 0 and a standard deviation of 1.

Next, the `build_keras_mode()` Python method creates a `Keras`-based model with two dense layers. Notice that the input layer has a size of 13, which is the number of columns in the dataframe X. The next code snippet compiles the model with an `adam` optimizer, the MSE loss function, and also specifies the MAE and accuracy for the metrics. The compiled model is then returned to the caller.

The next portion of Listing 4.6 initializes the `batch_size` variable to 32 and the epochs variable to 40, and specifies them in the code snippet that creates the model, as shown here:

```
model          =          tf.keras.wrappers.scikit_learn.
KerasRegressor(build_fn=build_keras_model,
batch_size=batch_size,epochs=epochs)
```

The short comment block that appears in Listing 4.6 explains the purpose of the preceding code snippet, which constructs our `Keras` model.

The next portion of Listing 4.6 invokes the `fit()` method to train the model and then invokes the `predict()` method on the `X_test` data to calculate a set of predictions and initialize the variable `y_pred` with those predictions.

The final portion of Listing 4.6 displays a scatter plot in which the horizontal axis includes the values in `y_test` (the actual values from the CSV file `housing.csv`) and the vertical axis is the set of the predicted values.

Figure 4.5 displays a scatter plot of points based on the test values and the predictions for those test values.

Listing 4.7 displays the first four rows of the CSV file `hous-`

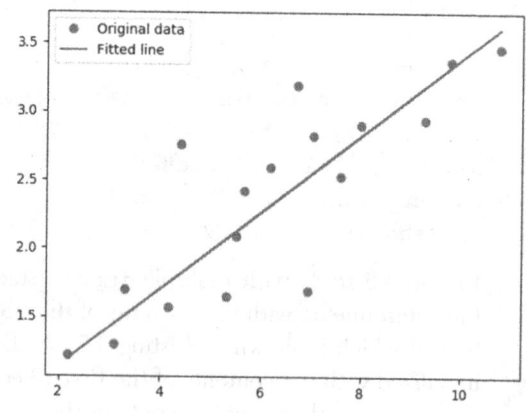

FIGURE 4.10 A Scatter Plot and a Best-Fitting Line

`ing.csv` used in the Python code in Listing 4.6.

LISTING 4.7 housing.csv

```
0.00632,18,2.31,0,0.538,6.575,65.2,4.09,1,296,15.3,396.
9,4.98,24
0.02731,0,7.07,0,0.469,6.421,78.9,4.9671,2,242,17.8,396
.9,9.14,21.6
0.02729,0,7.07,0,0.469,7.185,61.1,4.9671,2,242,17.8,392
.83,4.03,34.7
0.03237,0,2.18,0,0.458,6.998,45.8,6.0622,3,222,18.7,394
.63,2.94,33.4
```

Summary

This chapter introduced you to machine learning and concepts such as feature selection, feature engineering, data cleaning, training sets, and test sets. Next you learned about supervised, unsupervised, and semi-supervised learning. Then you learned about regression tasks, classification tasks, and clustering, as well as the steps that are typically required to prepare a dataset. These steps include feature selection or feature extraction that can be performed using various algorithms. Then you learned about issues that can arise with the data in datasets and how to rectify them.

In addition, you also learned about linear regression, along with a brief description of how to calculate a best-fitting line for a dataset of values in the Euclidean plane. You saw how to perform linear regression using NumPy in order to initialize arrays with data values, along with a perturbation technique that introduces some randomness for the y values. This technique is useful because you will know the correct values for the slope and y-intercept of the best-fitting line, which you can then compare with the trained values.

You then learned how to perform linear regression in code samples that involve Keras. In addition, you saw how to use Matplotlib to display line graphs for best-fitting lines and graphs that display the cost versus the number of iterations during the training-related code blocks.

## CHAPTER 5

WORKING WITH CLASSIFIERS

This chapter presents numerous classification algorithms in machine learning. These algorithms include the kNN (k Nearest Neighbor) algorithm, logistic regression (despite its name, it is a classifier), decision trees, random forests, SVMs, and Bayesian classifiers. The emphasis on algorithms is intended to introduce you to machine learning, and this chapter includes a tree-based code sample that relies on scikit-learn. The latter portion of this chapter contains Keras-based code samples for standard datasets.

Due to space constraints, this chapter does not cover other well-known algorithms (such as Linear Discriminant Analysis) and the k-Means algorithm (which is for unsupervised learning and clustering). However, there are many online tutorials available that discuss these and other algorithms in machine learning.

With the preceding points in mind, the first section of this chapter briefly discusses the classifiers that are mentioned in the introductory paragraph. The second section of this chapter provides an overview of activation functions, which will be very useful if you decide to learn about deep neural networks. In this section, you will learn how and why they are used in neural networks. This section also contains a list of the TensorFlow 2/ Keras APIs for activation functions, followed by a description of some of their merits.

The third section introduces logistic regression, which relies on the sigmoid function. Although neural networks often use the ReLU activation function, the sigmoid function (as well as the tanh function) is used in

RNNs (Recurrent Neural Networks) and LSTMs (Long Short Term Memory). The fourth part of this chapter contains a code sample involving logistic regression and the MNIST dataset.

In order to give you some context, classifiers are one of three major types of algorithms: regression algorithms (such as linear regression in Chapter 4), classification algorithms (discussed in this chapter), and clustering algorithms (such as k-Means, which is not discussed in this book).

The section pertaining to activation functions does involve a basic understanding of the hidden layers in a neural network. Depending on your comfort level, you might benefit from reading some preparatory material before diving into this section (there are many articles available online).

Finally, if you are unfamiliar with `Keras`, please read the `Keras`-related appendix that contains a simple introduction to `Keras`.

What is Classification?

Given a dataset that contains observations whose class membership is known, classification is the task of determining the class to which a new datapoint belongs. Classes refer to categories and are also called targets or labels. For example, spam detection for email service providers involves binary classification (only 2 classes). The MNIST dataset contains a set of images where each image is a single digit, which means there are 10 labels. Some applications in classification include credit approval, medical diagnosis, and target marketing.

What are Classifiers?

In the previous chapter, you learned that linear regression uses supervised learning in conjunction with numeric data. The goal is to train a model that can make numeric predictions (e.g., the price of stock tomorrow, the temperature of a system, its barometric pressure, and so forth). By contrast, classifiers use supervised learning in conjunction with non-numeric classes of data. The goal is to train a model that can make categorical predictions.

For instance, suppose that each row in a dataset is a specific wine, and each column pertains to a specific wine feature (tannin, acidity, and so forth). Suppose further that there are five classes of wine in the dataset: for simplicity, let's label them A, B, C, D, and E. Given a new data point, which is to say a new row of data, a classifier for this dataset attempts to determine the label for this wine.

Some of the classifiers in this chapter can perform categorical classification and also make numeric predictions (i.e., they can be used for regression as well as classification).

Common Classifiers

Some of the most popular classifiers for machine learning are listed here (in no particular order):

- linear classifiers
- kNN
- logistic regression
- decision trees
- random forests
- SVMs
- Bayesian classifiers
- CNNs (deep learning)

Keep in mind that different classifiers have different advantages and disadvantages, which often involve a trade-off between complexity and accuracy, similar to algorithms in fields that are outside of AI.

In the case of Deep Learning, CNNs (Convolutional Neural Networks) perform image classification, which makes them classifiers (they can also be used for audio and text processing).

The upcoming sections provide a brief description of the ML classifiers that are listed in the previous list.

Binary versus Multi-Class Classification

Binary classifiers work with datasets that have two classes, whereas multi-class classifiers (sometimes called multinomial classifiers) distinguish more than two classes. Random forest classifiers and naïve Bayes classifiers support multiple classes, whereas SVMs and linear classifiers are used as binary classifiers. Note that there are techniques in which SVMs can be used as multi-class classifiers.

In addition, some of the techniques for multi-class classification are based on binary classifiers: One-versus-All (OvA) and One-versus-One (OvO).

The OvA technique (also called One-versus-The-Rest) involves multiple binary classifiers that are equal to the number of classes. For example, if a dataset has five classes, then OvA uses five binary classifiers, each of which detects one of the five classes. In order to classify a datapoint in this particular dataset, select the binary classifier that outputs the highest score.

The OvO technique also involves multiple binary classifiers, but in this case, a binary classifier is used to train on a pair of classes. For instance, if the classes are A, B, C, D, and E, then 10 binary classifiers are required: one for A and B, one for A and C, one for A and D, and so forth, until we reach the last binary classifier for D and E.

In general, if there are n classes, then $n*(n-1)/2$ binary classifiers are required. Although the OvO technique requires considerably more binary classifiers (e.g., 190 are required for 20 classes) than the OvA technique (e.g., a mere 20 binary classifiers for 20 classes), the OvO technique has the advantage that each binary classifier is only trained on the portion of the dataset that pertains to its two chosen classes.

Multi-Label Classification

Multi-label classification involves assigning multiple labels to an instance from a dataset. Hence, multi-label classification generalizes multi-class classification (discussed in the previous section), where the latter involves assigning a single label to an instance belonging to a dataset that has multiple classes. An article involving multi-label classification that contains `Keras`-based code is here:

https://medium.com/@vijayabhaskar96/multi-label-image-classification-tutorial-with-keras-imagedatagenerator-cd541f8eaf24

You can also perform an online search for articles that involve scikit-learn or PyTorch for multi-label classification tasks.

What are Linear Classifiers?

A linear classifier separates a dataset into two classes. A linear classifier is a line for 2D points, a plane for 3D points, and a hyper plane (a generalization of a plane) for higher dimensional points.

Linear classifiers are often the fastest classifiers, so they are often used when the speed of classification is of high importance. Linear classifiers usually work well when the input vectors are sparse (i.e., mostly zero values) or when the number of dimensions is large.

What is kNN?

The kNN (k Nearest Neighbor) algorithm is a classification algorithm. In brief, data points that are near each other are classified as belonging to the same class. When a new point is introduced, it's added to the class of the majority of its nearest neighbor. For example, suppose that k equals 3, and a new data point is introduced. Look at the class of its 3 nearest neighbors: let's say they are A, A, and B. Then by majority vote, the new data point is labeled as a data point of class A.

The kNN algorithm is essentially a heuristic and not a technique with complex mathematical underpinnings, and yet it's still an effective and useful algorithm.

Try the kNN algorithm if you want to use a simple algorithm, or when you believe that the nature of your dataset is highly unstructured. The kNN algorithm can produce highly nonlinear decisions despite being very simple. You can use kNN in search applications where you are searching for similar items.

Measure similarity by creating a vector representation of the items, and then compare the vectors using an appropriate distance metric (such as the Euclidean distance). Some concrete examples of kNN search include searching for semantically similar documents.

How to Handle a Tie in kNN

An odd value for k is less likely to result in a tie vote, but it's not impossible. For example, suppose that k equals 7, and when a new data point is introduced, its 7 nearest neighbors belong to the set {A,B,A,B,A,B,C}. As you can see, there is no majority vote, because there are 3 points in class A, 3 points in class B, and 1 point in class C.

There are several techniques for handling a tie in kNN, as listed here:

- Assign higher weights to closer points.
- Increase the value of k until a winner is determined.
- Decrease the value of k until a winner is determined.
- Randomly select one class.

If you reduce k until it equals 1, it's still possible to have a tie vote: there might be two points that are equally distant from the new point, so you need a mechanism for deciding which of those two points to select as the 1-neighbor.

If there is a tie between classes A and B, then randomly select either class A or class B. Another variant is to keep track of the tie votes, and alternate round-robin style to ensure a more even distribution.

What are Decision Trees?

Decision trees are another type of classification algorithm that involve a tree-like structure. In a "generic" tree-based data structure, the placement of a data point is determined by conditional logic. As a simple illustration, suppose that a dataset contains a set of numbers that represents the ages of people, and let's also suppose that the first number is 50. This number is chosen as the root of the tree, and all numbers that are smaller than 50 are added on the left branch of the tree, whereas all numbers that are greater than 50 are added on the right branch of the tree.

For example, suppose we have the sequence of numbers of {50, 25, 70, 40}. Then we can construct a tree as follows: 50 is the root node; 25 is the left child of 50; 70 is the right child of 50; and 40 is the right child of 20. Each additional numeric value that we add to this dataset is processed to determine which direction to proceed ("left or right") at each node in the tree.

Listing 5.1 displays the content of sklearn_tree2.py, which defines a set of 2D points in the Euclidean plane, along with their labels, and then predicts the label (i.e., the class) of several other 2D points in the Euclidean plane.

LISTING 5.1 sklearn_tree2.py

```
from sklearn import tree

# X = pairs of 2D points and Y = the class of each point
X = [[0, 0], [1, 1], [2,2]]
Y = [0, 1, 1]

tree_clf = tree.DecisionTreeClassifier()
tree_clf = tree_clf.fit(X, Y)

#predict the class of samples:
print("predict class of [-1., -1.]:")
print(tree_clf.predict([[-1., -1.]]))

print("predict class of [2., 2.]:")
print(tree_clf.predict([[2., 2.]]))
```

```
# The percentage of training samples of the same class
# in a leaf node equals the probability of each class
print("probability of each class in [2.,2.]:")
print(tree_clf.predict_proba([[2., 2.]]))
```

Listing 5.1 imports the tree class from sklearn and then initializes the arrays X and y with data values. Next, the variable tree_clf is initialized as an instance of the DecisionTreeClassifier class, after which it is trained by invoking the fit() method with the values of X and y.

Now launch the code in Listing 5.3 and you will see the following output:

```
predict class of [-1., -1.]:
[0]
predict class of [2., 2.]:
[1]
probability of each class in [2.,2.]:
[[0. 1.]]
```

As you can see, the points [-1,-1] and [2,2] are correctly labeled with the values 0 and 1, respectively, which is probably what you expected.

Listing 5.2 displays the content of sklearn_tree3.py, which extends the code in Listing 5.1 by adding a third label, and also by predicting the label of three points instead of two points in the Euclidean plane (the modifications are shown in bold).

LISTING 5.2 sklearn_tree3.py

```
from sklearn import tree

# X = pairs of 2D points and Y = the class of each point
X = [[0, 0], [1, 1], [2,2]]
Y = [0, 1, 2]

tree_clf = tree.DecisionTreeClassifier()
tree_clf = tree_clf.fit(X, Y)

#predict the class of samples:
print("predict class of [-1., -1.]:")
print(tree_clf.predict([[-1., -1.]]))

print("predict class of [0.8, 0.8]:")
print(tree_clf.predict([[0.8, 0.8]]))

print("predict class of [2., 2.]:")
print(tree_clf.predict([[2., 2.]]))
```

```
# The percentage of training samples of the same class
# in a leaf node equals the probability of each class
print("probability of each class in [2.,2.]:")
print(tree_clf.predict_proba([[2., 2.]]))
```

Now launch the code in Listing 5.2 and you will see the following output:

```
predict class of [-1., -1.]:
[0]
predict class of [0.8, 0.8]:
[1]
predict class of [2., 2.]:
[2]
probability of each class in [2.,2.]:
[[0. 0. 1.]]
```

As you can see, the points [-1,-1], [0.8, 0.8], and [2,2] are correctly labeled with the values 0, 1, and 2, respectively, which is probably what you expected.

Listing 5.3 displays a portion of the dataset partial_wine.csv, which contains two features and a label column (there are three classes). The total row count for this dataset is 178.

LISTING 5.3 partial_wine.csv

```
Alcohol, Malic acid, class
14.23,1.71,1
13.2,1.78,1
13.16,2.36,1
14.37,1.95,1
13.24,2.59,1
14.2,1.76,1
```

Listing 5.4 displays content of tree_classifier.py, which uses a decision tree to train a model on the dataset partial_wine.csv.

LISTING 5.4 tree_classifier.py

```
import numpy as np
import matplotlib.pyplot as plt
import pandas as pd

# Importing the dataset
dataset = pd.read_csv('partial_wine.csv')
```

```
X = dataset.iloc[:, [0, 1]].values
y = dataset.iloc[:, 2].values

# split the dataset into a training set and a test set
from sklearn.model_selection import train_test_split
X_train, X_test, y_train, y_test = train_test_split(X,
y, test_size = 0.25, random_state = 0)

# Feature Scaling
from sklearn.preprocessing import StandardScaler
sc = StandardScaler()
X_train = sc.fit_transform(X_train)
X_test = sc.transform(X_test)

# ====> INSERT YOUR CLASSIFIER CODE HERE <====
from sklearn.tree import DecisionTreeClassifier
classifier                                     =
DecisionTreeClassifier(criterion='entropy',random_
state=0)
classifier.fit(X_train, y_train)
# ====> INSERT YOUR CLASSIFIER CODE HERE <====

# predict the test set results
y_pred = classifier.predict(X_test)

# generate the confusion matrix
from sklearn.metrics import confusion_matrix
cm = confusion_matrix(y_test, y_pred)
print("confusion matrix:")
print(cm)
```

Listing 5.4 contains some import statements and then populates the Pandas DataFrame dataset with the contents of the CSV file partial_wine. csv. Next, the variable X is initialized with the first two columns (and all the rows) of the dataset, and the variable y is initialized with the third column (and all the rows) of the dataset.

Next, the variables X_train, X_test, y_train, and y_test are populated with data from X and y using a 75/25 split proportion. Notice that the variable sc (which is an instance of the StandardScalar class) performs a scaling operation on the variables X_train and X_test.

The code block shown in bold in Listing 5.4 is where we create an instance of the DecisionTreeClassifier class, and then train the instance with the data in the variables X_train and X_test.

The next portion of Listing 5.4 populates the variable y_pred with a set of predictions that are generated from the data in the X_test variable. The last portion of Listing 5.4 creates a confusion matrix based on the data in y_test and the predicted data in y_pred.

Remember that all the diagonal elements of a confusion matrix are correct predictions (such as true positive and true negative); all the other cells contain a numeric value that specifies the number of predictions that are incorrect (such as false positive and false negative).

Now launch the code in Listing 5.4, and you will see the following output for the confusion matrix in which there are 36 correct predictions and 9 incorrect predictions (with an accuracy of 80%):

```
confusion matrix:
[[13  1  2]
 [ 0 17  4]
 [ 1  1  6]]
from sklearn.metrics import confusion_matrix
```

There is a total of 45 entries in the preceding 3x3 matrix, and the diagonal entries are correctly identified labels. Hence, the accuracy is 36/45 = 0.80.

What are Random Forests?

Random forests are a generalization of decision trees. This classification algorithm involves multiple trees (and the number of trees is specified by you). If the data involves making a numeric prediction, the average of the predictions of the trees is computed. If the data involves a categorical prediction, the mode of the predictions of the trees is determined.

By way of analogy, random forests operate in a manner similar to financial portfolio diversification: the goal is to balance the losses with higher gains. Random forests use a "majority vote" to make predictions, which operates under the assumption that selecting the majority vote is more likely to be correct (more often) than any individual prediction from a single tree.

You can easily modify the code in Listing 5.4 to use a random forest by replacing the two lines shown in bold with the following code:

```
from sklearn.ensemble import RandomForestClassifier
classifier  =  RandomForestClassifier(n_estimators  =  10,
criterion='entropy', random_state = 0)
```

Change this code, launch the code, and examine the confusion matrix to compare its accuracy with the accuracy of the decision tree in Listing 5.4.

What are SVMs?

Support Vector Machines involve a supervised machine learning algorithm and can be used for classification or regression problems. SVM can work with non-linearly separable data as well as linearly separable data. SVM uses a technique called the "kernel trick" to transform data and then finds an optimal boundary. The transform involves a higher dimensionality. This technique results in a separation of the transformed data, after which it's possible to find a hyperplane that separates the data into two classes.

SVMs are more common in classification tasks than in regression tasks. Some use cases for SVMs include:

- text classification tasks (category assignment)
- detecting spam/sentiment analysis
- image recognition (aspect-based recognition color-based classification)
- handwritten digit recognition (postal automation)

Tradeoffs of SVMs

Although SVMs are extremely powerful, there are tradeoffs involved. Some of the advantages of SVMs are listed here:

- high accuracy
- work well on smaller cleaner datasets
- can be more efficient because they use a subset of training points
- an alternative to CNNs in cases of limited datasets
- capture more complex relationships between data points

Despite the power of SVMs, there are some disadvantages of SVMs, which are listed here:

- not suited to larger datasets (the training time can be high)
- less effective on noisier datasets with overlapping classes

SVMs involve more parameters than decision trees and random forests.

Modify Listing 5.4 to use an SVM by replacing the two lines shown in bold with the following two lines shown in bold:

```
from sklearn.svm import SVC
classifier = SVC(kernel = 'linear', random_state = 0)
```

You now have an SVM-based model, simply by making the previous code update! Make the code change, then launch the code, and examine the confusion matrix to compare its accuracy with the accuracy of the decision tree model and the random forest model earlier in this chapter.

What is Bayesian Inference?

Bayesian inference is an important technique in statistics that involves statistical inference and Bayes' theorem to update the probability for a hypothesis as more information becomes available. Bayesian inference is often called "Bayesian probability," and it's important in the dynamic analysis of sequential data.

Bayes' Theorem

Given two sets A and B, let's define the following numeric values (all of them are between 0 and 1):

```
P(A) = probability of being in set A
P(B) = probability of being in set B
P(Both) = probability of being in A intersect B
P(A|B) = probability of being in A (given you're in B)
P(B|A) = probability of being in B (given you're in A)
```

Then the following formulas are also true:

```
P(A|B) = P(Both)/P(B)  (#1)
P(B|A) = P(Both)/P(A)  (#2)
```

Multiply the preceding pair of equations by the term that appears in the denominator and we get these equations:

```
P(B)*P(A|B) = P(Both)  (#3)
P(A)*P(B|A) = P(Both)  (#4)
```

Now set the left side of equations #3 and #4 equal to each another, which gives us this equation:

```
P(B)*P(A|B) = P(A)*P(B|A)  (#5)
```

Divide both sides of #5 by P(B), and we get this well-known equation:

```
P(A|B) = P(A)*P(A|B)/P(B)  (#6)
```

Some Bayesian Terminology

In the previous section, we derived the following relationship:

```
P(h|d) = (P(d|h) * P(h)) / P(d)
```

There is a name for each of the four terms in the preceding equation, as discussed below.

First, the *posterior probability* is `P(h|d)`, which is the probability of hypothesis h given the data d.

Second, `P(d|h)` is the probability of data d given that the hypothesis h was true.

Third, the prior probability of h is `P(h)`, which is the probability of hypothesis h being true (regardless of the data).

Finally, `P(d)` is the probability of the data (regardless of the hypothesis).

We are interested in calculating the posterior probability of `P(h|d)` from the prior probability `p(h)` with `P(d)` and `P(d|h)`.

What is MAP?

The maximum a posteriori (MAP) hypothesis is the hypothesis with the highest probability, which is the maximum probable hypothesis. This can be written as follows:

```
MAP(h) = max(P(h|d))
```

or:

```
MAP(h) = max((P(d|h) * P(h)) / P(d))
```

or:

```
MAP(h) = max(P(d|h) * P(h))
```

Why Use Bayes' Theorem?

Bayes' Theorem describes the probability of an event based on the prior knowledge of the conditions that might be related to the event. If we know the conditional probability, we can use the Bayes' rule to find out the reverse probabilities. The previous statement is the general representation of the Bayes' rule.

What is a Bayesian Classifier?

A Naive Bayes (NB) classifier is a probabilistic classifier inspired by the Bayes' theorem. An NB classifier assumes the attributes are conditionally independent and it works well even when assumption is not true. This assumption greatly reduces computational cost, and it's a simple algorithm to implement that only requires linear time. Moreover, an NB classifier is easily scalable to larger datasets and good results are obtained in most cases. Other advantages of an NB classifier are as follows:

- can be used for binary and multi-class classification
- provides different types of NB algorithms
- a good choice for Text Classification problems
- a popular choice for spam email classification
- can be easily trained on small datasets

As you can probably surmise, NB classifiers do have some disadvantages, as listed below:

- all features are assumed unrelated
- it cannot learn relationships between features
- it can suffer from "the zero probability problem"

The "zero probability problem" refers to the case when the conditional probability is zero for an attribute, so it fails to give a valid prediction. However, it can be fixed explicitly using a Laplacian estimator.

Types of Naïve Bayes Classifiers

There are three major types of NB classifiers:

- Gaussian Naive Bayes
- Multinomial NB Naive Bayes
- Bernoulli Naive Bayes

Details of these classifiers are beyond the scope of this chapter, but you can perform an online search for more information.

Training Classifiers

Some common techniques for training classifiers are:

- holdout method
- k-fold cross-validation

The *holdout method* is the most common method, which starts by dividing the dataset into two partitions called train and test (80% and 20%, respectively). The train set is used for training the model, and the test data tests its predictive power.

The *k-fold cross-validation* technique is used to verify that the model is not over-fitted. The dataset is randomly partitioned into k mutually-exclusive subsets, where each partition is of equal size. One partition is for testing, and the other partitions are for training. You iterate throughout the whole of the k folds.

Evaluating Classifiers

Whenever you select a classifier for a dataset, it's obviously important to evaluate the accuracy of that classifier. Some common techniques for evaluating classifiers are:

- Precision and Recall
- ROC curve (Receiver Operating Characteristics)

Precision and recall are discussed in Chapter 2 and reproduced here for your convenience. Let's define the following variables:

```
TP = the number of true positive results
FP = the number of false positive results
TN = the number of true negative results
FN = the number of false negative results
```

Then the definitions of precision, accuracy, and recall are given by the following formulas:

```
precision = TP/(TN + FP)
accuracy  = (TP + TN)/[P + N]
recall    = TP/[TP + FN]
```

The *ROC (Receiver Operating Characteristics) curve* is used for the visual comparison of classification models that shows the trade-off between the true positive rate and the false positive rate. The area under the ROC curve is a measure of the accuracy of the model. When a model is closer to the diagonal, it is less accurate. A model with perfect accuracy will have an area of 1.0.

The ROC curve plots the True Positive Rate versus the False Positive Rate. Another type of curve is the PR curve that plots the Precision versus

Recall. When dealing with highly skewed datasets (a strong class imbalance), the Precision-Recall (PR) curves give good results.

Later in this chapter, you will see many of the `Keras`-based classes (located in the tf.keras.metrics namespace) that correspond to common statistical terms, which include some of the terms in this section.

This concludes the portion of the chapter pertaining to statistical terms and techniques for measuring the validity of a dataset. Now let's look at activation functions in machine learning, which is the topic of the next section.

What are Activation Functions?

An activation function is (usually) a non-linear function that introduces non-linearity into a neural network, thereby preventing a "consolidation" of the hidden layers in neural network. Suppose that every pair of adjacent layers in a neural network involves just a matrix transformation *without* an activation function. Such a network is a linear system, which means that its layers can be consolidated into a much smaller system.

First, we can use a matrix to represent the weights of the edges that connect the input layer with the first hidden layer: let's call it W1. Next, we can use another matrix to represent the weights of the edges that connect the first hidden layer with the second hidden layer: let's call it W2. Repeat this process until we reach the edges that connect the final hidden layer with the output layer: let's call this matrix Wk. Since we do not have an activation function, we can simply multiply the matrices W1, W2, ..., Wk together and produce one matrix: let's call it W. We have now replaced the original neural network with an equivalent neural network that contains one input layer, a single matrix of weight W, and an output layer. In other words, we no longer have our original multi-layered neural network!

Fortunately, we can prevent the previous scenario from happening when we specify an activation function between every pair of adjacent layers. In other words, an activation function at each layer prevents this "matrix consolidation." Hence, we can maintain all the intermediate hidden layers during the process of training the neural network.

For simplicity, let's assume that we have the same activation function between every pair of adjacent layers (we'll remove this assumption shortly). The process for using an activation function in a neural network is described as follows:

1) Start with an input vector x1 of numbers.

2) Multiply x1 by the matrix of weight W1 that represents the edges that connect the input layer with the first hidden layer: the result is a new vector x2.

3) "Apply" the activation function to each element of x2 to create another vector x3.

Now we repeat Steps 2 and 3, except that we use the "starting" vector x3 and the weights matrix W2 for the edges that connect the first hidden layer with the second hidden layer (or just the output layer if there is only one hidden layer).

After completing the preceding process, we have "preserved" the neural network, which means that it can be trained on a dataset. One other thing: instead of using the same activation function at each step, you can replace each activation function by a different activation function (the choice is yours).

Why do we Need Activation Functions?

The previous section outlines the process for transforming an input vector from the input layer and then through the hidden layers until it reaches the output layer. The purpose of activation functions in neural networks is vitally important, so it's worth repeating here: *activation functions "maintain" the structure of neural networks and prevent them from being reduced to an input layer and an output layer.*

Hence, if we include a non-linear activation function between every pair of consecutive layers, then the neural network cannot be reduced with a neural network that contains fewer layers unless you explicitly remove them.

Without a non-linear activation function, we simply multiply a weight matrix for a given pair of consecutive layers with the output vector that is produced from the previous pair of consecutive layers. We repeat this simple multiplication until we reach the output layer of the neural network. After reaching the output layer, we have effectively replaced multiple matrices with a single matrix that "connects" the input layer with the output layer.

How do Activation Functions Work?

If this is the first time you have encountered the concept of an activation function, it's probably confusing, so here's an analogy that might be helpful. Suppose you're driving your car late at night and there's nobody else on the highway. You can drive at a constant speed for as long as there are no obstacles (stop signs, traffic lights, and so forth). On the other hand, suppose you drive into the parking lot of a large grocery store. When you approach a speed bump you must slow down, cross the speed bump, and increase speed again, and repeat this process for every speed bump.

Think of the non-linear activation functions in a neural network as the counterpart to the speed bumps: you simply cannot maintain a constant speed, which (by analogy) means that you cannot first multiply all the weight matrices together and "collapse" them into a single weight matrix. Another analogy involves a road with multiple toll booths: you must slow down, pay the toll, and then resume driving until you reach the next toll booth. These are only analogies (and hence imperfect) to help you understand the need for non-linear activation functions.

Common Activation Functions

Although there are many activation functions (and you can define your own if you know how to do so), here is a list of common activation functions, followed by brief descriptions:

- Sigmoid
- Tanh
- ReLU
- ReLU6
- ELU
- SELU

The `sigmoid` activation function is based on Euler's constant e, with a range of values between 0 and 1, and its formula is shown here:

```
1/[1+e^(-x)]
```

The `tanh` activation function is also based on Euler's constant e, and its formula is shown here:

```
[e^x - e^(-x)]/[e^x+e^(-x)]
```

One way to remember the preceding formula is to note that the numerator and denominator have the same pair of terms: they are separated by a "-" sign in the numerator and a "+" sign in the denominator. The tanh function has a range of values between -1 and 1.

The ReLU (Rectified Linear Unit) activation function is straightforward: if x is negative, then ReLU(x) is 0; for all other values of x, ReLU(x) equals x. ReLU6 is specific to TensorFlow, and it's a variation of ReLU(x): the additional constraint is that ReLU(x) equals 6 when x >= 6 (hence its name).

ELU is Exponential Linear Unit, and it's the exponential "envelope" of ReLU, which replaces the two linear segments of ReLU with an exponential activation function that is differentiable for all values of x (including x = 0).

SELU is an acronym for Scaled Exponential Linear Unit, and it's slightly more complicated than the other activation functions (and used less frequently). For a thorough explanation of these and other activation functions (along with graphs that depict their shape), navigate to the following Wikipedia link:

https://en.wikipedia.org/wiki/Activation_function

The preceding link provides a long list of activation functions as well as their derivatives.

Activation Functions in Python

Listing 5.5 displays content of the file `activations.py`, which contains the formulas for the various activation functions.

LISTING 5.5 activations.py

```
import numpy as np

# Python sigmoid example:
z = 1/(1 + np.exp(-np.dot(W, x)))

# Python tanh example:
z = np.tanh(np.dot(W,x))

# Python ReLU example:
z = np.maximum(0, np.dot(W, x))
```

Listing 5.5 contains Python code that uses NumPy methods to define a sigmoid function, a `tanh` function, and a ReLU function. Note that you need to specify values for x and W to launch the code in Listing 5.5.

Keras Activation Functions

TensorFlow (and many other frameworks) provide implementations for many activation functions, which saves you the time and effort when writing your own implementation of activation functions.

Here is a list of TensorFlow 2/Keras APIs activation functions that are located in the tf.keras.layers namespace:

- tf.keras.layers.leaky_relu
- tf.keras.layers.relu
- tf.keras.layers.relu6
- tf.keras.layers.selu
- tf.keras.layers.sigmoid
- tf.keras.layers.sigmoid_cross_entropy_with_logits
- tf.keras.layers.softmax
- tf.keras.layers.softmax_cross_entropy_with_logits_v2
- tf.keras.layers.softplus
- tf.keras.layers.softsign
- tf.keras.layers.softmax_cross_entropy_with_logits
- tf.keras.layers.tanh
- tf.keras.layers.weighted_cross_entropy_with_logits</UL>

The following subsections provide additional information regarding some of the activation functions in the preceding list. Keep the following point in mind: for general neural networks, use ReLU as your first choice.

The ReLU and ELU Activation Functions

Currently, ReLU is often the preferred activation function. Previously, the preferred activation function was tanh (and before tanh, it was sigmoid). ReLU behaves similarly to a linear unit and provides the best training accuracy and validation accuracy.

ReLU is like a switch for linearity: it's "off" if you don't need it, and its derivative is 1 when it's active, which makes ReLU the simplest of all the current activation functions. Note that the second derivative of the function is 0 everywhere: it's a very simple function that simplifies optimization. In addition, the gradient is large whenever you need large values, and it never "saturates" (i.e., it does not shrink to zero on the positive horizontal axis).

Rectified linear units and generalized versions are based on the principle that linear models are easier to optimize. Use the ReLU activation function or one of its related alternatives (discussed later).

The Advantages and Disadvantages of ReLU

The following list contains the advantages of the ReLU activation function:

- does not saturate in the positive region
- very efficient in terms of computation
- models with ReLU typically converge faster those with other activation functions

However, ReLU does have a disadvantage when the activation value of a ReLU neuron becomes 0: then the gradients of the neuron will also be 0 during back-propagation. You can mitigate this scenario by judiciously assigning the values for the initial weights as well as the learning rate.

ELU

ELU is an acronym for *exponential linear unit* that is based on ReLU: the key difference is that ELU is differentiable at the origin (ReLU is a continuous function, but it is not differentiable at the origin). However, keep in mind several points. First, ELUs trade computational efficiency for "immortality" (immunity to dying). Read the following paper for more details: *arxiv.org/abs/1511.07289*. Secondly, ReLUs are still popular and preferred over ELU because the use of ELU introduces an additional new hyper-parameter.

Sigmoid, Softmax, and Hardmax Similarities

The `sigmoid` activation function has an output range in $(0,1)$, and it saturates and "kills" gradients for large input values (be they positive or negative). Unlike the tanh activation function, `sigmoid` outputs are not zero-centered. In addition, both `sigmoid` and `softmax` (discussed later) are discouraged for vanilla feed forward implementation (see Chapter 6 of the online book, *Deep Learning*, by Ian Goodfellow et al.). However, the `sigmoid` activation function is still used in LSTMs (specifically for the forget gate, input gate, and the output gate), GRUs (Gated Recurrent Units), and probabilistic models. Moreover, some autoencoders have additional requirements that preclude the use of piecewise linear activation functions.

Softmax

The `softmax` activation function maps the values in a dataset to another set of values that are between 0 and 1, and whose sum equals 1. Thus, `softmax` creates a probability distribution. In the case of image classification with Convolutional Neural Networks (CNNs), the `softmax` activation function "maps" the values in the final hidden layer to the 10 neurons in the output layer. The index of the position that contains the largest probability is matched with the index of the number 1 in the one-hot encoding of the input image. If the index values are equal, then the image has been classified, otherwise it's considered a mismatch.

Softplus

The `softplus` activation function is a smooth (i.e., differentiable) approximation to the ReLU activation function. Recall that the origin is the only non-differentiable point of the ReLU function, which is "smoothed" by the `softmax` activation whose equation is here:

```
f(x) = ln(1 + e^x)
```

Tanh

The `tanh` activation function has a range in (-1,1), whereas the `sigmoid` function has a range in (0,1). Both of these two activations saturate, but unlike the `sigmoid` neuron, the tanh output is zero-centered. Therefore, in practice, the `tanh` non-linearity is always preferred over the `sigmoid` nonlinearity.

The `sigmoid` and `tanh` activation functions appear in LSTMs (sigmoid for the three gates and tanh for the internal cell state) as well as GRUs (Gated Recurrent Units) during the calculations pertaining to the input gates, forget gates, and output gates (discussed in more detail in the next chapter).

Sigmoid, Softmax, and HardMax Differences

This section briefly discusses some of the differences among these three functions. First, the `sigmoid` function is used for binary classification in the logistic regression model, as well as the gates in LSTMs and GRUs. The `sigmoid` function is used as an activation function while building neural networks, but keep in mind that the sum of the probabilities is *not* necessarily equal to 1.

Second, the softmax function generalizes the sigmoid function: it's used for multi-classification in the logistic regression model. The softmax function is the activation function for the "fully connected layer" in CNNs, which is the right-most hidden layer and the output layer. Unlike the sigmoid function, the sum of the probabilities *must* equal 1. You can use either the sigmoid function or softmax for binary (n=2) classification.

Third, the so-called "hardmax" function assigns 0 or 1 to output values (similar to a step function). For example, suppose that we have three classes {c1, c2, c3} whose scores are [1, 7, 2], respectively. The hardmax probabilities are [0, 1, 0], whereas the softmax probabilities are [0.1, 0.7, 0.2]. Notice that the sum of the hardmax probabilities is 1, which is also true of the sum of the softmax probabilities. However, the hardmax probabilities are all-or-nothing, whereas the softmax probabilities are analogous to receiving "partial credit."

What is Logistic Regression?

Despite its name, logistic regression is a classifier and a linear model with a binary output. Logistic regression works with multiple independent variables and involves a sigmoid function for calculating probabilities. Logistic regression is essentially the result of "applying" the sigmoid activation function to linear regression in order to perform binary classification.

Logistic regression is useful in a variety of unrelated fields. Such fields include machine learning, various medical fields, and social sciences. Logistic regression can be used to predict the risk of developing a given disease based on various observed characteristics of the patient. Other fields that use logistic regression include engineering, marketing, and economics.

Logistic regression can be binomial (only two outcomes for a dependent variable), multinomial (three or more outcomes for a dependent variable), or ordinal (dependent variables are ordered). For instance, suppose that a dataset consists of data that belong either to class A or to class B. If you are given a new data point, logistic regression predicts whether that new data point belongs to class A or to class B. By contrast, linear regression predicts a numeric value, such as the next-day value of a stock.

Setting a Threshold Value

The threshold value is a numeric value that determines which data points belong to class A and which points belong to class B. For instance, a pass/

fail threshold might be 0.70. A pass/fail threshold for passing a written driver's test in California is 0.85.

As another example, suppose that p = 0.5 is the "cutoff" probability. Then we can assign class A to the data points that occur with probability > 0.5 and assign class B to data points that occur with probability <= 0.5. Since there are only two classes, we do have a classifier.

A similar (yet slightly different) scenario involves tossing a well-balanced coin. We know that there is a 50% chance of throwing heads (let's label this outcome as class A) and a 50% chance of throwing tails (let's label this outcome as class B). If we have a dataset that consists of labeled outcomes, then we have the expectation that approximately 50% of them are class A and class B.

On the other hand, we have no way to determine (in advance) what percentage of people will pass their written driver's test, or the percentage of people who will pass their course. Datasets containing outcomes for these types of scenarios need to be trained, and logistic regression can be a suitable technique for doing so.

Logistic Regression: Important Assumptions

Logistic regression requires the observations to be independent of each other. In addition, logistic regression requires little or no multi-collinearity among the independent variables. Logistic regression handles numeric, categorical, and continuous variables, and also assumes linearity of independent variables and log odds, which is defined here:

```
odds = p/(1-p) and logit = log(odds)
```

This analysis does not require the dependent and independent variables to be related linearly; however, another requirement is that independent variables are linearly related to the log odds.

Logistic regression is used to obtain the odds ratio in the presence of more than one explanatory variable. The procedure is quite similar to multiple linear regression, with the exception that the response variable is binomial. The result is the impact of each variable on the odds ratio of the observed event of interest.

Linearly Separable Data

Linearly separable data is data that can be separated by a line (in 2D), a plane (in 3D), or a hyperplane (in higher dimensions). Linearly non-separable data is data (clusters) that cannot be separated by a line or a hyperplane. For example, the XOR function involves data points that cannot be separated by a line. If you create a truth table for an XOR function with two inputs, the points (0,0) and (1,1) belong to class 0, whereas the points (0,1) and (1,0) belong to class 1 (draw these points in a 2D plane to convince yourself). The solution involves transforming the data in a higher dimension so that it becomes linearly separable, which is the technique used in SVMS (discussed earlier in this chapter).

Keras, Logistic Regression, and Iris Dataset

Listing 5.6 displays the content of tf2-keras-iris.py, which defines a Keras-based model to perform logistic regression.

LISTING 5.6 tf2-keras-iris.py

```
import tensorflow as tf
import matplotlib.pyplot as plt

from sklearn.datasets import load_iris
from sklearn.model_selection import train_test_split
from    sklearn.preprocessing    import    OneHotEncoder,
StandardScaler

iris = load_iris()
X = iris['data']
y = iris['target']

#you can view the data and the labels:
#print("iris data:",X)
#print("iris target:",y)

# scale the X values so they are between 0 and 1
scaler = StandardScaler()
X_scaled = scaler.fit_transform(X)

X_train, X_test, y_train, y_test = train_test_split(X_
scaled, y, test_size = 0.2)

model = tf.keras.models.Sequential()
model.add(tf.keras.layers.Dense(activation='relu',
input_dim=4,units=4, kernel_initializer='uniform')) .
```

```
model.add(tf.keras.layers.Dense(activation='relu',
units=4, kernel_initializer='uniform'))
model.add(tf.keras.layers.Dense(activation='sigmoid',
units=1,kernel_initializer='uniform'))
#model.add(tf.keras.layers.Dense(1,
activation='softmax'))

model.compile(optimizer='adam',        loss='mean_squared_
error', metrics=['accuracy'])

model.fit(X_train, y_train, batch_size=10, epochs=100)

# Predicting values from the test set
y_pred = model.predict(X_test)

# scatter plot of test values-vs-predictions
fig, ax = plt.subplots()
ax.scatter(y_test, y_pred)
ax.plot([y_test.min(), y_test.max()], [y_test.min(), y_
test.max()], 'r*--')
ax.set_xlabel('Calculated')
ax.set_ylabel('Predictions')
plt.show()
```

Listing 5.6 starts with an assortment of `import` statements, and then initializes the variable `iris` with the `Iris` dataset. The variable X contains the first three columns (and all the rows) of the `Iris` dataset, and the variable y contains the fourth column (and all the rows) of the `Iris` dataset.

The next portion of Listing 5.6 initializes the training set and the test set using an 80/20 data split. Next, the `Keras`-based model contains three `Dense` layers, where the first two specify the ReLU activation function and the third layer specifies the sigmoid activation function.

The next portion of Listing 5.6 compiles the model, trains the model, and then calculates the accuracy of the model via the test data. Launch the code in Listing 5.6 and you will see the following output:

```
Train on 120 samples
Epoch 1/100
120/120 [==============================] - 0s 980us/sam-
ple - loss: 0.9819 - accuracy: 0.3167
Epoch 2/100
```

```
120/120 [==============================] - 0s 162us/sam-
ple - loss: 0.9789 - accuracy: 0.3083
Epoch 3/100
120/120 [==============================] - 0s 204us/sam-
ple - loss: 0.9758 - accuracy: 0.3083
Epoch 4/100
120/120 [==============================] - 0s 166us/sam-
ple - loss: 0.9728 - accuracy: 0.3083
Epoch 5/100
120/120 [==============================] - 0s 160us/sam-
ple - loss: 0.9700 - accuracy: 0.3083
// details omitted for brevity
Epoch 96/100
120/120 [==============================] - 0s 128us/sam-
ple - loss: 0.3524 - accuracy: 0.6500
Epoch 97/100
120/120 [==============================] - 0s 184us/sam-
ple - loss: 0.3523 - accuracy: 0.6500
Epoch 98/100
120/120 [==============================] - 0s 128us/sam-
ple - loss: 0.3522 - accuracy: 0.6500
Epoch 99/100
120/120 [=============================] - 0s 187us/sam
ple - loss: 0.3522 - accuracy: 0.6500
Epoch 100/100
120/120 [==============================] - 0s 167us/sam-
ple - loss: 0.3521 - accuracy: 0.6500
```

Figure 5.1 displays a scatter plot of points based on the test values and the predictions for those test values.

The accuracy is admittedly poor (abysmal?), and yet it's quite possible that you will encounter this type of situation. Experiment with a different number of hidden layers and replace the final hidden layer with a Dense layer that specifies a softmax activation function – or some other activation function – to see if this change improves the accuracy.

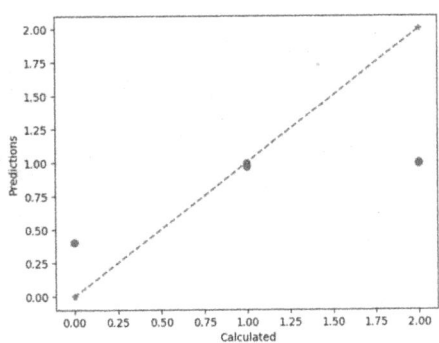

FIGURE 5.1 A Scatter Plot and a Best-Fitting Line

Summary

This chapter started with an explanation of classification and classifiers, followed by a brief explanation of commonly used classifiers in machine learning.

Next you learned about activation functions, why they are important in neural networks, and also how they are used in neural networks. Then you saw a list of the TensorFlow 2/Keras APIs for various activation functions, followed by a description of some of their merits.

You also learned about logistic regression that involves the sigmoid activation function, followed by a Keras-based code sample involving logistic regression.

## CHAPTER 6

ANGULAR AND TENSORFLOW.JS

This chapter provides a very fast-paced introduction to TensorFlow. js. You will find various code samples that use TensorFlow.js and `tfjs-vis` for data visualization, along with a code sample that uses TensorFlow.js to perform linear regression in an Angular 8 application. After learning the basic sequence of steps for creating machine learning models in TensorFlow.js, you can learn how to create more complex models from online blog posts and tutorials. If you are familiar with TF 2/Keras, then the TensorFlow.js code in this chapter will look familiar to you.

The first part of this chapter provides a quick introduction to TensorFlow. js, along with some of its features. You will learn about the TensorFlow. js APIs that are needed in order to create, compile, and train a machine learning model in TensorFlow.js, as well as an API for making predictions. You will see an example of how to use TensorFlow.js to perform linear regression in an HTML Web page.

The second part of this chapter contains examples of rendering various charts and graphs with tfjs-vis, including a line graph, bar chart, scatter plot, and a heat map. The third portion of this chapter contains a code sample that combines TensorFlow.js and `tfjs-vis` to perform linear regression in an HTML Web page. The final portion of this chapter shows you how to combine TensorFlow.js and `tfjs-vis` in an Angular 8 application to perform linear regression, render the data points, and make a prediction.

Please keep in mind a few details before you read this chapter. First, you do need a basic understanding of HTML and JavaScript for this chapter.

You also need to be comfortable with the keywords `async` and `await` that are used in the code samples. This chapter does not provide any tutorial-like material for these topics, but you can easily find many online tutorials that explain the HTML and JavaScript used in this chapter.

Second, this chapter assumes that you have read the material in earlier chapters pertaining to linear regression, as well as the `Keras`-related material in the appendix. Specifically, this chapter assumes that you have at least a basic understanding of the terms activation functions, optimizers, MSE, SGD, loss function, and metrics, all of which are discussed in Chapter 4.

Third, the code samples in this chapter are not intended for production-ready code: you need to follow the best practices for TensorFlow.js that are available online. As you will see, the description of each code sample is cursory, and a minimal set of TensorFlow.js APIs is discussed in this chapter. If you want to delve more deeply into TensorFlow.js, please navigate to the official website containing the TensorFlow.js APIs:

https://js.tensorflow.org/api/latest/

What is TensorFlow.js?

As you can undoubtedly guess, TensorFlow.js is TensorFlow for modern browsers, which includes Chrome and Firefox, and most of the features of TensorFlow are available in TensorFlow.js. This chapter illustrates an example of TensorFlow.js in a stand-alone HTML Web page, as well as how to use TensorFlow.js as part of an Angular 8 application.

TensorFlow.js leverages the power of WebGL to train models in a browser session. Some of the APIs in TensorFlow.js are listed here:

The tf.fromPixels() API that creates a Tensor from an image.
The tf.linspace() API that is the counterpart to the np.linspace() API in NumPy.
The tf.oneHot() API that performs a one-hot encoding.
The tf.flatten() API that is the counterpart to flatten() in tf.data.

Keep in mind that some of the Tensorflow.js APIs return a Promise, and some methods are synchronous. Beyond the usual set of APIs, there are two other important APIs that are specific to TensorFlow.js: the `tf.tidy()` method and the `tf.dispose()` method. The `tf.tidy()` method essentially acts like a garbage collector, which is unavailable in WebGL. The tf.dispose() method performs similar functionality for objects that contain tensors.

Incidentally, one convenient aspect of TensorFlow.js APIs is that they have package names that are parallel to the corresponding APIs in TensorFlow. For instance, the TensorFlow package `tf.keras.layers` corresponds to the TensorFlow.js package `tf.layers`. You can now infer that the TensorFlow.js API `tf.layers.dense` corresponds to the API `tf.keras.layers.Dense` in TensorFlow.

Although it's not necessary right now (perhaps at some point later in this chapter), it's worth your while to spend some time perusing the detailed list of the TensorFlow.js APIs at this URL:

https://js.tensorflow.org/api/latest/

ML Models in TensorFlow.js

TensorFlow.js gives you several options for working with TensorFlow models in a browser:

- Import trained models.
- Retrain models.
- Create models in a browser.

If you already have a TensorFlow model, you can convert that model to the TensorFlow.js format and then use that model in a Web browser. The details of model conversion are here:

https://www.tensorflow.org/js/guide/conversion

Another possibility is to take advantage of transfer learning: you start with a previously trained model and then perform some (hopefully minimal) additional training with your own data.

> **NOTE** *The code samples in this chapter involve models that have been developed in Firefox version 72.0.1.*

A Simple HTML Web Page with TensorFlow.js

Listing 6.1 displays the content of `tfjs-hello.html`, which illustrates how to reference the JavaScript code that pertains to TensorFlow.js and display a simple message.

LISTING 6.1 *tfjs-hello.html*

```
<html>
  <head>
    <!-- Load TensorFlow.js -->
```

```
<script
   src="https://cdn.jsdelivr.net/npm/@tensorflow/tfjs/
dist/tf.min.js">
   </script>
   </head>
   <body>
      Hello
   </body>
</html
```

Listing 6.1 contains a `<script>` element that references the TensorFlow.js code, which does nothing in this example. The Web page displays the word "Hello" and nothing more.

Working with Tensors in TensorFlow.js

TensorFlow.js provides several methods for working with tensors. The `tensor()` method supports multi-dimensional data points, but does not indicate the dimensionality of the data. Fortunately, TensorFlow.js provides dimension-specific APIs, such as the `tensor2d()` method for 2D data points, the `tensor3d()` method for 3D data points, and so forth, up to the `tensor6d()` method for data points of dimension 6.

For example, the following code snippet defines a 2-dimensional tensor that has a "shape" of 4x1:

```
const xs = tf.tensor2d([1, 2, 3, 4], [4, 1]);
```

The term "shape" refers to the dimensionality of the elements in a tensor. Thus, the preceding code snippet specifies 4 samples, each of which contains a single value.

You learned in the machine learning chapter that linear regression involves a set of data points and a set of labels. For example, suppose we define the following array of input values:

```
var inputV = [[1,3], [2,6], [3,9]];
```

The corresponding tensor would be defined like the following:

```
const inputT = tf.tensor2d(inputV, [inputV.length, 1]);
```

Similarly, suppose that the corresponding labels are defined as follows:

```
var labelV = [[10], [20], [30]];
```

The corresponding tensor for the labels would be defined like the following:

```
const labelT = tf.tensor2d(labelV, [labelV.length, 1]);
```

As you can see in the definition of `inputT` and `labelT`, the first argument is the actual data and the second argument specifies the shape of the data.

Machine Learning APIs in TensorFlow.js

This section contains some of the TensorFlow.js APIs for defining machine learning models in TensorFlow.js. As you learned from earlier chapters, there are several steps involved in training a machine learning model (illustrated with `Keras`-based APIs in the appendix). In this section, we'll see an example of creating a very rudimentary model in TensorFlow.js that implements the sequence of steps shown below:

- Define a model.
- Add one or more layers to the model.
- Compile the model.
- Initialize some data values.
- Fit (train) the model.
- Make some predictions.

Let's see how to implement the preceding steps, starting with the simplest definition of a model in TensorFlow.js:

```
const model = tf.sequential();
```

The `tf.sequential()` API is for a model in which the outputs from one layer are the inputs to the next adjacent layer (in a left-to-right direction). TensorFlow.js also supports another model via the `tf.model()` API, and you can learn about this model from the TensorFlow.js documentation.

Next, the following code snippet adds a dense (i.e., fully connected) layer to the defined model:

```
model.add(tf.layers.dense({units:32,inputShape:[64]}));
```

The first layer (which is the preceding code snippet) *must* specify the input shape, which in this case is 64. TensorFlow.js uses automatic shape inference to determine the shape of the subsequent layers in a model.

Now initialize the tensors xs and ys that represent the input and output values, respectively:

```
const xs = tf.tensor2d([1,2,3,4,5,6,7,8,],    [8,1]);
const ys = tf.tensor2d([3,6,9,12,15,18,21,24],[8,1]);
```

Now we can train this sequential model by invoking the fit() method, as shown here:

```
model.fit(xs, ys);
```

At this point our model has been trained with the training data, so we can make a prediction with this code snippet:

```
model.predict(tf.tensor2d([10], [1, 1])).print()
```

You now know the basic sequence of steps that are necessary in order to create, compile, and train a model in TensorFlow.js, as well as make predictions with that trained model.

Now let's look at an HTML Web page that uses TensorFlow.js to train a linear regression model and displays the result, which is the topic of the next section.

Linear Regression with TensorFlow.js

Listing 6.2 displays the content of tfjs-linreg1.html, which illustrates how to perform linear regression with TensorFlow.js.

LISTING 6.2 tfjs-linreg1.html

```
<html>
  <head>
    <script src="https://cdn.jsdelivr.net/npm/@tensor-
flow/tfjs/dist/tf.min.js"> </script>
    <title>Hello from TensorFlowJS!</title>
  </head>

  <body>
    <h3>Linear Regression and Some Predictions</h3>
    <ul id="mylist"></ul>

    <script>
      async function LinearRegression(){
        // 1) DEFINE THE MODEL:
        const model = tf.sequential();
```

```
model.add(
    tf.layers.dense({
        units:1,
        inputShape:[1],
        bias: true
    })
);

// 2) COMPILE THE MODEL:
// specify the loss, optimizer, and metrics:
model.compile({
    loss:'meanSquaredError',
    optimizer: 'sgd',
    metrics: ['mse']
});

// 3) FIT/TRAIN THE MODEL:
// y = 2*x+1 (relationship between xs and ys)
const xs = tf.tensor1d([1,2,3,4,5,6,7,8,9,10]);
const ys = tf.tensor1d([3,5,7,9,11,13,15,17,19,21]);
await model.fit(xs, ys, {epochs:100});

// 4) MAKE SOME PREDICTIONS
// 4a) PREDICT Y for X=-30:
var list1 = document.getElementById('mylist');
var item1 = document.createElement('li');
 var pred1 = model.predict(tf.tensor1d([-30])).
dataSync();
        var data1 = document.createTextNode("Pre-
dict(-30):"+pred1);
        item1.appendChild(data1);
        list1.appendChild(item1);
        // 4a) PREDICT Y for X=50:
        var item2 = document.createElement('li');
         var pred2 = model.predict(tf.tensor1d([50])).
dataSync();
  vardata2=document.createTextNode("Predict(50):"+pred2);
        item2.appendChild(data2);
        list1.appendChild(item2);
        // 4c) PREDICT Y for X=100:
        var item3 = document.createElement('li');
         var pred3 = model.predict(tf.tensor1d([100])).
dataSync();
```

```
        var data3 = document.createTextNode("Pre-
dict(100):"+pred3);
        item3.appendChild(data3);
        list1.appendChild(item3);
      }

    LinearRegression();
    </script>
  </body>
</html>
```

Listing 6.2 starts with a <script> element that references the TensorFlow.js code, followed by a <body> element that contains four main sections, as shown here:

```
// 1) DEFINE THE MODEL:
// 2) COMPILE THE MODEL:
// 3) FIT/TRAIN THE MODEL:
// 4) MAKE SOME PREDICTIONS
```

The first section defines the variable model as an instance of the TensorFlow.js Sequential model, which resembles tf.keras.layers.Sequential that is discussed in the Keras-related appendix. Next, the model variable adds a single layer via the dense API in TensorFlow.js.

The second section specifies three parameter values, as shown here:

```
model.compile({
    loss:'meanSquaredError',
    optimizer: 'sgd',
    metrics: ['mse']
});
```

The purpose of these parameters has been discussed in previous chapters, and you can review that material if you need to refresh your memory.

The third section initializes the variables xs and ys and then invokes the fit() method of the model variable in order to train this model.

The fourth section contains three predictions for the value of Y when the value of X is –30, 50, and 100. The key idea is to invoke the predict() method of the model variable, once for each of the preceding values of X. For instance, this code snippet predicts the value of Y when the value of X is –30:

```
var pred1 = model.predict(tf.tensor1d([-30])).dataSync();
```

If need be, you can enhance the HTML code to create a more aesthetically pleasing effort (or you can simplify the code as well).

Launch this Web page in a browser and you will see the following output:

```
Linear Regression and Some Predictions
Predict(-30):-61.6697998046875
Predict(50):104.10870361328125
Predict(100):207.7202606201172
```

According to the formula y = 2*x + 1, the correct values for –30, 50, and 100 are –59, 101, and 201, respectively. As you can see, the predictions are less accurate for larger positive (and negative) values of x.

Now let's see how to combine TensorFlow.js with Angular, which is the topic of the next section.

Angular, TensorFlow.js, and Linear Regression

This section contains an example of combining TensorFlow.js with Angular, and then training a model via linear regression. Copy the directory NGTFJSLinReg from the companion files into a convenient location. Listing 6.3 displays the content of app.component.ts, which uses a good portion of the code from the previous section.

LISTING 6.3 app.component.ts

```
import { Component } from '@angular/core';
import * as tf        from '@tensorflow/tfjs';

// remember: npm install @tensorflow/tfjs --save

@Component({
  selector: 'app-root',
  styleUrls: ['./app.component.css'],
  template: `
    <h3>Prediction for Value 50:</h3>
    <div id="mydiv">
      {{predict}}
    </div>
  `
})
export class AppComponent {
```

```
title = 'NGTFJSLinReg';
public predict = "";

constructor() {
    this.LinearRegression();
}

private async LinearRegression(){
    // 1) DEFINE THE MODEL:
    const model = tf.sequential();
    model.add(
      tf.layers.dense({
          units:1,
          inputShape:[1]
      })
    );

    // 2) COMPILE THE MODEL:
    // specify the loss, optimizer, and metrics:
    model.compile({
        loss:'meanSquaredError',
        optimizer: 'sgd',
        metrics: ['mse']
    });

    // 3) FIT/TRAIN THE MODEL:
    // y = 2*x+1 (relationship between xs and ys)
    const xs = tf.tensor1d([1,2,3,4,5,6,7,8,9,10]);
    const ys = tf.tensor1d([3,5,7,9,11,13,15,17,19,21]);
    await model.fit(xs, ys, {epochs:100});

    // 4) MAKE SOME PREDICTIONS
    // 4a) PREDICT Y for X=50:
    var mydiv = document.getElementById('mydiv');
    mydiv.innerText += model.predict(tf.tensor1d([50]));
  }
}
```

Listing 6.3 contains an `import` statement for `Component`, followed by another import statement for the `tfjs` code. Note the comment with an npm command to install TensorFlow.js in this Angular application.

The next section contains boilerplate code, except for the template property, which includes an HTML `<div>` element that will be populated with the output from the prediction (performed in Step 4 below).

The next portion of Listing 6.3 defines an empty constructor that invokes a private method that contains all the TensorFlow-related functionality. Notice that the method `LinearRegression` (which is invoked in the constructor) is defined with the following signature:

```
private async LinearRegression(){. . .}
```

The preceding signature is slightly different from what you saw in the previous section, as shown here:

```
function async LinearRegression(){. . .}
```

The `LinearRegression` method has four main sections, as shown here:

```
// 1) DEFINE THE MODEL:
// 2) COMPILE THE MODEL:
// 3) FIT/TRAIN THE MODEL:
// 4) MAKE SOME PREDICTIONS
```

The first section defines the variable `model` as an instance of the TensorFlow.js `Sequential` model, which resembles `tf.keras.layers.Sequential` (discussed in the `Keras`-related appendix). Next, the `model` variable adds a single `tf.layers.dense` layer that specifies an input shape of size 1.

Notice that the `tf.layers.dense` API does not support the `bias` property that is specified in the code in the preceding section.

The second section specifies three parameter values, as shown here:

```
model.compile({
    loss:'meanSquaredError',
    optimizer: 'sgd',
    metrics: ['mse']
});
```

The purpose of these parameters has been discussed in previous chapters, and you can review that material if you need to refresh your memory.

The third section initializes the variables `xs` and `ys` and then invokes the `fit()` method of the `model` variable in order to train this model. The fourth section contains a prediction for the value of `Y` when the value of `X` is 50 by invoking the `predict()` method of the variable `model`. Now launch this Web page in a browser and you will see the following output:

```
Prediction for Value 50:
Tensor
[[104.7459564],]
```

According to the formula $y = 2*x + 1$, the correct value for 50 is 101, and the predicted value differs from the exact value by more than three.

Now that you know how to create basic code samples with TensorFlow.js and also how to combine TensorFlow.js in an Angular application, let's look at tfjs-vis, which gives you the ability to display line graphs, bar charts, histograms, and so forth in an HTML Web page.

Creating Line Graphs in tfjs-vis

Listing 6.4 displays the content of tfjsvis-linegraph.js, which contains the data for a line graph. Listing 6.3 displays the content of tfjs-vis-linegraph.html, which illustrates how to use tfjs-vis to display a line graph.

LISTING 6.4 tfjsvis-linegraph.js

```
// define the data points
values = [
   [{x: 10, y: 20}, {x: 20, y: 30}, {x: 30, y: 5}, {x:
40, y: 12}],
   [{x: 10, y: 40}, {x: 20, y: 0}, {x: 30, y: 50}, {x:
40, y: -5}]
];

// legend-related information
let series = ['Dataset1', 'Dataset2'];

// render the line graph
tfvis.render.linechart(document.getElementBy-
Id('plot1'), {values, series}, {
  xLabel: 'x-axis',
  yLabel: 'y-axis'
});
```

Listing 6.4 defines the variables values with data points and the variable series that contains the strings to display in a legend. The final portion of Listing 6.4 invokes the tfvis API for rendering a line graph in the HTML <div> element whose class value is plotted.

LISTING 6.5 tfjsvis-linegraph.html

```html
<html>
  <head>
      <script src="https://cdn.jsdelivr.net/npm/@tensor-
flow/tfjs@latest"> </script>
      <script src="https://cdn.jsdelivr.net/npm/@tensor-
flow/tfjs-vis@latest"> </script>

    <style>
      .plot {
        display: inline-block;
        width: 50%;
        margin: 10px;
      }
    </style>
  </head>
  <body>
    <div class="plot" id="plot1"></div>
  </body>

  <script src="tfjsvis-barchart.js"> </script>
</html>
```

Listing 6.5 contains a `<head>` element with two `<script>` elements that reference the necessary `tfjs-vis` JavaScript code for rendering charts and graphs. The `<style>` element specifies some properties for layout purposes.

The next portion of Listing 6.5 defines a `<div>` element where the line graph will be rendered, and the final code snippet in Listing 6.5 is a `<script>` element that references the code in `tfjsvis-barchart.js`.

Figure 6.1 shows a line graph that is displayed when you launch the code in Listing 6.5.

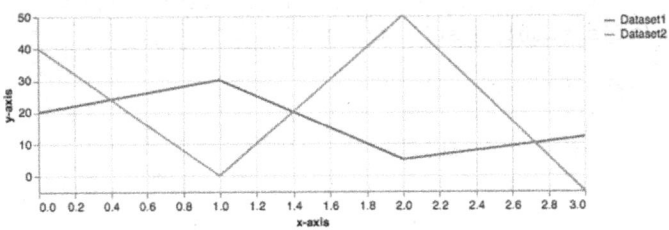

FIGURE 6.1 A Line Graph

Creating Bar Charts in tfjs-vis

Listing 6.6 displays the content of `tfjsvis-barchart.js`, which contains the data for a bar chart. Listing 6.7 displays the content of `tfjs-vis-barchart.html`, which illustrates how to use `tfjs-vis` to display a bar chart.

LISTING 6.6 tfjsvis-barchart.js

```
// define the data points
const data = [
    {index: 'foo', value: 1}, {index: 'bar', value: 7},
    {index: 3, value: 3}, {index: 5, value: 6}];

// render the bar chart
tfvis.render.barchart(document.getElementById('plot1'),
data, {
  yLabel: 'y-axis',
  width:   400
});
```

Listing 6.5 defines the variables `values` with data points and the `data` series that contains the strings to display in a legend. The final portion of Listing 6.5 invokes the `tfvis.render.barchart` API for rendering a bar chart in the HTML `<div>` element whose `class` value is plotted.

LISTING 6.7 tfjsvis-barchart.html

```
<html>
  <head>
    <script src="https://cdn.jsdelivr.net/npm/@tensor-
flow/tfjs@latest"> </script>
    <script src="https://cdn.jsdelivr.net/npm/@tensor-
flow/tfjs-vis@latest"> </script>

    <style>
      .plot {
        display: inline-block;
        width: 50%;
        margin: 10px;
      }
    </style>
  </head>
```

```
<body>
  <div class="plot" id="plot1"></div>
</body>

<script src="tfjsvis-barchart.js"> </script>
</html>
```

Listing 6.7 contains a `<head>` element with two `<script>` elements that reference the necessary `tfjs-vis` JavaScript code for rendering charts and graphs. The `<style>` element specifies some properties for layout purposes.

The next portion of Listing 6.7 defines a `<div>` element where the line graph will be rendered, and the final code snippet in Listing 6.7 is a `<script>` element that references the code in `tfjsvis-barchart.js`.

Figure 6.2 shows a bar chart that is displayed when you launch the code in Listing 6.7.

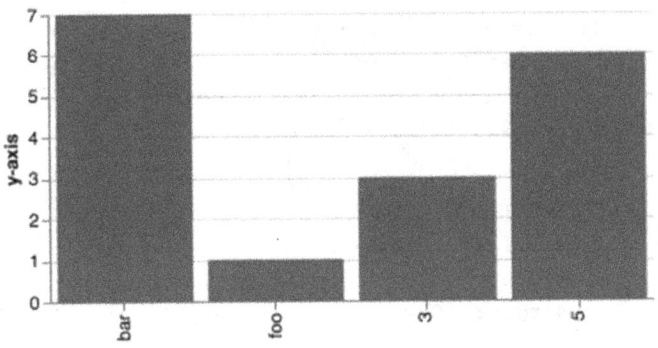

FIGURE 6.2 A Bar Chart

Creating Scatter Plots in tfjs-vis

Listing 6.8 displays the content of `tfjsvis-scatterplot.js`, which contains the data for a scatter plot. Listing 6.9 displays the content of the HTML Web page `tfjsvis-scatterplot.html`, which illustrates how to use `tfjs-vis` to display a scatter plot.

LISTING 6.8 tfjsvis-scatterplot.js

```
// define the data points
const data = [
```

```
    {index: 'foo', value: 1}, {index: 'bar', value: 7},
    {index: 3, value: 3}, {index: 5, value: 6}}];
// render the bar chart
tfvis.render.barchart(document.getElementById('plot1'),
data, {
  yLabel: 'y-axis',
  width:   400
});
```

Listing 6.8 defines the variables `values` with data points and the `data` series that contains the strings to display in a legend. The final portion of Listing 6.8 invokes the `tfvis.render.barchart` API for rendering a bar chart in the HTML `<div>` element whose `class` value is `plotted`.

LISTING 6.9 tfjsvis-scatterplot.html

```
<html>
  <head>
      <script src="https://cdn.jsdelivr.net/npm/@tensor-
flow/tfjs@latest"> </script>
      <script src="https://cdn.jsdelivr.net/npm/@tensor-
flow/tfjs-vis@latest"> </script>

    <style>
      .plot {
        display: inline-block;
        width: 50%;
        margin: 10px;
      }
    </style>
  </head>

  <body>
    <div class="plot" id="plot1"></div>
  </body>

  <script src="tfjsvis-barchart.js"> </script>
</html>
```

Listing 6.9 contains a `<head>` element with two `<script>` elements that reference the necessary `tfjs-vis` JavaScript code for rendering charts and graphs. The `<style>` element specifies some properties for layout purposes.

The next portion of Listing 6.9 defines a `<div>` element where the scatter plot will be rendered, and the final code snippet in Listing 6.9 is a `<script>` element that references the code in `tfjsvis-scatterplot.js`.

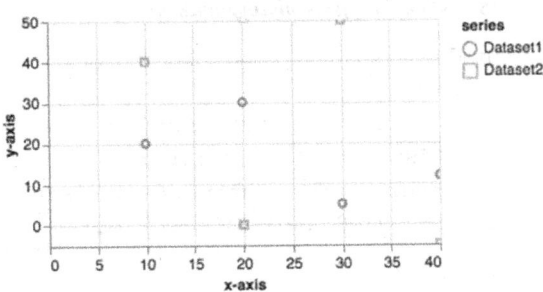

FIGURE 6.3 A Scatter Plot

Figure 6.3 shows a scatter plot that is displayed when you launch the code in Listing 6.9.

Creating Histograms in tfjs-vis

Listing 6.10 displays the content of `tfjsvis-histogram.js`, which contains the data for a histogram. Listing 6.11 displays the content of the HTML Web page `tfjsvis-histogram.html`, which illustrates how to use `tfjs-vis` to display a histogram.

LISTING 6.10 tfjsvis-histogram.js

```
// define the data points
data = [1, 5, 12, 12, 5, 10, -2, -8];

// render the histogram
tfvis.render.histogram(document.getElementBy-
Id('plot1'), data, {
  maxBins: 5,
  width: 400
});
```

Listing 6.10 defines the variables `values` with data points and the `data` series that contains the strings to display in a legend. The final portion of Listing 6.10 invokes the `tfvis.render.histogram` API for rendering a histogram in the HTML `<div>` element whose `class` value is plotted.

LISTING 6.11 tfjsvis-histogram.html

```html
<html>
  <head>
      <script src="https://cdn.jsdelivr.net/npm/@tensor-
flow/tfjs@latest"> </script>
      <script src="https://cdn.jsdelivr.net/npm/@tensor-
flow/tfjs-vis@latest"> </script>

    <style>
      .plot {
        display: inline-block;
        width: 50%;
        margin: 10px;
      }
    </style>
  </head>

  <body>
    <div class="plot" id="plot1"></div>
  </body>

  <script src="tfjsvis-histogram.js"> </script>
</html>
```

Listing 6.11 contains a `<head>` element with two `<script>` elements that reference the necessary `tfjs-vis` JavaScript code for rendering charts and graphs. The `<style>` element specifies some properties for layout purposes.

The next portion of Listing 6.11 defines a `<div>` element where the histogram will be rendered, and the final code snippet in Listing 6.10 is a `<script>` element that references the code in `tfjs-vis-histo-gram.js`.

Figure 6.4 shows a histogram that is displayed when you launch the code in Listing 6.11.

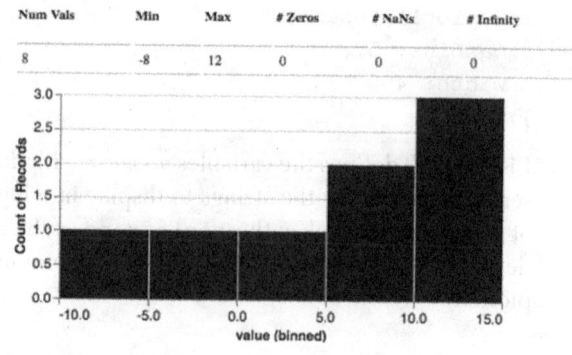

Num Vals	Min	Max	# Zeros	# NaNs	# Infinity
8	-8	12	0	0	0

FIGURE 6.4 A Histogram

Creating Heat Maps in tfjs-vis

Listing 6.12 displays the content of `tfjsvis-heatmap.js`, which contains the data for a heat map. Listing 6.13 displays the content of the HTML Web page `tfjsvis-heatmap.html`, which illustrates how to use `tfjs-vis` to display a heat map.

LISTING 6.12 tfjsvis-heatmap.js

```
// render the heat map
tfvis.render.heatmap(document.getElementById('plot1'),
{
  values: [[1,0,0], [0,0.5,0.8], [0,0.8,0.5]],
  xTickLabels: ['Tall', 'Medium', 'Short'],
  yTickLabels: ['Tall', 'Medium', 'Short']
}, {
  width: 500,
  height: 500,
  xLabel: 'TypeA',
  yLabel: 'TypeB',
  colorMap: 'reds'
});
```

Listing 6.12 defines the variable `values` with data points and two strings to display in the horizontal and vertical axes of the heat map. The final portion of Listing 6.12 invokes the `tfvis.render.heatmap` API for rendering a heat map in the HTML <div> element whose `class` value is plotted.

LISTING 6.13 tfjsvis-heatmap.html

```
<html>
  <head>
      <script src="https://cdn.jsdelivr.net/npm/@tensor-
flow/tfjs@latest"> </script>
      <script src="https://cdn.jsdelivr.net/npm/@tensor-
flow/tfjs-vis@latest"> </script>

    <style>
      .plot {
        display: inline-block;
        width: 50%;
        margin: 10px;
      }
```

```
    </style>
  </head>

  <body>
    <div class="plot" id="plot1"></div>
  </body>

  <script src="tfjsvis-heatmap.js"> </script>
</html>
```

Listing 6.13 contains a `<head>` element with two `<script>` elements that reference the necessary `tfjs-vis` JavaScript code for rendering charts and graphs. The `<style>` element specifies some properties for layout purposes.

The next portion of Listing 6.13 defines a `<div>` element where the heat map will be rendered, and the final code snippet in Listing 6.13 is a `<script>` element that references the code in `tfjsvis-heatmap.js`.

Figure 6.5 shows a heat map that is displayed when you launch the code in Listing 6.13.

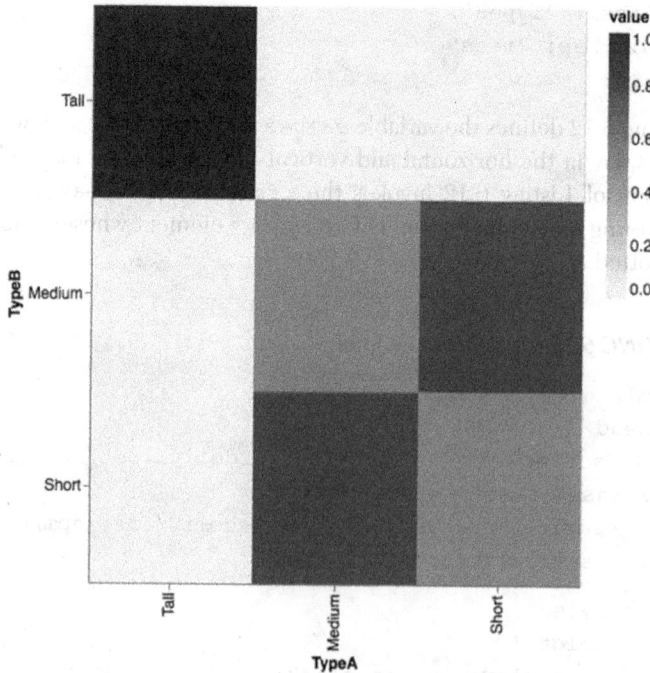

FIGURE 6.5 A Heat Map

This concludes the portion of the chapter pertaining to some of the data visualization functionality that is available in `tfjs-vis`. The next portion of the chapter contains a code sample that combines TensorFlow.js and `tfjs-vis` in an Angular application that performs linear regression.

TensorFlow.js, tfjs-vis, and Linear Regression

Listing 6.14 displays the content of `tfjs-vis-linreg1.html`, which illustrates how to generate a set of random-like values and then use machine learning and linear regression to determine the best-fitting line.

LISTING 6.14 tfjs-vis-linreg1.html

```
<html>
  <head>
     <script src="https://cdn.jsdelivr.net/npm/@tensor-
flow/tfjs@latest">
     </script>
     <script
       src="https://cdn.jsdelivr.net/npm/@tensorflow/tfjs-
vis@latest">
     </script>

     <style>
        .plot {
           width: 100%;
           height: 40%;
           margin: 4px;
        }

        .btn {
           display: float-left;
        }
     </style>
  </head>

  <body>
     <div id="mydiv"></div>

     <div>
        <button class="btn" type="button" onclick="trainLin-
earModel()">Train the Model</button>
```

```
    </div>
    <!-- the scatterplot is displayed here: -->
    <div class="plot" id="plot1"></div>
  </body>

  <script>
   async function trainLinearModel() {
     //---------------------------------
     // Define a simple model that
     // 1) has a single input (numeric value)
     // 3) is connected to the output layer
     // 4) is an output layer of one neuron
     //---------------------------------

     const model = tf.sequential();
       model.add(tf.layers.dense({units: 1, inputShape:
[1]}));
     model.compile({
        loss: 'meanSquaredError',
        optimizer: 'sgd'
     });

     var epochs  = 100
     var maxRand = 30
     var count   = 100
     items1 = []
     itemsX = []
     itemsY = []
     values = []

     // define the data points
     for(var i=0; i<count; i++) {
       x = i
       y = 2*x + 1 + Math.random()*maxRand

       items1.push({"x":x, "y":y})
       itemsX.push(x)
       itemsY.push(y)
     }

     values.push(items1)

     const xs = tf.tensor1d([1,2,3,4,5,6,7,8,9,10]);
    const ys = tf.tensor1d([3,5,7,9,11,13,15,17,19,21]);
```

```
    // legend-related information
    let series1 = ['Dataset1', 'Dataset2'];

    // render the scatter plot in the 'plot1' element:
        tfvis.render.scatterplot(document.getElementBy-
Id('plot1'), {values,series1}, {
        width:  600,
        xLabel: 'x-axis',
        yLabel: 'y-axis'
    })

    // train the model:
    await model.fit(xs, ys, {epochs: epochs});

    // predict the value of y when x = 52.5:
    var mydiv = document.getElementById('mydiv');
    mydiv.innerText += "Prediction for 52.5: "+
                model.predict(tf.tensor1d([50]));

    }
  </script>
</html>
```

Listing 6.14 contains a <head> element with <script> elements that reference the necessary tfjs-vis JavaScript code for rendering charts and graphs and for the TensorFlow.js code. The <style> element specifies some properties for layout purposes.

The next portion of Listing 6.14 defines a <div> element that contains a <button> element for invoking the training process. Another <div> element specifies where the scatter plot will be rendered for the data points in this example.

The next portion of Listing 6.14 contains a <script> element with the function trainLinearModel(), which contains all the code to perform linear regression. As you can see, the next block of code defines the variable model, adds a single layer, and then compiles the model, just like you have seen in previous code samples.

Before we can train the model via the fit() method, we need to generate some data values. In this example, a for loop iterates through the x values, which are the integers from 1 to 100, and then calculates the corresponding y values, as shown here:

```
// define the data points
for(var i=0; i<count; i++) {
```

```
x = i
y = 2*x + 1 + Math.random()*maxRand

items1.push({"x":x, "y":y})
itemsX.push(x)
itemsY.push(y)
}
```

The arrays `itemsX` and `itemsY` contain the x values and y values, respectively, and the array `items1` contains the value pairs `(x,y)`.

The next portion of Listing 6.13 contains the code for rendering a scatter plot, which is virtually identical to the code that you saw in an earlier example.

The next code snippet trains the model via the `fit()` method, in exactly the same way as previous code samples, as shown here:

```
await model.fit(xs, ys, {epochs: epochs});
```

Finally, the last portion of Listing 6.14 invokes the `predict()` method of the variable model in order to predict the value of y when the value of x is 52.5, and then populates this value in the appropriate `<div>` element, as shown here:

```
// predict the value of y when x = 52.5:
var mydiv = document.getElementById('mydiv');
mydiv.innerText += "Prediction for 52.5: "+
                   model.predict(tf.tensor1d([50]));
```

Figure 6.6 displays the contents of the Web page after you launch the code in Listing 6.14 and click on the top-most button.

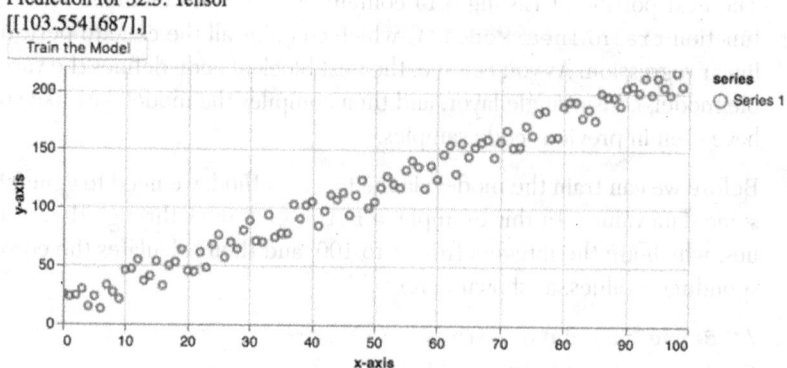

FIGURE 6.6 A Machine Learning Prediction

Summary

This chapter started with a quick introduction to some aspects TensorFlow.js, along with an example of performing linear regression in an HTML Web page with TensorFlow.js.

Next, you saw an assortment of examples of charts and graphs using `tfjs-vis`, including a line graph, a bar chart, a scatter plot, and a heat map.

In addition, you learned how to combine TensorFlow.js and `tfjs-vis` to perform linear regression in an HTML Web page. Finally, you saw how to combine TensorFlow.js and `tfjs-vis` in an Angular 8 application to perform linear regression, render the data points, and make a prediction.

INTRODUCTION TO KERAS

This appendix introduces you to `Keras`, along with code samples that illustrate how to define basic neural networks and deep neural networks with various datasets, such as `MNIST` and `cifar10`.

The first part of this appendix briefly discusses some of the important namespaces (such as `tf.keras.layers`) and their contents, as well as a simple `Keras`-based model.

The second section contains an example of performing linear regression with `Keras` and a simple CSV file. You will also see a `Keras`-based MLP neural network that is trained on the `MNIST` dataset.

The third section contains a simple example of training a neural network with the `cifar10` dataset. This code sample is similar to training a neural network on the `MNIST` dataset, and requires a very small code change.

The final section contains two examples of `Keras`-based models that perform early stopping, which is convenient when the model exhibits minimal improvement (that is determined by you) during the training process.

What is Keras?

If you are already comfortable with `Keras`, you can skim this section to learn about the new namespaces and what they contain. Then proceed to the next section that contains details for creating a `Keras`-based model.

If you are new to `Keras`, you might be wondering why this section is included in this appendix. First, `Keras` is well-integrated into TF 2, and it's in the `tf.keras` namespace. Second, `Keras` is well-suited for defining models to solve a myriad of tasks, such as linear regression and logistic regression, as well as deep learning tasks involving the CNNs, RNNs, and LSTMs.

The next several subsections contain lists of bullet items for various `Keras`-related namespaces, and they will be very familiar if you have worked with TF 1.x. If you are new to TF 2, you'll see examples of some of the classes in subsequent code samples.

Working with Keras Namespaces in TF 2

TF 2 provides the `tf.keras` namespace, which in turn contains the following namespaces:

- tf.keras.layers
- tf.keras.models
- tf.keras.optimizers
- tf.keras.utils
- tf.keras.regularizers

The preceding namespaces contain various layers in `Keras` models, different types of `Keras` models, optimizers (Adam et al.), utility classes, and regularizers (such as L1 and L2).

Currently, there are three ways to create `Keras`-based models, via the

- Sequential API
- Functional API
- Model API

The `Keras`-based code samples in this book use primarily the `Sequential` model (it's the most intuitive and straightforward). The `Sequential` model enables you to specify a list of layers, most of which are available in the `tf.keras.layers` namespace (discussed later).

The `Keras`-based models that use the functional API involve specifying layers that are passed as function-like elements in a pipeline-like fashion. Although the functional API provides some additional flexibility, you will probably use the Sequential API to define `Keras`-based models if you are a TF 2 beginner.

The model-based API provides the greatest flexibility, and it involves defining a Python class that encapsulates the semantics of your `Keras` model. This class is a subclass of the `tf.model.Model` class, and you must implement the two methods __init__ and `call` in order to define a `Keras` model in this subclass.

Perform an online search for more details regarding the Functional API and the Model API.

Working with the tf.keras.layers Namespace

The most common (and also the simplest) `Keras`-based model is the `Sequential()` class that is in the `tf.keras.models` namespace. This model is comprised of various layers that belong to the `tf.keras.layers` namespace, as shown here:

- tf.keras.layers.Conv2D()
- tf.keras.layers.MaxPooling2D()
- tf.keras.layers.Flatten()
- tf.keras.layers.Dense()
- tf.keras.layers.Dropout()
- tf.keras.layers.BatchNormalization()
- tf.keras.layers.embedding()
- tf.keras.layers.RNN()
- tf.keras.layers.LSTM()
- tf.keras.layers.Bidirectional

The `Conv2D()` and `MaxPooling2D()` classes are used in `Keras`-based models for CNNs. Generally speaking, the next six classes in the preceding list can appear in models for CNNs as well as models for machine learning. The `RNN()` class is for simple RNNs and the LSTM class is for LSTM-based models. The `Bidirectional()` class is a bi-directional LSTM that you will often see in models for solving NLP (Natural Language Processing) tasks. Two very important NLP frameworks that use bidirectional LSTMs were released as open source (on GitHub) in 2018: ELMo from Facebook and BERT from Google.

Working with the tf.keras.activations Namespace

Machine learning and deep learning models require activation functions. For `Keras`-based models, the activation functions are in the `tf.keras.activations` namespace, some of which are listed here:

- tf.keras.activations.relu
- tf.keras.activations.selu
- tf.keras.activations.linear

- `tf.keras.activations.elu`
- `tf.keras.activations.sigmoid`
- `tf.keras.activations.softmax`
- `tf.keras.activations.softplus`
- `tf.keras.activations.tanh`

The ReLU/SELU/ELU functions are closely related, and they often appear in ANNs (Artificial Neural Networks) and CNNs. Before the `relu()` function became popular, the `sigmoid()` and `tanh()` functions were used in ANNs and CNNs. However, they are still important, and they are used in various gates in GRUs and LSTMs. The `softmax()` function is typically used in the pair of layers consisting of the right-most hidden layer and the output layer.

Working with the keras.tf.datasets Namespace

For your convenience, TF 2 provides a set of built-in datasets in the `tf.keras.datasets` namespace, some of which are listed here:

- `tf.keras.datasets.boston_housing`
- `tf.keras.datasets.cifar10`
- `tf.keras.datasets.cifar100`
- `tf.keras.datasets.fashion_mnist`
- `tf.keras.datasets.imdb`
- `tf.keras.datasets.mnist`
- `tf.keras.datasets.reuters`

The preceding datasets are popular for training models with small datasets. The `mnist` dataset and `fashion_mnist` dataset are both popular when training CNNs, whereas the `boston_housing` dataset is popular for linear regression. The Titanic dataset is also popular for linear regression, but it's not currently supported as a default dataset in the `tf.keras.datasets` namespace.

Working with the tf.keras.experimental Namespace

The `contrib` namespace in TF 1.x has been deprecated in TF 2, and its successor is the `tf.keras.experimental` namespace, which contains the following classes (among others):

- `tf.keras.experimental.CosineDecay`
- `tf.keras.experimental.CosineDecayRestarts`
- `tf.keras.experimental.LinearCosineDecay`

- `tf.keras.experimental.NoisyLinearCosineDecay`
- `tf.keras.experimental.PeepholeLSTMCell`

If you are a beginner, you probably won't use any of the classes in the preceding list. Although the `PeepholeLSTMCell` class is a variation of the LSTM class, there are limited use cases for this class.

Working with Other tf.keras Namespaces

TF 2 provides a number of other namespaces that contain useful classes, some of which are listed here:

- `tf.keras.callbacks`   (early stopping)
- `tf.keras.optimizers`   (Adam et al.)
- `tf.keras.regularizers` (L1 and L2)
- `tf.keras.utils`   (to_categorical)

The `tf.keras.callbacks` namespace contains a class that you can use for early stopping, which is to say that it's possible to terminate the training process if there is an insufficient reduction in the loss function in two successive iterations.

The `tf.keras.optimizers` namespace contains the various optimizers that are available for working in conjunction with the loss functions, which includes the popular `Adam` optimizer.

The `tf.keras.regularizers` namespace contains two popular regularizers: the L1 regularizer (also called `LASSO` in machine learning) and the L2 regularizer (also called the `Ridge` regularizer in machine learning). L1 is for the MAE (Mean Absolute Error) and L2 is for the MSE (Mean Squared Error). Both of these regularizers act as penalty terms that are added to the chosen loss function to reduce the influence of the features in a machine learning model. Note that `LASSO` can drive values to zero, with the result that features are actually eliminated from a model. Hence, it is related to the feature selection in machine learning.

The `tf.keras.utils` namespace contains an assortment of functions, including the `to_categorical()` function for converting a class vector into a binary class.

Although there are other namespaces in TF 2, the classes listed in all the preceding subsections will probably suffice for the majority of your tasks if you are a beginner at TF 2 and machine learning.

TF 2 Keras versus "Standalone" Keras

The original `Keras` is actually a specification, with various backend frameworks such as TensorFlow, Theano, and CNTK. Currently, `Keras` standalone does not support TF 2, whereas the implementation of `Keras` in `tf.keras` has been optimized for performance.

`Keras` standalone will live in perpetuity in the `keras.io` package, which is discussed in detail at the `Keras` website: *keras.io*.

Now that you have a high-level view of the TF 2 namespaces for `Keras` and the classes that they contain, let's find out how to create a `Keras`-based model, which is the subject of the next section.

Creating a Keras-Based Model

The following list of steps describe the high-level sequence involved in creating, training, and testing a `Keras` model:

Step 1: Determine a model architecture (the number of hidden layers, various activation functions, and so forth).
Step 2: Invoke the compile() method.
Step 3: Invoke the fit() method to train the model.
Step 4: Invoke the evaluate() method to evaluate the trained model.
Step 5: Invoke the predict() method to make predictions.

Step 1 involves determining the values of a number of hyperparameters, including:

- the number of hidden layers
- the number of neurons in each hidden layer
- the initial values of the weights of the edges
- the loss function
- the optimizer
- the learning rate
- the dropout rate
- the activation function(s)

Steps 2 through 4 involve the training data, whereas Step 5 involves the test data, which are included in the following, more detailed, sequence of steps for the preceding list:

- Specify a dataset (if necessary, convert the data to numeric data).
- Split the dataset into training data and test data (usually an 80/20 split).

- Define the Keras model (such as the `tf.keras.models.Sequential()` API).
- Compile the `Keras` model (the `compile()` API).
- Train (fit) the `Keras` model (the `fit()` API).
- Make a prediction (the `prediction()` API)

Note that the preceding bullet items skip some steps that are part of a real `Keras` model, such as evaluating the `Keras` model on the trained model, as well as dealing with issues such as overfitting.

The first bullet item states that you need a dataset, which can be as simple as a CSV file with 100 rows of data and just 3 columns (or even smaller). In general, a dataset is substantially larger: it can be a dataset with 1,000,000 rows of data and 10,000 columns in each row. We'll look at a concrete dataset in a subsequent section.

Next, a Keras model is in the `tf.keras.models` namespace, and the simplest (and also very common) Keras model is `tf.keras.models.Sequential`. In general, a Keras model contains layers that are in the `tf.keras.layers` namespace, such as `tf.keras.Dense` (which means that two adjacent layers are completely connected).

Here's a code block of the `Keras` model that's described in the preceding paragraphs (which covers the first four bullet points):

```
import tensorflow as tf

model = tf.keras.models.Sequential([
    tf.keras.layers.Dense(512,activation=tf.keras.activations.relu),
])
```

We have three more bullet items to discuss, starting with the compilation step. `Keras` provides a `compile()` API for this step, an example of which is here:

```
model.compile(optimizer='adam',
              loss='sparse_categorical_crossentropy',
              metrics=['accuracy'])
```

Next we need to specify a training step, and `Keras` provides the `fit()` API (as you can see, it's not called `train()`), an example of which is here:

```
model.fit(x_train, y_train, epochs=5)
```

The final step is the prediction that is performed via the `predict()` API, an example of which is here:

```
pred = model.predict(x_test)
```

Keep in mind that the `evaluate()` method is used for evaluating a trained model, and the output of this method is accuracy or loss. The `predict()` method makes predictions from the input data.

Listing A.1 displays the content of `tf2_basic_keras.py`, which combines the code blocks in the preceding steps into a single code sample.

LISTING A.1 tf2_basic_keras.py

```
import tensorflow as tf

# NOTE: we need the train data and test data

model = tf.keras.models.Sequential([
  tf.keras.layers.Dense(1, activation=tf.nn.relu),
])

model.compile(optimizer='adam',
              loss='sparse_categorical_crossentropy',
              metrics=['accuracy'])

model.fit(x_train, y_train, epochs=5)
model.evaluate(x_test, y_test)
```

Listing A.1 contains no new code, and we've essentially glossed over some of the terms, such as the *optimizer* (an algorithm that is used in conjunction with a loss function), the *loss* (the type of loss function) and the *metrics* (how to evaluate the efficacy of a model).

The explanations for these details cannot be condensed into a few paragraphs (alas), but the good news is that you can find a plethora of detailed online blog posts that discuss these terms.

Keras and Linear Regression

This section contains a simple example of creating a `Keras`-based model to solve a task involving linear regression: given a positive number representing kilograms of pasta, predict its corresponding price. Listing A.2 displays the content of `pasta.csv` and Listing A.3 displays the content of `keras_pasta.py` that performs this task.

LISTING A.2 pasta.csv

```
weight,price
5,30
```

```
10,45
15,70
20,80
25,105
30,120
35,130
40,140
50,150
```

LISTING A.3 keras_pasta.py

```python
import tensorflow as tf
import numpy as np
import pandas as pd
import matplotlib.pyplot as plt

# price of pasta per kilogram
df = pd.read_csv("pasta.csv")

weight = df['weight']
price  = df['price']

model = tf.keras.models.Sequential([
   tf.keras.layers.Dense(units=1,input_shape=[1])
])

# MSE loss function and Adam optimizer
model.compile(loss='mean_squared_error',
              optimizer=tf.keras.optimizers.Adam(0.1))

# train the model
history   =   model.fit(weight,   price,   epochs=100,
verbose=False)

# graph the # of epochs versus the loss
plt.xlabel('Number of Epochs')
plt.ylabel("Loss Values")
plt.plot(history.history['loss'])
plt.show()

print("Cost for 11kg:",model.predict([11.0]))
print("Cost for 45kg:",model.predict([45.0]))
```

Listing A.3 initializes the Pandas Dataframe df with the contents of the CSV file pasta.csv, and then initializes the variables weight and cost with the first and second columns, respectively, of df.

The next portion of Listing A.3 defines a `Keras`-based model that consists of a single `Dense` layer. This model is compiled and trained, and then a graph is displayed that shows the number of epochs on the horizontal axis and the corresponding value of the loss function for the vertical axis. Launch the code in Listing A.3 and you will see the following output:

```
Cost for 11kg: [[41.727108]]
Cost for 45kg: [[159.02121]]
```

Figure A.1 displays a graph of the epochs versus the loss during the training process.

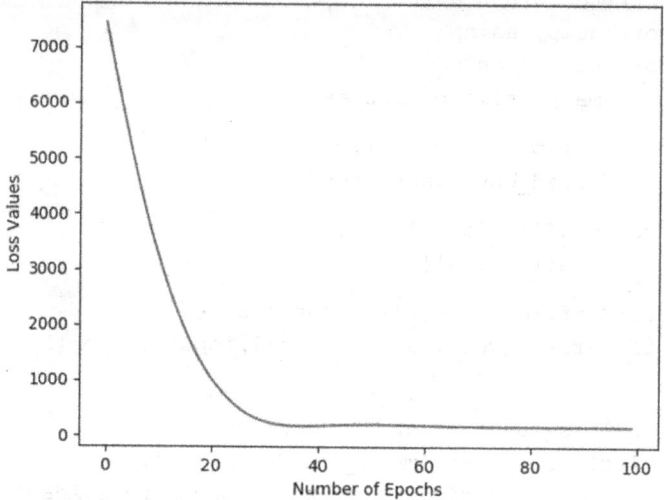

FIGURE A.1 A Graph of Epochs versus Loss

Keras, MLPs, and MNIST

This section contains a simple example of creating a `Keras`-based model that will be trained with the `MNIST` dataset. Listing A.4 displays the content of `keras_mlp_mnist.py` that performs this task.

LISTING A.4 keras_mlp_mnist.py

```
import tensorflow as tf
import numpy as np

# instantiate mnist and load data:
mnist = tf.keras.datasets.mnist
```

```
(x_train, y_train), (x_test, y_test) = mnist.load_data()

# one-hot encoding for all labels to create 1x10
# vectors that are compared with the final layer:
y_train = tf.keras.utils.to_categorical(y_train)
y_test  = tf.keras.utils.to_categorical(y_test)

image_size = x_train.shape[1]
input_size = image_size * image_size

# resize and normalize the 28x28 images:
x_train = np.reshape(x_train, [-1, input_size])
x_train = x_train.astype('float32') / 255
x_test  = np.reshape(x_test, [-1, input_size])
x_test  = x_test.astype('float32') / 255

# initialize some hyper-parameters:
batch_size = 128
hidden_units = 128
dropout_ratea = 0.20

# define a Keras-based model:
model = tf.keras.models.Sequential()
model.add(tf.keras.layers.Dense(hidden_units,
input_dim=input_size))
model.add(tf.keras.layers.Activation('relu'))
model.add(tf.keras.layers.Dropout(dropout_rate))
model.add(tf.keras.layers.Dense(hidden_units))
model.add(tf.keras.layers.Activation('relu'))
model.add(tf.keras.layers.Dense(10))
model.add(tf.keras.layers.Activation('softmax'))

model.summary()

model.compile(loss='categorical_crossentropy',
              optimizer='adam',
              metrics=['accuracy'])

# train the network on the training data:
model.fit(x_train,          y_train,          epochs=10,
batch_size=batch_size)

# calculate and then display the accuracy:
loss,   acc   =   model.evaluate(x_test,   y_test,
batch_size=batch_size)
print("\nTest accuracy: %.1f%%" % (100.0 * acc))
```

Listing A.4 contains the usual `import` statements and then initializes the variable `mnist` as a reference to the `MNIST` dataset. The next portion of Listing A.4 contains some typical code that populates the training dataset and the test dataset and converts the labels to numeric values via the technique known as one-hot encoding.

Next, several hyperparameters are initialized, and a `Keras`-based model is defined that specifies three `Dense` layers and the `relu` activation function. This model is compiled and trained, and the accuracy on the test dataset is computed and then displayed. Launch the code in Listing A.4 and you will see the following output:

```
Model: "sequential"
```

Layer (type)	Output Shape	Param #
dense (Dense)	(None, 256)	200960
activation (Activation)	(None, 256)	0
dropout (Dropout)	(None, 256)	0
dense_1 (Dense)	(None, 256)	65792
activation_1 (Activation)	(None, 256)	0
dropout_1 (Dropout)	(None, 256)	0
dense_2 (Dense)	(None, 10)	2570
activation_2 (Activation)	(None, 10)	0

```
Total params: 269,322
Trainable params: 269,322
Non-trainable params: 0

Train on 60000 samples
Epoch 1/10
60000/60000 [==============================] - 4s 74us/
sample - loss: 0.4281 - accuracy: 0.8683
Epoch 2/10
```

```
60000/60000 [==============================] - 4s 66us/
sample - loss: 0.1967 - accuracy: 0.9417
Epoch 3/10
60000/60000 [==============================] - 4s 63us/
sample - loss: 0.1507 - accuracy: 0.9547
Epoch 4/10
60000/60000 [==============================] - 4s 63us/
sample - loss: 0.1298 - accuracy: 0.9600
Epoch 5/10
60000/60000 [==============================] - 4s 60us/
sample - loss: 0.1141 - accuracy: 0.9651
Epoch 6/10
60000/60000 [==============================] - 4s 66us/
sample - loss: 0.1037 - accuracy: 0.9677
Epoch 7/10
60000/60000 [==============================] - 4s 61us/
sample - loss: 0.0940 - accuracy: 0.9702
Epoch 8/10
60000/60000 [==============================] - 4s 61us/
sample - loss: 0.0897 - accuracy: 0.9718
Epoch 9/10
60000/60000 [==============================] - 4s 62us/
sample - loss: 0.0830 - accuracy: 0.9747
Epoch 10/10
60000/60000 [==============================] - 4s 64us/
sample - loss: 0.0805 - accuracy: 0.9748
10000/10000 [==============================] - 0s 39us/
sample - loss: 0.0654 - accuracy: 0.9797
Test accuracy: 98.0%
```

Keras, CNNs, and cifar10

This section contains a simple example of training a neural network with the cifar10 dataset. This code sample is similar to training a neural network on the MNIST dataset and requires a very small code change.

Keep in mind that images in MNIST have the dimensions 28x28, whereas images in cifar10 have the dimensions 32x32. Always ensure that images have the same dimensions in a dataset, otherwise the results will be unpredictable.

Make sure that the images in your dataset have the same dimensions.

Listing A.5 displays the content of `keras_cnn_cifar10.py`, which trains a neural network with the `cifar10` dataset.

LISTING A.5 keras_cnn_cifar10.py

```
import tensorflow as tf

batch_size = 32
num_classes = 10
epochs = 100
num_predictions = 20

cifar10 = tf.keras.datasets.cifar10

# The data, split between the train and test sets:
(x_train, y_train), (x_test, y_test) = cifar10.load_data()
print('x_train shape:', x_train.shape)
print(x_train.shape[0], 'train samples')
print(x_test.shape[0], 'test samples')

# Convert class vectors to binary class matrices
y_train    =     tf.keras.utils.to_categorical(y_train,
num_classes)
y_test     =      tf.keras.utils.to_categorical(y_test,
num_classes)

model = tf.keras.models.Sequential()
model.add(tf.keras.layers.Conv2D(32,(3,3),padding=
'same',input_shape=x_train.shape[1:]))
model.add(tf.keras.layers.Activation('relu'))
model.add(tf.keras.layers.Conv2D(32, (3, 3)))
model.add(tf.keras.layers.Activation('relu'))
model.add(tf.keras.layers.MaxPooling2D(pool_size=(2,
2)))
model.add(tf.keras.layers.Dropout(0.25))

# you can also duplicate the preceding code block here

model.add(tf.keras.layers.Flatten())
model.add(tf.keras.layers.Dense(512))
model.add(tf.keras.layers.Activation('relu'))
model.add(tf.keras.layers.Dropout(0.5))
```

```
model.add(tf.keras.layers.Dense(num_classes))
model.add(tf.keras.layers.Activation('softmax'))

# use RMSprop optimizer to train the model
model.compile(loss='categorical_crossentropy',
              optimizer=opt,
              metrics=['accuracy'])
x_train = x_train.astype('float32')
x_test = x_test.astype('float32')
x_train /= 255
x_test /= 255

model.fit(x_train, y_train,
          batch_size=batch_size,
          epochs=epochs,
          validation_data=(x_test, y_test),
          shuffle=True)

# evaluate and display results from test data
scores = model.evaluate(x_test, y_test, verbose=1)
print('Test loss:', scores[0])
print('Test accuracy:', scores[1])
```

Listing A.5 contains the usual `import` statement and then initializes the variable `cifar10` as a reference to the `cifar10` dataset. The next section of code is similar to the contents of Listing A.4: *the main difference is that this `Keras`-based model defines a CNN instead of an MLP.* Hence, the first layer is a convolutional layer, as shown here:

```
model.add(tf.keras.layers.Conv2D(32,(3,3),padding=
'same',input_shape=x_train.shape[1:]))
```

Note that a "vanilla" CNN involves a convolutional layer (which is the purpose of the preceding code snippet), followed by the ReLU activation function, and a max pooling layer, both of which are displayed in Listing A.5. In addition, the final layer of the `Keras` model is the soft-max activation function, which converts the 10 numeric values in the fully connected layer to a set of 10 non-negative numbers between 0 and 1, whose sum equals 1 (this gives us a probability distribution).

This model is compiled and trained, and then evaluated on the test dataset. The last portion of Listing A.5 displays the value of the test-related loss and accuracy, both of which are calculated during the preceding evaluation step. Launch the code in Listing A.5 and you will see the following output (note that the code was stopped after partially completing the second epoch):

```
x_train shape: (50000, 32, 32, 3)
50000 train samples
10000 test samples

Epoch 1/100
50000/50000 [==============================] - 285s 6ms/
sample - loss: 1.7187 - accuracy: 0.3802 - val_loss:
1.4294 - val_accuracy: 0.4926
Epoch 2/100
 1888/50000 [>.............................] - ETA: 4:39
- loss: 1.4722 - accuracy: 0.4635
```

Resizing Images in Keras

Listing A.6 displays the content of keras_resize_image.py, which illustrates how to resize an image in Keras.

LISTING A.6: keras_resize_image.py

```
import tensorflow as tf
import numpy as np
import imageio
import matplotlib.pyplot as plt

# use any image that has 3 channels
inp = tf.keras.layers.Input(shape=(None, None, 3))
out = tf.keras.layers.Lambda(lambda image: tf.image.
resize(image, (128, 128)))(inp)

model = tf.keras.Model(inputs=inp, outputs=out)
model.summary()

# read the contents of a PNG or JPG
X = imageio.imread('sample3.png')

out = model.predict(X[np.newaxis, ...])

fig, axes = plt.subplots(nrows=1, ncols=2)
axes[0].imshow(X)
axes[1].imshow(np.int8(out[0,...]))

plt.show()
```

Listing A.6 contains the usual `import` statements and then initializes the variable `inp` so that it can accommodate a color image, followed by the variable `out` that is the result of resizing `inp` so that it has dimensions 28x23. Next, `inp` and `out` are specified as the values of `inputs` and `outputs`, respectively, for the `Keras` model, as shown in this code snippet:

```
model = tf.keras.Model(inputs=inp, outputs=out)
```

Next, the variable `X` is initialized as a reference to the result of reading the contents of the image `sample3.png`. The remainder of Listing A.6 involves displaying two images: the original image and the resized image. Launch the code in Listing A.6 and you will see a graph of an image and its resized image, as shown in Figure A.2.

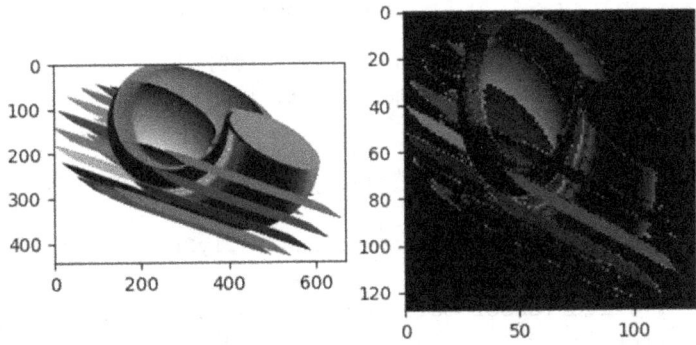

FIGURE A.2 A Graph of an Image and its Resized Image

Keras and Early Stopping (1)

After specifying the training set and the test set from a dataset, you also specify the number of training epochs. A value that's too large can lead to overfitting, whereas a value that's too small can lead to underfitting. Moreover, model improvement can diminish and subsequent training iterations will become redundant.

Early stopping is a technique that allows you to specify a large value for the number of epochs, and yet the training will stop if the model performance improvement drops below a threshold value.

There are several ways that you can specify early stopping, and they involve the concept of a *callback function*. Listing A.7 displays the content of `tf2_keras_callback.py`, which performs early stopping via a callback mechanism.

LISTING A.7 tf2_keras_callback.py

```
import tensorflow as tf
import numpy as np

model = tf.keras.Sequential()
model.add(tf.keras.layers.Dense(64, activation='relu'))
model.add(tf.keras.layers.Dense(64, activation='relu'))
model.add(tf.keras.layers.Dense(10,
activation='softmax'))

model.compile(optimizer=tf.keras.optimizers.Adam(0.01),
              loss='mse',         # mean squared error
            metrics=['mae'])   # mean absolute error

data   = np.random.random((1000, 32))
labels = np.random.random((1000, 10))

val_data   = np.random.random((100, 32))
val_labels = np.random.random((100, 10))

callbacks = [
  # stop training if "val_loss" stops improving for over
2 epochs
          tf.keras.callbacks.EarlyStopping(patience=2,
monitor='val_loss'),
  # write TensorBoard logs to the ./logs directory
  tf.keras.callbacks.TensorBoard(log_dir='./logs')
]

model.fit(data,    labels,    batch_size=32,    epochs=50,
callbacks=callbacks,
          validation_data=(val_data, val_labels))

model.evaluate(data, labels, batch_size=32)
```

Listing A.7 defines a `Keras`-based model with three hidden layers and then compiles the model. The next portion of Listing A.7 uses the `np.random.random` function in order to initialize the variables `data`, `labels`, `val_data`, and `val_labels`.

The interesting code involves the definition of the `callbacks` variable that specifies the `tf.keras.callbacks.EarlyStopping` class with a value of 2 for `patience`, which means that the model will stop training if there is an insufficient reduction in the value of `val_loss`. The callbacks variable includes the `tf.keras.callbacks.TensorBoard` class to specify the `logs` subdirectory as the location for the TensorBoard files.

Next, the `model.fit()` method is invoked with a value of 50 for the epochs (shown in bold), followed by the `model.evaluate()` method. Launch the code in Listing A.7, and you will see the following output:

```
Epoch 1/50
1000/1000 [==============================] - 0s 354us/
sample - loss: 0.2452 - mae: 0.4127 - val_loss: 0.2517 -
val_mae: 0.4205
Epoch 2/50
1000/1000 [==============================] - 0s 63us/
sample - loss: 0.2447 - mae: 0.4125 - val_loss: 0.2515 -
val_mae: 0.4204
Epoch 3/50
1000/1000 [==============================] - 0s 63us/
sample - loss: 0.2445 - mae: 0.4124 - val_loss: 0.2520 -
val_mae: 0.4209
Epoch 4/50
1000/1000 [==============================] - 0s 68us/
sample - loss: 0.2444 - mae: 0.4123 - val_loss: 0.2519 -
val_mae: 0.4205
1000/1000 [==============================] - 0s 37us/
sample - loss: 0.2437 - mae: 0.4119
(1000, 10)
```

Notice that the code stopped training after four epochs, even though 50 epochs are specified in the code.

Keras and Early Stopping (2)

The previous section contains a code sample with minimalistic functionality with respect to the use of the callback function in `Keras`. However, you can also define a custom class that provides a finer-grained functionality that uses a callback mechanism.

Listing A.8 displays the content of `tf2_keras_callback2.py`, which performs early stopping via a callback mechanism (the new code is shown in bold).

LISTING A.8 tf2_keras_callback2.py

```
import tensorflow as tf
import numpy as np
```

```
model = tf.keras.Sequential()
model.add(tf.keras.layers.Dense(64, activation='relu'))
model.add(tf.keras.layers.Dense(64, activation='relu'))
model.add(tf.keras.layers.Dense(10,
activation='softmax'))

model.compile(optimizer=tf.keras.optimizers.Adam(0.01),
              loss='mse',        # mean squared error
              metrics=['mae'])   # mean absolute error

data   = np.random.random((1000, 32))
labels = np.random.random((1000, 10))

val_data   = np.random.random((100, 32))
val_labels = np.random.random((100, 10))

class MyCallback(tf.keras.callbacks.Callback):
  def on_train_begin(self, logs={}):
    print("on_train_begin")

  def on_train_end(self, logs={}):
    print("on_train_begin")
    return

  def on_epoch_begin(self, epoch, logs={}):
    print("on_train_begin")
    return

  def on_epoch_end(self, epoch, logs={}):
    print("on_epoch_end")
    return

  def on_batch_begin(self, batch, logs={}):
    print("on_batch_begin")
    return

  def on_batch_end(self, batch, logs={}):
    print("on_batch_end")
    return

callbacks = [MyCallback()]

model.fit(data,labels,batch_size=32,epochs=50,call-
backs=callbacks,validation_data=(val_data,val_labels))

model.evaluate(data, labels, batch_size=32)
```

The new code in Listing A.8 differs from Listing A.7, and the difference is the code block that is displayed in bold. This new code defines a custom Python class with several methods, each of which is invoked during the appropriate point during the Keras lifecycle execution. The six methods consist of three pairs of methods for the start event and end event associated with the training, epochs, and batches, as listed here:

- `def on_train_begin()`
- `def on_train_end()`
- `def on_epoch_begin()`
- `def on_epoch_end()`
- `def on_batch_begin()`
- `def on_batch_end()`

The preceding methods contain just a `print()` statement in Listing A.8, and you can insert any code you wish in any of these methods. Launch the code in Listing A.8 and you will see the following output:

```
on_train_begin
on_train_begin
Epoch 1/50
on_batch_begin
on_batch_end
   32/1000 [..............................] - ETA: 4s -
loss: 0.2489 - mae: 0.4170on_batch_begin
on_batch_end
on_batch_begin on_batch_end
// details omitted for brevity
on_batch_begin
on_batch_end
on_batch_begin
on_batch_end
992/1000 [=============================>.] - ETA: 0s -
loss: 0.2468 - mae: 0.4138on_batch_begin
on_batch_end
on_epoch_end
1000/1000 [==============================] - 0s 335us/
sample - loss: 0.2466 - mae: 0.4136 - val_loss: 0.2445 -
val_mae: 0.4126
on_train_begin
Epoch 2/50
on_batch_begin
```

```
on_batch_end
  32/1000 [...............................] - ETA: 0s -
loss: 0.2465 - mae: 0.4133on_batch_begin
on_batch_end
on_batch_begin
on_batch_end
// details omitted for brevity
on_batch_end
on_epoch_end
1000/1000 [==============================] - 0s 51us/
sample - loss: 0.2328 - mae: 0.4084 - val_loss: 0.2579 -
val_mae: 0.4241
on_train_begin
  32/1000 [...............................] - ETA: 0s -
loss: 0.2295 - mae: 0.4030
1000/1000 [==============================] - 0s 22us/
sample - loss: 0.2313 - mae: 0.4077
(1000, 10)
```

Keras and Metrics

Many `Keras`-based models only specify "the accuracy" as the metric for evaluating a trained model, as shown here:

```
model.compile(optimizer='adam',
              loss='sparse_categorical_crossentropy',
              metrics=['accuracy'])
```

However, there are many other built-in metrics available, each of which is encapsulated in a `Keras` class in the `tf.keras.metrics` namespace. A list of many such metrics are displayed in the following list:

- class Accuracy: how often the predictions match the labels
- class BinaryAccuracy: how often the predictions match the labels
- class CategoricalAccuracy: how often the predictions match the labels
- class FalseNegatives: the number of false negatives
- class FalsePositives: the number of false positives
- class Mean: the (weighted) mean of the given values
- class Precision: the precision of the predictions with respect to the labels
- class Recall: the recall of the predictions with respect to the labels
- class TrueNegatives: the number of true negatives
- class TruePositives: the number of true positives

Perform an online search for code samples that use the metrics in the preceding list.

Saving and Restoring Keras Models

Listing A.9 displays the content of tf2_keras_save_model.py, which creates, trains, and saves a Keras-based model, then creates a new model that is populated with the data from the saved model.

LISTING A.8 tf2_keras_save_model.py

```
import tensorflow as tf
import os
def create_model():
  model = tf.keras.models.Sequential([
    tf.keras.layers.Flatten(input_shape=(28, 28)),
    tf.keras.layers.Dense(512, activation=tf.nn.relu),
    tf.keras.layers.Dropout(0.2),
    tf.keras.layers.Dense(10, activation=tf.nn.softmax)
  ])

model.compile(optimizer=tf.keras.optimizers.Adam(),
loss=tf.keras.losses.sparse_categorical_crossentropy,-
metrics=['accuracy'])

  return model

# Create a basic model instance
model = create_model()
model.summary()

checkpoint_path = "checkpoint/cp.ckpt"
checkpoint_dir = os.path.dirname(checkpoint_path)

# Create checkpoint callback
cp_callback            =            tf.keras.callbacks.
ModelCheckpoint(checkpoint_path,
save_weights_only=True, verbose=1)

# => model #1: create the first model
model = create_model()

mnist = tf.keras.datasets.mnist
(X_train, y_train),(X_test, y_test) = mnist.load_data()
```

```
X_train, X_test = X_train / 255.0, X_test / 255.0
print("X_train.shape:",X_train.shape)

model.fit(X_train, y_train,  epochs = 2,
          validation_data = (X_test,y_test),
          callbacks = [cp_callback])  # pass callback to
training

# => model #2: create a new model and load saved model
model = create_model()
loss, acc = model.evaluate(X_test, y_test)
print("Untrained      model,      accuracy:      {:5.2f}%".
format(100*acc))

model.load_weights(checkpoint_path)
loss,acc = model.evaluate(X_test, y_test)
print("Restored      model,      accuracy:      {:5.2f}%".
format(100*acc))
```

Listing A.8 starts with the `create_model()` Python function that creates and compiles a `Keras`-based model. The next portion of Listing A.8 defines the location of the file that will be saved, as well as the checkpoint callback, as shown here:

```
checkpoint_path = "checkpoint/cp.ckpt"
checkpoint_dir = os.path.dirname(checkpoint_path)

# Create checkpoint callback
cp_callback=tf.keras.callbacks.ModelCheckpoint
(checkpoint_path,save_weights_only=True,verbose=1)
```

The next portion of Listing A.8 trains the current model using the `MNIST` dataset, and also specifies `cp_callback` so that the model can be saved.

The final code block in Listing A.8 creates a new `Keras`-based model by invoking the Python method `create_model()` again, evaluating this new model on the test-related data, and displaying the value of the accuracy. Next, the model is loaded with the saved model weights via the `load_weights()` API. The relevant code block is reproduced here:

```
model = create_model()
loss, acc = model.evaluate(X_test, y_test)
print("Untrained      model,      accuracy:      {:5.2f}%".
format(100*acc))

model.load_weights(checkpoint_path)
```

```
loss,acc = model.evaluate(X_test, y_test)
print("Restored    model,    accuracy:    {:5.2f}%".
format(100*acc))
```

Now launch the code in Listing A.8, and you will see the following output:

```
on_train_begin
Model: "sequential"
```

Layer (type)	Output Shape	Param #
flatten (Flatten)	(None, 784)	0
dense (Dense)	(None, 512)	401920
dropout (Dropout)	(None, 512)	0
dense_1 (Dense)	(None, 10)	5130

```
Total params: 407,050
Trainable params: 407,050
Non-trainable params: 0

Train on 60000 samples, validate on 10000 samples
Epoch 1/2
59840/60000 [============================>.] - ETA: 0s -
loss: 0.2173 - accuracy: 0.9351
Epoch 00001: saving model to checkpoint/cp.ckpt
60000/60000  [==============================]  -  10s
168us/sample - loss: 0.2170 - accuracy: 0.9352 - val_
loss: 0.0980 - val_accuracy: 0.9696
Epoch 2/2
59936/60000 [============================>.] - ETA: 0s -
loss: 0.0960 - accuracy: 0.9707
Epoch 00002: saving model to checkpoint/cp.ckpt
60000/60000  [==============================]  -  10s
174us/sample - loss: 0.0959 - accuracy: 0.9707 - val_
loss: 0.0735 - val_accuracy: 0.9761
10000/10000 [==============================] - 1s 86us/
sample - loss: 2.3986 - accuracy: 0.0777
Untrained model, accuracy:  7.77%
```

```
10000/10000 [==============================] - 1s 67us/
sample - loss: 0.0735 - accuracy: 0.9761
Restored model, accuracy: 97.61%
```

The directory where you launched this code sample contains a new sub-directory called checkpoint whose contents are shown here:

```
-rw-r--r--  1 owner  staff     1222 Aug 17 14:34 cp.ckpt.
index
-rw-r--r--  1 owner  staff  4886716 Aug 17 14:34 cp.ckpt.
data-00000-of-00001
-rw-r--r--  1 owner  staff       71 Aug 17 14:34 checkpoint
```

Summary

This appendix introduced you to some of the features of Keras and an assortment of Keras-based code samples involving basic neural networks with the MNIST and cifar10 datasets. You learned about some of the important namespaces (such as tf.keras.layers) and their contents.

Next, you saw an example of performing linear regression with Keras and a simple CSV file. Then you learned how to create a Keras-based MLP neural network that is trained on the MNIST dataset.

In addition, you saw examples of Keras-based models that perform early stopping, which is convenient when the model exhibits miznimal improvement (that is specified by you) during the training process.

INDEX